JESSIE TAFT

Therapist and
Social Work Educator

Jessie Taft, June, 1959

JESSIE TAFT

Therapist and Social Work Educator

❧

A Professional Biography

❧

Edited by

VIRGINIA P. ROBINSON

Philadelphia

University of Pennsylvania Press

7321

Printed in the United States of America

THE ALUMNI ASSOCIATION of the University of Pennsylvania School of Social Work is privileged to share in this memorial to Dr. Jessie Taft. Her death in June 1960 called forth from the alumni a spontaneous and widely expressed wish to honor her as teacher and writer. Officers and Executive Committee of the Alumni Association, the membership at large, and the School faculty agreed that the publication of a volume of her assembled writings would express most fittingly their appreciation of Dr. Taft and at the same time add significantly to the literature of social work.

In Miss Virginia Robinson's editorship of this book, the Alumni Association is fortunate indeed. Her long and close collaboration with Dr. Taft in social work education, her distinguished skills as teacher, writer, and editor combine to make this tribute to Dr. Taft all that the Alumni had envisioned, and more. In these pages former students of Dr. Taft will find expression of the thought and spirit which imparted so much meaning to their professional education. All readers will find that the re-statement of her original approach to helping in the social work setting is as vital and evocative today as when she taught and wrote.

The Alumni Association's wholehearted response to the

5

advance underwriting of this publication, the devoted help of Dean Ruth E. Smalley and the School faculty, together with Miss Robinson's gifted editorship now bring into being a biography that will long stand as a living memorial to a beloved teacher—Dr. Jessie Taft.

Florence Silverblatt,
Alumni Representative
for the Jessie Taft Memorial

July 19, 1961

Foreword

It was Ralph Waldo Emerson who wrote: "An institution is the lengthened shadow of one man." Anyone associated with an institution, and certainly with that specific institution, a school of social work, knows how integral and vital to its on-going life are the separate and combined efforts of all who are a part of it. Yet, distinctive and vigorous institutions do bear the special mark of the particularly strong and gifted, the giants, who over a considerable period of time, poured their life and gifts into the institution's life. No institution among schools of social work has been more blessed in its "giants" than the School of Social Work of the University of Pennsylvania, whose faculty has included such men and women as Karl de Schweinitz, Kenneth Pray, and, in a very special and central way—Virginia Robinson and Jessie Taft.

In this volume there evolves the strong, forthright, deeply compassionate, immediately and humanly responsive scholar, psychotherapist and social work educator who was Jessie Taft. Through her own writings and through the story of her life, which becomes their context, so comprehendingly and movingly told by Virginia Robinson, her lifelong friend and companion, she is here revealed as an always powerful, developing, and then fully developed professional self. The interaction of these two

7

women, which served as spark to the genius of each, and
which resulted in a contribution second to none in social
work, is illustrated and exemplified in the production of
this book.

Strikingly confirmed here are the words of the citation
presented by the Alumni to Dr. Taft on the occasion of
the School's celebration of its Fiftieth Anniversary in
1959: "Much that comprises the strength and distinction
of the University of Pennsylvania School of Social Work
originated in her thinking, teaching, and writing." With
humility and a deep sense of responsibility, the present
School honors and seeks to comprehend ever more fully
and to use ever more creatively in its continuing development, the heritage in which Dr. Taft and Dr. Robinson
shared so centrally. For the School's alumni, the publication of this book, an undertaking initiated and spon-
sored by them, has special meaning, for their lives were
deeply touched by the living presence of Dr. Taft. For the
profession as a whole it makes available in one place and
preserves for all time a theory of social casework, unique
and powerful in character, whose impact on social work
practice and social work education, already great, even
revolutionary, promises to continue to be just as great as
the profession will let it be. "To have great poets there
must be great audiences too," and the depths to which
readers will take what is here written, and let it be for
them a moving and direction-giving experience in their
own lives, must depend on the readers themselves.

What Dr. Taft said of the writings of Otto Rank might
be said of her own: ". . . as to the importance of his relation to social work, he gave to a limited group of social

workers the secret of helping. But it is not understood except by those who have felt its effects. It will never be popular; it is too hard to live up to." Here I dare to be more confident and optimistic than Dr. Taft—about the capacity and the courage of social workers generally, both to understand and to live up to the hard yet deeply rewarding doctrine of discipline and responsibility, and necessity to live life fully and in the present moment—a doctrine full of life and promise—which constitutes the core of the contribution of both Dr. Rank and Dr. Taft, and through them and Dr. Robinson, of the School of Social Work of the University of Pennsylvania.

Dr. Taft lived positively, *for* and not *against; for* life richly and responsibly lived, *for* a belief in the wish and capacity of each to so live his own life, *for* defining and then using a psychology of help through human relationship, functionally determined and moving in time, as true for education for social work as for its practice. She was the living exponent of her own credo of the power of the positive will, a lover and liver of life. As she *was* so, she *emerges* so, in these pages, from her earliest beginnings to her own quietly affirmed ending with life, although the form and content of her professional contribution were influenced and confirmed by Dr. Otto Rank and her long friendship with Dr. Robinson. "The professional self is the immortal self," said Dr. Taft. Here is her immortality, and more. Here is the immortality of "Miss Robinson and Dr. Taft" as they were lovingly known.

As present Dean of the School she served so brilliantly, it is my privilege to commend this volume not only to members of the social work profession who will find in it for their own and their profession's use all of the vigor, the penetrating psychological insight, and the clarity of Dr. Taft, but to any reader who may wish to restore and renew the life in himself through association with a life fully, abundantly, and most generously lived.

RUTH E. SMALLEY, *Dean*
School of Social Work
University of Pennsylvania

July 7, 1961

Editor's Preface

When, in the fall of 1958, Dr. Ruth Smalley, Dean of the University of Pennsylvania School of Social Work, asked me to write a history of the School for presentation at the Fiftieth Anniversary celebration of the School in the spring of 1959 there began for me and for Jessie Taft, my lifelong companion, an exploration into our past going back to 1917. In that year I came to the faculty of the School; in the year following, Jessie Taft came to Philadelphia to develop a mental hygiene program for children under the Seybert Institution. She soon became an authority on mental hygiene and problems of children in this community, speaking and writing on these subjects, and teaching a course in psychology for students in the Pennsylvania School of Social Work. From that time on, our interest in defining and creating professional education for social work had been absorbing. For purposes of writing this history we had not only our own memories to depend on but published and unpublished speeches, correspondence, catalogues of the School, curriculum studies and all the papers that collect in the files of teachers. Those that bore clearly upon the history of the School were in order by the time the paper was delivered in June, 1959.

When we returned from vacation in Vermont in the fall of 1959, Dr. Taft decided to continue with the process

11

of organizing our past by putting her separate papers in order. These included copies of all of her published speeches, early reports of her work in children's agencies, several records of office interviews with difficult children, copies of some pieces of teaching material and case illustrations. It was characteristic of her to answer, often by return mail and in longhand, personal letters from friends and former students and to destroy these letters. The correspondence relating to writing and publishing her last book, a biography of Otto Rank, and current professional correspondence was preserved. In January, February, and March she worked regularly on this material with great satisfaction in seeing her professional past in perspective. She finished this task in March, 1960.

In undertaking the editorship of a Memorial Volume to be drawn from these papers, I recognize my handicap in my own involvement, personal and professional, in this history. This involvement has left open no possibility of choice of editorship either to the alumni or to myself. It has made the work of editing this volume at times painful, but always deeply rewarding. It has been my aim to present only such biographical material as is necessary to follow the development of a professional person in the field of mental hygiene and social casework in the first half of this century. Jessie Taft always said "the professional self is the real self, the self that carries value, the immortal self." This was never said to deny that it was also for her the human self. Nothing she ever wrote from the slightest comment on a student's paper to a national conference address was written or spoken perfunctorily or from the level of intellect alone; every utterance came from a whole self responding spontaneously and humanly as well as responsibly to the person or situation before her. For this reason her papers as published in this volume constitute a biography.

Without the sponsorship of the alumni and faculty of the University of Pennsylvania School of Social Work this volume could not have been undertaken. Their interest and concern expressed in contributions to the Memorial Fund and in meetings with me through Florence Silverblatt, President of the Alumni Association, Dr. Ruth Smalley, Dean of the School and Dr. Isabel Carter, the faculty representative, have been a source of stimulation and support on which I have relied throughout my work as editor. Anita Faatz has given me invaluable help as consultant through her intimate knowledge of the material we were using, her discriminating judgment in selecting papers, and her special editorial and bibliographical skills. The work of compiling the bibliography is hers. To Mrs. Grace Seeburger, my first secretary in the School and presently the able secretary of the Alumni Association, belong my sincere thanks for her unfailing patience and skill in typing and retyping the manuscript.

VIRGINIA P. ROBINSON

Flourtown, Pennsylvania
June, 1961

Acknowledgments

For PERMISSION to reprint, acknowledgment is made to the Family Service Association of America for articles appearing in *The Family* and *Social Casework;* the National Conference on Social Welfare for papers printed in the *Proceedings;* the World Federation for Mental Health, United States Committee for discussion from the *Proceedings of the First International Conference on Mental Hygiene;* the *Journal of Jewish Communal Service* for a paper from the *Jewish Social Service Quarterly;* the American Academy of Political and Social Science for an article from *The Annals;* the University of Pennsylvania Press and School of Social Work for quotations from their *Journals;* the Child Study Association of America for an article appearing in *Child Study;* the John Dewey Society for an article published in *Progressive Education;* the University of Chicago Alumni Association for the quotation from *University of Chicago Magazine;* the Division of Pupil Personnel and Counseling of the Philadelphia School District for a paper delivered at its meeting; to Alfred A. Knopf for reprinting excerpts from *Will Therapy and Truth and Reality;* to the Julian Press, for excerpts from *Otto Rank, a Biographical Study.* In each instance, full details of publication are given in the bibliography at the end of this volume.

For permission to quote from correspondence and other

materials thanks are due to: Miss Phoebe Crosby, Dr. Florence Clothier Wislocki, Mr. Edward Solenberger, Miss Anita J. Faatz, Mr. Arthur Ceppos, Mr. Roland Baughman, Mrs. Margorie Mohan Turville, Dr. Frederick H. Allen, Dr. Fay B. Karpf, Dr. John N. Shlien, Mr. Jack Jones; and to Miss Laura Taft and Mrs. Lorraine Taft Warner, for permission to use family pictures.

Contents

Forewords   Florence Silverblatt and
  Ruth E. Smalley   5

Editor's Preface   Virginia P. Robinson   11

Acknowledgments   15

❧

PART I
Des Moines and Chicago, 1882–1913   23

PART II
New York and Mental Hygiene,
  1913–1918   41
  THE RELATION OF PSYCHIATRY TO SOCIAL WORK   56

PART III
Philadelphia and Children's Work,
  1918–1934   67
  PROBLEMS OF SOCIAL CASEWORK WITH CHILDREN   76
  THE SOCIAL WORKER'S OPPORTUNITY   90
  WHAT IT MEANS TO BE A FOSTER PARENT   98

THE USE OF THE TRANSFER WITHIN THE LIMITS
OF THE OFFICE INTERVIEW   105
THE FUNCTION OF A MENTAL HYGIENIST IN A
CHILDREN'S AGENCY   108

PART IV

Association with Rank, 1926–1939   121

DISCUSSION OF A PAPER DELIVERED BY DR. OTTO
RANK   135
LIVING AND FEELING   140
FOREWORD FROM "THE DYNAMICS OF THERAPY
IN A CONTROLLED RELATIONSHIP"   154
THE TIME ELEMENT IN THERAPY   157
THE FORCES THAT MAKE FOR THERAPY   177

PART V

Functional Casework and Teaching, 1934–1950   193

THE RELATION OF FUNCTION TO PROCESS IN SOCIAL
CASEWORK   206
SOCIAL CASEWORK WITH CHILDREN   226
FOSTER HOME CARE FOR CHILDREN   232
SOME SPECIFIC DIFFERENCES IN CURRENT THEORY
AND PRACTICE   246
A FUNCTIONAL APPROACH TO FAMILY CASEWORK   260
A PHILOSOPHY OF HELPING IN SOCIAL WORK   273
THE FUNCTION OF THE PERSONALITY COURSE IN
THE PRACTICE UNIT   291

PART VI

Final Statement of Philosophy, 1949–1950

305

TIME AS THE MEDIUM OF THE HELPING PROCESS   305

A CONCEPTION OF THE GROWTH PROCESS UNDER-
LYING SOCIAL CASEWORK PRACTICE   325

PART VII

Retirement and Biography of Otto Rank, 1950–1960

345

Selections from correspondence relating to the
Rank collection and work on the biography

Bibliography

371

A complete bibliography of the writings of
Jessie Taft, in chronological sequence, com-
piled by Anita J. Faatz

The illustrations appear as a group after
page 192.

In the last analysis, therapy as a qualitative affair must depend upon the personal development of the therapist and his ability to use consciously for the benefit of his client, the insight and self-discipline which he has achieved in his own struggle to accept self, life, and time as limited, and to be experienced fully only at the cost of fear, pain, and loss. I do not mean that knowledge is not necessary, that technical skill is not necessary; they are, but they are of no value therapeutically without the person. To make casework therapeutic, incidentally or deliberately, one must be a therapist and only to the extent that this is true are the relationships one sets up therapeutic, regardless of the label, the number of the visits, or the interpretation recorded in the dictation.

JESSIE TAFT, The Dynamics of Therapy
in a Controlled Relationship, 1933.

The possibility of providing for the individual in need, an artificial growth-producing situation, is, in my opinion, the epoch-making psychological discovery of our era, a discovery that may yet be found to be more momentous for the future of civilization than the unlocking of the forces in the atom.

JESSIE TAFT, A Conception of the Growth Process
Underlying Social Casework Practice, 1950.

PART I

Des Moines and Chicago

1882-1913

☙❧ AT ONE TIME in her life, shortly after retirement from the compelling work at the University of Pennsylvania School of Social Work, Jessie Taft considered the possibility of writing her autobiography for her own interest, not for publication. This impulse was short-lived; in its place a biography of Otto Rank absorbed her for several years and satisfied the desire to follow a lifelong process through to conclusion. But in the experiences of her own childhood she retained a keen interest, and she delighted to talk of them in conversation with friends.

From Dubuque, Iowa, where she was born June 24, 1882, the family moved to Des Moines, where they maintained a home until her father's death in 1917. She was the oldest of three girls. On both sides of her family there were Vermont backgrounds, the father coming as a boy from Dummerston, Vermont, not far from Townshend, the original home of the distinguished Taft family with its many famous offspring to whom this Iowa family traced no known connection.

From Vermont, her father brought his knowledge and skill in apple growing and established a prosperous wholesale fruit business in Des Moines. The home was comfortable but not luxurious and lacked cultural interests. Jessie Taft described it and her background as typically Midwestern. Social life in the home was limited by her mother's deafness, increasing with the birth of each child, but the children were free to find and develop social life in the community as they wished. For the oldest child, it was school that offered the greatest resources in companionship, and she used them to the full. Her ability and her eager responsiveness to books and lessons easily placed her among the first in her classes, where there were other able students. The family was without church affiliations, and she tells how in adolescence she found her own church connection by trying out all the ministers in town. She chose the Unitarian Church as suitable for her purpose at that time. For recreation there were Sunday rides behind her father's horses, of which the family were very proud, and later, as the first bicycles came to town, the family rode separately and together.

Ordinary as the external conditions of her family in these years would seem to have been, she has described an inner life of rich and meaningful experience. This experience contributed to her sensitivity to the children she was to work with later in children's agencies, and to her capacity to describe them movingly in the case illustrations in speeches written in this period.

There are only a few direct references to this inner life of childhood in her papers. One such reference from an unpublished paper is memorable.

How well I can remember in very early childhood the painful shock attending the discovery of my own impotence, when some magic plan met the check of an unbending reality. I remember once waking with a sense of something creative in the air, and an idea which I had had the night before struggled into consciousness. It was a sudden appreciation of the infinite possibilities of the piano keys. One could sit down and combine them in different ways forever and ever; what a richness of potential activity, what a glow of warm feeling it shed over my day. I shall never forget my efforts to connect this impulse with reality. I went boldly to the piano, sat down, put my fingers on the keys and waited for the miracle to happen. With humiliation and bitter disappointment, I found that the piano keys were not combined into melodies by mere desire. It is such impulses towards action on the environment, impulses charged with more working energy than all the indirect fear, punishment, and reward motivations in the world, that are the school's responsibility and opportunity."[1]

A similar memory of early childhood that came to mind often was her passionate desire to paint on black velvet. Like the piano keys, it offered such infinite possibilities in imagination, doomed to disappointment in reality. The only criticism she ever made of her parents, the only real regret she ever expressed about her childhood, was that she was taught so little skill with her hands. Her mother was too competent a cook herself to want the children bothering her in the kitchen, and her father did no work around the house in which the children could share. The piano was the only musical instrument in the home, and, as was the custom of the times, she had piano lessons from a good teacher and learned to play and to care about music and kept a relation to the piano for the rest of her life. As she grew older there was singing around the piano at home and in the home of two musical Dutch friends. She played

[1] Jessie Taft, "Mental Hygiene and Education," unpublished. Note on paper reads: "Fall of 1922 for Educational Committee of Chicago Women's Club and Abraham Lincoln Center Group, Chicago."

by sight and enjoyed playing accompaniments, and German songs learned at this period became old friends for life.

Always a precocious child, she matured early and appeared fully grown in high school. Loving food, she took on weight too fast and was painfully sensitive to being overweight and outsize. In retrospect, adolescence flattened out into a long desert waste marked by evenings of boredom spent on the porch in the intense heat of an Iowa summer. Illuminating this dark picture, there were memories of a succession of romantic projections on her part, from the trolley car driver in early childhood to the principal of the high school later.

There were real friends, too, neighbor children at first, then in high school and Drake University, friends of her own choosing: a man with whom she read and discussed philosophy in pursuit of questions about space and time, which absorbed her as early as she could remember; and an older woman, a competent and successful doctor in Des Moines who, attracted to this young girl so eager for life and experience, opened many doors to her through her knowledge of medicine and an extensive practice which included obstetrical work in the Salvation Army maternity home. The relationship with the philosopher friend ended when she found in her classes at the University of Chicago all the opportunity she craved for an exploration of philosophical questions.

A year of study at the University of Chicago seems to have been a natural next step in an educational process to follow the Bachelor of Arts program completed at Drake University in 1904. There seems to have been no financial problem and no obstacle of any kind put in her path. Her father's brief letters, which she saved over the years, show his unfailing affection and willingness to have her find her own way and to support her choice. His own preference was to have his girls stay at home where he would willingly have supported them. He never sought to understand the strange determination in this oldest daughter that took her away from home, but followed her movements with pride in her accomplishments, and turned his own desire to do for her into occasional dinner parties with steak and champagne at a big Chicago hotel for her and her friends when a business trip brought him to that city. She always expressed warm affection and admiration for him, and felt herself identified with his background in Dummerston, Vermont, his knowledge of apples and apple growing, and with a romantic impulsive streak that appeared along with his solid business accomplishment. She never shared her mother's apprehension of his business judgment when he speculated in strange ventures. One of these speculations uprooted the family for a journey to a piece of land he had bought in the Florida lake country. The children delighted in the new experiences—the trip to school by rowboat across the lake or by mule over a track around the sandy shore. Their mother's impatience with the discomforts and difficulties in getting food supplies brought them back to Iowa before the year was out.

In the separation from home and family that came when Jessie Taft went to Chicago in 1905, her guilt was focused on leaving the aunt who, with her invalid husband, had always lived with the family, sharing responsibility as a grandmother might do. She functioned in this role particularly for the oldest child whose love and devotion to her was lifelong. Like the father she put no pressure on this girl who must have felt like her own child, but trusted her with the freedom to find her own way.

After a year of study at the University of Chicago and a Ph.B. degree, she returned to Des Moines to a teaching position in the West Des Moines High School, where she remained on the faculty for four years, teaching mathematics, Latin and, at times, German. Teaching never seemed more than a temporary job for her, and when a fellowship in philosophy was offered her at the University of Chicago she returned to work for a doctor's degree.

It was at the University of Chicago in the summer of 1908 that I first met Jessie Taft. I had finished a year of teaching in the Louisville Girl's High School, after five years and a master's degree from Bryn Mawr College, and was eager for a summer of study. When the suggestion of summer school at Chicago came to me through the person who had been assistant in the psychological laboratory at Bryn Mawr in my graduate year, I was immediately responsive to it. She had been given the house of Dr. Tufts, professor of philosophy, for the summer and was asking several summer school students to share it with her as boarders. Among them was Jessie Taft. She was 26, I was 25. We were thrown together at first it seemed by chance through our acquaintance with the person in charge of the house. Neither of us had known her well or intimately, but in her role as manager of this house where a few students were boarders, she became a stranger whose erratic actions were inexplicable. We spent hours of time in trying to understand what she was doing to us; at the same time we were drawn together through the more positive bonds of our interest in philosophy and the several courses we attended together. We explored our likenesses and differences—she from the Midwest and a small coeducational university, I from the South and Bryn Mawr College—and made the most of all that Chicago offered, walking on the Midway, rowing on the lagoon in Jackson Park. For both of us, in spite of the eccentricities of the person in charge of the house, it was a lovely summer.

My own impressions of Chicago University and of Jessie Taft I find in two letters written to a Bryn Mawr classmate. On June 22, 1908, I wrote:

> The atmosphere here at Chicago University is not that of the quiet and dignity and repose produced by grey stone buildings covered with ivy and students wearing gowns but one of hurry and confusion resulting from too many buildings in too small a space and too many people thronging hither and thither—not distinctly students. It's a university in perfection—crowds and crowds of people of every type and nationality eager to grasp a little knowledge, school teachers from rural districts, country preachers intent on getting a modern idea or two. And no matter where you go the modern idea is there. Pragmatism is in the air and everybody starts with it as a basis. I do not know how I shall escape the influence. I have registered for five courses: Primitive Social Control with W. I. Thomas; Absolutism, Realism, Pragmatism, Moore; Psychology of the Educational Process, Angell; Psychology of Religion, Ames; Philosophy of Religion, Foster. . . .
>
> I simply sit and gasp as one by one the old standbys—the arguments we staked our life on and accepted as truisms in philosophy at Bryn Mawr—are cast aside as so much dead wood.

The letter goes on to describe the person who brought me to Chicago, the head of the house we lived in. I write that her point of view so different from my own makes me quiver. Then the letter continues:

> One other person, Jessie Taft, a friend of M——, about as unlike her as I, or more. A joy to me. She's large and ungainly, and Western but with the kindest eyes I've ever seen. There is no escaping the appeal of her good, straightforward common sense and understanding of things. She feels somewhat towards M——as I do. Cares more I think. She discusses her with me in the frankest way. I've never met such frankness in mortal being. Yet you would trust her utterly, strange to say. She likes me.

In a letter dated July 14 this description appears:

> Jessie Taft has been a strong rock for me. She is so frank and sincere and free from conventionality that she compels you to a like frankness, and you find yourself telling her things in the most natural, matter-of-course manner. Things get straighter when you talk to her, too. She sees them in such a clear, straight way without warping them. I do appreciate that ability especially when I seem to be seeing things so wrong myself.

After this summer I did not see Jessie Taft again until the summer of 1910 when I stopped in Chicago for a few days to visit her on my way East. But we had kept in touch with each other's thinking and experience, comparing our discontent with teaching, and affirming our intention to see each other again. In 1910 she was already engaged in a program of work towards a doctor's degree in philosophy, while I had only a hope but no prospect of such a program for myself in the immediate future.

My letters to the college friend reveal my growing dissatisfaction with teaching, my feeling of not being able to find any connection between the English literature, the content of the courses that I loved to teach, and the children's indifferent response. The children and I remained apart, and I described my sense of frustration and despair in detail. I seem never to have heard of social work in my community, but to this friend who is living at Hartley House Settlement in New York and taking courses at the New York School of Social Work, I write of my interest in getting to know more about "real people."

Meanwhile, in addition to teaching, I am very active in the Suffrage movement in Kentucky and speak and debate the "cause" of equality for women eagerly. An interesting indication of a beginning realization of the value of "function" in group contacts I find in another letter written January 15, 1912, to this same friend, describing a meeting where I addressed a group of women in a small town near Louisville.

I talked first, and then they asked questions and gave their opinions, and the last were highly illuminating. I am sure that the only reason I've learned to care for "people" is because I've gotten really acquainted with some through suffrage work. How infinitely much better such a meeting is where conversation is to a point and with a purpose and where each person really says something, than a tea or a reception where conversation is always scattered and marked by inanity only. I may be singularly unsuccessful at social gatherings where no one ever said anything more significant to me than "it's a pretty day." And my remarks are no better. While at the suffrage meeting people give me their most sincere convictions, often their deepest emotions. Hasten the time when an invitation to tea will read, "Discussion of Charlotte Perkins Gilman's latest book"—or some novel even. Anything to concentrate discussion.

In a later letter I find mention of the opportunity that was to offer me a way out of the irksome limitations in high school teaching and that promised to open up a road to a more real experience with "people." It had come to me, strange to say, from the person with whom Jessie Taft and I had boarded in the summer of 1908, and who was now in New York State in charge of a new project for the investigation of criminal women; a project being developed by Katherine Bement Davis, superintendent of the State Reformatory for Women at Bedford Hills, New York, financed by John D. Rockefeller, Jr. Searching for investigators to interview women committed to the Bedford Reformatory and institutions in New York City, she had turned to me and to Jessie Taft. For me it would necessitate a leave of absence from my teaching position for the rest of the school year. For Jessie Taft, while it would mean a temporary giving up of her doctoral work, it would offer actually the next step in the educational program she was pursuing—the chance for real experience outside of books. The chance to work together played no small part in our decision to go if I could get a leave and make arrangements in my personal responsibilities. The only flaw in this situation was our continuing distrust of the person who was recommending us for this job. An interview with Katharine Bement Davis, the truly remarkable head of the New York State Reformatory and the prime mover in this project, resolved all our doubts. That we brought no qualifications for working with criminal women except interest did not disturb Miss Davis, nor did it disturb us. This was our chance for vital gripping experience, and we plunged into it without a qualm and with no regrets.

We began work in New York City on April 1, 1912, living in a furnished room at 7 West 16th Street, setting out in the early mornings to catch a boat across the East River to Blackwell's Island where, in a cell converted into an office, we interviewed the drunks and prostitutes committed from Night Court. Evenings were spent observing the prostitutes soliciting on 14th Street or being brought into Night Court, and week ends in Bedford getting acquainted with that institution and talking with Miss Davis about our experiences. Miss Davis, herself, unique and wonderful person that she was, contributed not the least of the exciting new experiences of that summer. We felt ourselves to be only at the beginning in assimilation of these experiences, and our choice was soon made to leave teaching and to stay in this field of work with people, a choice that included staying together and working together.

Meanwhile Jessie Taft had every intention of returning to Chicago to finish her work for the doctor's degree. She hoped to complete this by April, 1913, and to come back to Bedford for a job in the Reformatory under Miss Davis. I accepted the job that was offered me for the following year as fieldworker in the research project at Bedford, now known as The Laboratory of Social Hygiene, and resigned my position in the Louisville Girls' High School. As preparation for this fieldworker job, Jessie Taft and I spent our vacation in August of 1912 at Cold Spring Harbor, Long Island, where Dr. Charles B. Davenport conducted a summer school in eugenics. Nothing remains in my memory from the classes; but field trips through the sandy paths of the New Jersey pine woods in intense heat, in search of "Pineys" to interview, are unforgettable. These trips and the charts of family histories we constructed from them were valuable preparation for the field trips in Rockland and Dutchess Counties (New York) in the following year, as eugenics fieldworkers from the Laboratory of Social Hygiene—which Jessie Taft describes amusingly in her paper, "The Relation of Mental Hygiene to Social Work," in 1926.

Among the letters of Jessie Taft's that I had saved in 1912–1913, I found several that described the problems and struggle of writing a dissertation and maintaining an individual program of reading and study for the examinations. Her coursework had then been completed. I quote from two of these, the first written in November, 1912.

> Please walk into my room this morning. Once more I am all unpacked and as neat as I will ever be again. The little room isn't half bad—about as large as Miss F.'s room at Bedford—with a white maple dresser, a little desk with shelves below—very convenient—a brass bed, one stiff chair (I pray for a rocker) and a good closet. I think I'll invest in a secondhand table or maybe a rocker. The curtains are pretty, the room is light and cheerful, and I found last night there was plenty of air. The people, a German woman and her two daughters, one of whom goes to the University, seem to be very nice, quiet people. The flat is large and new and well furnshed, with a piano at my service, but I haven't tried it yet.

They gave me breakfast this morning. [She goes on to tell what was served.] Don't know whether I could stand breakfast like that every morning or not. [She plans to get lunch anywhere and dinner with a fellow student at a good place a block away.] It seems so queer to be settled in a strange place without you or anybody I know. But it ought to be great for work. Nobody to interrupt or to tempt to sin.

A letter written in mid-December, 1912, before she leaves college to spend a week off with her family at Christmas, is full of guilt and discouragement.

This is a wail about me and my good-for-nothingness. Maybe if I tell you just how hopeless I am I'll feel better. I feel as if this whole week had been wasted, and here I am taking a week off for Christmas. I have read down at the Crerar Library every day, and I've also fooled away a lot of time, and the reading hasn't counted for much. J—— is certainly the worst squanderer I've ever run up against, and the two of us are simply awful. But I can't blame it all on her—as the Bedford girls say, "Nobody can make you go wrong unless you want to." I'll be glad to get back into the routine of the Hall. Even if I do lose a little time I can't possibly lose so much. I just hate and despise myself. But this coming week I promise you I'm going to write every day, and by the time I leave for home a week from tomorrow I'll have the first section of this thesis ready to hand in or give up.

She struggled during this period, and in later years, with a troublesome physical problem, ligaments that went out of place in the sacroiliac and neck, and osteopathic treatments were resorted to.

A third letter from the year 1912–1913 gives a description of the oral examinations for the doctor's degree, when she was questioned by distinguished members of the departments of philosophy and psychology under whom she had studied. She felt satisfied with what she had done except in answer to the questioning of Professor Mead. With him she had expected to have trouble because "it usually takes a week or two of hard work to answer any of his questions. You can never answer him automatically. I felt that my application of Mead's point of view was far from brilliant." The day is summed up in this letter: "It doesn't seem possible that I really sailed through as I did, and it must be true or they wouldn't have mentioned it so conspicuously. I wasn't conscious of strain at the time, but afterwards I was dead to the world."

In an article about Professor Mead from the University of Chicago magazine which she had clipped and saved over the years the quality of Mead's influence on students is described in these words:

> His wisdom was not to be measured in minutes of listening to him but in a lifetime of realizing the significance of his ideas. . . . It is fitting that the influence of such a personality should have been highly personal. He wrote a number of articles that easily could be made into books, but chiefly his writing was the only kind that Plato thought really serious—that which is done directly on the minds of men. Thesis after thesis was written under him by students who were fired to develop ideas of his. When they went to him for advice he always had time to confer with them, but it never took much time. When he squared around to face them they knew the

truth of his saying that to feel a human being look at you is the most powerful stimulus known.[2]

The examinations were successfully over, but work on her dissertation continued into the spring of 1913. There are no letters preserved from this period, but I have vivid memories of her description of her despair, of the moment when she destroyed everything she had written and began again on the stimulus of a question raised by Professor Mead. The simple "note" with which she prefaces the dissertation in its published form (1915) acknowledges indebtedness to "Professor James H. Tufts and Professor George H. Mead for their advice and counsel in the writing of this thesis and to Miss Virginia P. Robinson and Miss Margaret Snodgrass for their aid in revising the manuscript." Her own references to it in later years were light, indicating amusement at herself writing with so much assurance out of "books and intellect" without firsthand experience. But its significance in her development goes beyond her comment. It is surely her own effort to establish for herself her worth as a woman in the world of men. And in this connection it is interesting to note that all of her teachers in the departments of psychology and philosophy were men, and that of nineteen Doctors of Philosophy awarded by the University of Chicago in 1913, only two were women.

Her degree was awarded "magna cum laude," and from

[2] Van Meter Ames, "George Herbert Mead, an Appreciation," *University of Chicago Magazine*, XXIII, No. 8 (June, 1931), 370.

A fine photograph of Mead hung on the wall of her office in the School, together with one of Rank, the only photographs she ever had framed and hung.

letters then and later written to her by teachers in the departments, it is evident that she was recognized as a promising, able student.

The long months spent in the university libraries had given her contact with the most articulate voices of the women writers of the period: with Olive Schreiner, Ellen Key, Charlotte Perkins Gilman, and Ida Tarbell; with the Abbotts: Grace, whose master's thesis for the University of Chicago, 1909, was entitled *The Legal Position of Married Women in the United States,* and Edith, who had published *Women in Industry* in 1910.

Classroom contact with the profound and stimulating thinking of her teachers, and extensive reading in the philosophical and psychological writing of that day—William James, John Dewey, Josiah Royce, and Havelock Ellis—supplied the material out of which she was forced to develop her own point of view, to state "a satisfactory view of emotion from functional psychology" and a social theory of the self as the background for an understanding of the woman movement. For her own thinking, she had worked out a fundamental philosophical basis solid and deep enough to furnish the ground she could stand on as she confronted the problems ahead of her in moving out of the academic world's protected environment into the world of social work.

PART II

New York and Mental Hygiene
1913-1918

THE POSITION offered to Jessie Taft by Katharine Bement Davis on the completion of her doctoral work at Chicago was an assistant superintendentship at the New York State Reformatory for Women. Nothing in her education or experience had given her any preparation for institutional work nor for understanding the court-committed inmates of a reformatory, and no process of introduction to the requirements of the job could be provided. One must plunge into the situation as a whole and meet its problems head-on; nothing but one's own inner strength could serve one. To this challenge Jessie Taft responded with all that was in her. She was quick to perceive the human relationships among the girls, to discriminate the different qualities in the staff members, to learn to abide by the necessary rules and regulations by which such an institution must maintain itself. Where these seemed too harsh or mechanical, Miss Davis' courage and freedom to try something new and her faith in the individual girl, were a source of stimulation and renewal for the hard-worked staff. Responsive to Miss Davis' belief in the institution, Jessie Taft accepted the function of assistant superintendent without rebellion. She schooled herself to put handcuffs on a girl who "smashed out" and to accompany her and the guard to the disciplinary building and solitary confinement. There she could visit the girl daily and help her work out some of the problems that had led to her behavior. She could maintain order during Sunday services

41

in a crowded auditorium full of restless occupants by the sheer force of her eyes upon them. She knew well her lack of muscular strength in the face of violence, but her courage was always greater than her fear of physical attack. The girls felt this strength in her intuitively and recognized her willingness to listen, to try to work out a fair solution. As one of the girls in the honor cottage expressed it: "Miss Taft listens to both sides and weighs it. If she hands it to a girl it is all right."

A long letter written to her while she was away from Bedford on vacation in January, 1915, by a girl whose behavior kept her in the disciplinary building indicates a recognition of her concern for the girl herself. E——writes that she is trying hard to have a good record when Miss Taft returns. The letter ends with these words:

> If you only knew how much you help me and even your mail comes at moments that do most good. I did not know you were a teacher. Maybe that is why you understand girls so well because you have been with them before even if they were not the same kind of girls. So I will say goodnight and God bless you and bring you back (most of all to bring you back). From your grateful though troublesome pupil.

Twenty years later in 1935 a letter came from this girl written from New York City to Jessie Taft in Philadelphia. It read as follows:

> I wonder if you will be able to recall a girl whom you befriended years ago? In 1913 I was sent to Bedford for masquerading as a boy. I was known by the nickname of Jack, right name E——. You were very kind to me in

my unruly childishness, and above all you never lied to me, so you have always remained in my memory. You see that up till now I've not lived either a normal life or one within the law.

The letter goes on to tell how she is now making an effort to come back to normal living through help given her from an institution and concludes with this paragraph:

I honestly don't know just what I mean in writing to you, but I think it is this; you have always been such a vivid memory and knowing the work you are interested in, and having some idea of me you would know just what a struggle I have ahead of me, and I thought your letters would be of a very great help with advice and *you.* Or is it possible that knowing me as you did and knowing what a mess I made of life that you think I am trying a hopeless act. You see you probably knew me better than I knew myself.

There is no copy of Jessie Taft's reply to this letter, but I am sure she sent one in longhand immediately. On her side, too, the memory of this powerful girl with the build and strength of a man, whose struggle to survive in Bedford kept her in the disciplinary building in solitary confinement almost constantly, was vivid and filled with compassion.

A factual line-a-day book which Jessie Taft kept from January 1 to June 24 of 1915 builds up a picture of a job of such pressing and varied demands that one wonders how anyone could have coped with it. It became impossible when Katherine Bement Davis resigned her administrative job as superintendent to become Commissioner of Charities and Corrections in New York City, leaving the institution in the irresponsible hands of her first assistant. Miss Davis' withdrawal could not fail to be upsetting to the institution, and when the acting superintendent's adeptness in shirking responsibility became apparent to the girls as well as to the staff, conditions deteriorated rapidly and the State Board instituted an investigation. Jessie Taft's decision to resign had been made earlier; however she had no choice but to stay through the investigation and at times had to carry the responsibility which the acting superintendent evaded. When she left in the summer of 1915 it was without a recommendation which she would not have accepted from the acting superintendent under any circumstances; a sad ending to what had been a valuable and successful two years of hard and devoted work. She was ready to leave the field of delinquency and already interested in the new mental hygiene movement, but where to find the next job was not clear to her.

In search of advice on job opportunities she made an appointment with Mary Richmond who in her position in the Russell Sage Foundation in New York was at that time the authority on social casework in the country. Her qualifications apparently did not impress Miss Richmond who told her she would need training in a good casework agency under a competent supervisor, suggesting Johanna Colcord. Jessie Taft was in no mood to consider subjecting herself to a beginner's position as a learner under anybody. In this dark moment when she did not know where to turn and could even speak of the temptation to go home and "live off father," the one job that was right for her interest and ability became vacant when Katharine Tucker, director of the Mental Hygiene Committee of the State Charities Aid Association of New York, resigned to become director of the Visiting Nurse Society of Philadelphia.

The last entry in the line-a-day book from Bedford Reformatory is on her birthday, June 24, 1915. By the fall of that year we had set up housekeeping in New York at 420 West 20th Street in a third floor rear apartment. The street in those days was quiet and little traveled. Across the way were the old grey stone buildings of the General Theological Seminary whose chimes told the hours morning and evening. Jessie Taft could walk across town to the office of the State Charities Aid Association in the United Charities Building at 22nd and Lexington.

The Mental Hygiene Committee carried on an educational program for mental hygiene in state hospitals and other institutions. As director of its Social Service Department, her first responsibility was to seek and fulfill speaking engagements in behalf of mental hygiene in institutions and communities in New York State. No assignment could have been more favorable to her needs at that time. In addition to this opportunity to speak on what was becoming in the words of her diary "a new philosophy of life" to us, she spent one day a week in the Cornell Clinic of Psychopathology, the first mental hygiene clinic in New York City.

My work that year was with the Public Education Association, where a small group of dedicated people were attempting to find a way of helping children in the public schools, the beginning of the visiting teacher or school counseling movement. I felt little but futility in my own efforts to help the children referred to me from a school located in the theatrical district, but I was intrigued with the problem of defining a function for a visiting teacher or social worker in the public school, and caught up in the excitement of the "new philosophy of life" we were discovering.

Early speaking engagements for Jessie Taft were often informal social occasions with board members of an institution or members of a woman's club meeting in the home of the president, and no record remains of them except newspaper clippings. Others were to professional organizations, doctors or nurses, teachers or social workers. Only a few were published; a few were reprinted and distributed by the State Charities Aid Association. The titles of these early papers indicate the dramatic nature of the content and her approach to it. Among them were the following titles: "Is There Anything the Matter with Your Child's Mind?" *Housewives League Magazine* (1916); "Fortifying the Child Against Mental Disease," *American Education* (1917); "Mental Pitfalls in Industry and How to Avoid Them," *Medicine and Surgery* (1917); "How Can We Safeguard the Child Against Mental Disease?" Paper read at the Annual Meeting of the Medical Society of the State of New York, April 26, 1917. Her first National Conference paper, "Supervision of the Feebleminded in the Community," delivered at St. Louis in 1918, speaks for the concern of the State Charities Aid Association with broad social problems, but contains a new emphasis on the role of the caseworker in the adjustment of the individual case, which was her own contribution.

A paper, published in *Medicine and Surgery* under the bold title "The Limitations of the Psychiatrist" gives a vivid picture of her struggle to find a place for herself as social worker in the Mental Hygiene Clinic at Cornell Hospital. In spite of the title of the article it was not critical of psychiatry or psychiatrists, but gave voice to a desperate sense of the need for treatment of the difficult cases that found their way to this clinic, where often the diagnosis alone was all that could be given them. She describes *herself* in this paper when, in answer to the psychiatrist's "Oh, you can't do much harm and you may do some good. Go ahead. Do anything you like" she writes of the social worker who "finds herself in the position of doing the work of the psychiatrist in the life of this patient because it is impossible for the patient to be abandoned, and because the psychiatrist cannot follow the patient into his home to bring about the conditions which, theoretically, he believes might stimulate this shut-in individual to a renewal of his attack on reality."

Jessie Taft never hesitated to follow these patients into the home for whatever it took to help them renew their "attack on reality." She did not preserve any record of these cases, but some of them live in my memory as they lived with us in actuality in the years 1916 to 1918. Some showed "startling results" quickly, but with the more obdurate ones her patience and ingenuity in trying one approach after another were inexhaustible. For a girl with a diagnosis of beginning dementia praecox who refused to talk, she set up a schedule of daily walks and pursued this regularly until communication was established between them. This girl married later and for many years kept in touch with her social worker by letters and Christmas gifts. For another brilliant girl, who was threatening suicide in high school, she gave her own intense life and positive conviction to pull her out of her depression and later helped arrange for a college education for her, using the first money that came to her by inheritance from her father's will. There were failures, of course, and from them we both learned something about the strength and unmoving determination of the neurotic will. For the life and belief in life that radiated from Jessie Taft acted like a magnet on the negative neurotic will, and she had not learned how to protect herself from this projection.

While she was working intensively with individual cases, she was searching for another way of helping the children who were referred to the Cornell Children's Clinic because of their inability to adjust in school. It seemed to her that a change of environment instead of individual treatment was of first importance, and with the help of the psychiatrist in the Children's Clinic she developed a plan which won the support and cooperation of the Public Education Association and Hartley House Settlement. The small Farm School that she established in New Jersey convenient to New York City took children referred by the Children's Clinic, by the Visiting Teachers Association, and by Hartley Settlement, and accomplished a remarkable change in some of these children. The school closed when the consulting psychiatrist had to leave for war duty, but not before it had accomplished its purpose as an experimental school.

In the final report which Jessie Taft gave to the Committee on Mental Hygiene of the State Charities Aid Association at the time of her resignation in 1918, she described the accomplishment of the Farm School experiment. In this report she said in part:

I would like to tell you, if I can, two things this experiment has meant to me. First, one of the most important things is not so much to help individual children—we could always have done that—but this kind of a plan meant that nine well-equipped people, nine trained workers already in the schools, got as much as we could give them of our point of view. Nine teachers went with Dr. Blumgart once a month to the School, and those were fine meetings. A spirit of give and take prevailed, and I believe we all learned more than we ever expected to learn about what we could do for children who are making difficulties in school. I think we started something we did not see the end of. We started nine people doing mental hygiene work for us in schools and that is something.

There was one thing we found out, and that was that it is not as difficult as we thought to change children. I had a feeling that perhaps we could not do anything with them, that it would take so much work on each child that we simply could not give it; that it was almost a hopeless task to put the amount of time required on each individual case. As a matter of fact, we found that ten out of eleven children from two to six months away from their old environment, with a reasonable amount of effort, actually changed their attitude, so that it was not an insoluble problem. . . . If you can supply the right attitude on the part of the person who is in charge of the child, you can get a change in that child's conduct and we did that. . . .

It seems to me that if it is possible to do that in a limited experiment like this we have found one way to get at the whole problem of the neurotic child in the school. It is not a hopeless problem. It is a problem of educating teachers to an entirely different attitude toward the children they teach.

Two years with the Mental Hygiene Committee of the New York State Charities Aid Association had given Jessie Taft invaluable experience with the mental hygiene movement and social work. The necessity of closing the Farm School with the withdrawal for war service of Dr. Leonard Blumgart, the psychiatrist whose part in the development of the program had been so valuable, was an important factor in her own decision to resign in the year 1918. We were both looking for the job opportunity where we could be together, and which would offer a permanent commitment for our interests and abilities. In search of this I had left the position with the Public Education Association in New York and accepted a job with Carson College, a new institution to be developed for orphan girls in Flourtown, Pennsylvania, near Philadelphia. It soon became apparent that there was no function I could fill before the institution was ready to take children, and I was glad to accept for the spring semester of 1918 a position on the staff of the Pennsylvania School of Social Work, whose small staff had been drawn off into war work. I soon found in the School all the challenge and opportunity I could ask for my teaching interest, and in the Philadephia social work community I found promise as a place where we could live and work together. From several opportunities open in Philadelphia, Jessie Taft decided on one offered by the Seybert Foundation for a mental hygienist to work with its children in shelter care. In preparing herself for a position as mental hygienist she saw the advantage that a psychologist's training in the techniques of mental testing could give her and seized the opportunity to get this experience under the competent supervision of Dr. Mabel Fernald at the Laboratory of Social Hygiene in Bedford Hills, New York. She worked six months from the Laboratory headquarters gaining experience in testing girls from a number of institutions—hard, gruelling work but invaluable training and discipline.

Many changes in circumstances and in herself combined to make the summer of 1918 a critical one for her. The change in herself, a fundamental change of commitment and direction, focused in the summer school of the Smith College training course for psychiatric social workers in August, 1918, where she was asked to speak and to present a case. I was spending my vacation month of August with my parents in California and was out of reach of mail while returning to Philadelphia by way of a stopover in Louisville, Kentucky. Among the very few letters I have saved in my life I find three from her written just before and after her speech at Smith. These letters were sent in one bundle to reach me in Louisville. Their very appearance, written in pencil on any paper that was available, reveals the intensity of the pressures within her.

The first letter, on paper bearing the letterhead of Hartley House Settlement where she was living in 1918, is dated "Monday before Smith." After a complaint about the problem of communication between us (between New York and California), "no letters for several days then three from you in one day" she goes on:

> I am all played out again tonight. No reason. But I'm simply exhausted. Just can't write you the letter I want to. And here it is Monday night and I haven't touched

the record of Margaret yet. Got a very nice note from Mrs. R—— asking me to spend the weekend (I can't) and telling me that all the students are at sea on the mental side of casework—says Miss Jarrett doesn't touch it. Wish I could do it right but I feel so limp and helpless. I'm so tired of the mess in my mind. I get such terrific organic reactions. . . .

I think my general state now is partly due to dreading and yet wanting to go to Smith. I have felt so miserable physically, but that may be effect and not cause. I feel so cowardly and good for nothing. But I brace up soon. It isn't like this all the time.

I am so glad to write to Louisville—that at least isn't off the earth. What would writing to Europe be?

The second letter dated Tuesday night begins:

Feel much better. Not nearly so gloomy. Feel as if I might tackle Smith with some courage. Certainly was all in last night though.

This has been a funny week. Every connection I ever had has turned up—I mean all the very personal ones. Today Miss T——[a staff member at Bedford Reformatory] is on her way to Europe. I had a most unusual time with her. Something has changed her. All at once after all these years she was able to talk, freely without embarrassment, and for the first time I felt not self-conscious and uncomfortable with her. It was as if something greater than her own self-consciousness had come in and taken possession. She spoke frankly of her nervousness—her sense of inferiority—her feeling for me—her desire to get hold of herself and make something of herself—all so simply that I was touched as I seldom have been. I felt ashamed that I had never had the courage or the interest to break down the barrier and help her. I could have, for my own attitude was sure. I went away feeling very solemn inside and very much under obligation to be the kind of person these people need since I seem to be able to reach them. Don't laugh at me. It isn't conceit but a tremendous reverence for this thing that seems to have been given to me. Here too is N—— who, with all I have done that was thoughtless and inconsiderate, still says I have helped—that she can at least talk a little—isn't so repressed. She talked almost freely, but she is so restless and unhappy. Wants and wants and wants and gets nothing. Her work at summer school gave her nothing. Psychiatry helped not at all—she got nothing real or life-giving. She wants to see me. I've promised to see everybody I know next week! . . .

I have finally begun on Margaret's record. I am much in the dark but am trusting the Lord—I know I can tell them something when the time comes. Wish I had your criticism of my presentation. The case is so involved— hard to separate the different factors. Margaret herself is in fine shape—more than coming along.

I'll write you all about Smith and put all my letters together and send them when you start Friday so that they will be waiting for you in Louisville. Tell me about when and where to meet you in Philadelphia. Are you coming Friday or Saturday? I can come any time.

The third letter, dated "on the train back from Smith"

I just can't wait to see you and I just can't spoil all my wonderful experiences by trying to write them—want to tell it all—will take hours too. So excited!

Smith was a success in every way beyond my wildest dreams. And all the Philadelphia students spoke to me about how they like you and how glad they will be to have Miss Robinson and Miss Taft for their "guides" next year. . . .

A few pages were added after she got back to Hartley House and found my letters. The letter ends:

> Where are my letters anyway? I write every other day at least. Now I'll pick up a few bits from your letters. Isn't it great about the School. I'm not sure I wouldn't rather run the School with you than do the shelter job for Seybert. I am so excited about teaching since Smith that I can hardly refrain. It is going to be a fine opportunity for you. [This evidently refers to the fact that I had been offered and had accepted the assistant directorship of the School.]
>
> I'll meet you Saturday at Broad Street Station any time and let's stay somewhere where we can talk before we join K. and E. We'll look for a house this weekend.

This ended a year of separation that had been difficult for both of us. We stayed at the old College Club in Philadelphia at 13th and Spruce Streets until we found an apartment at 1700 Pine Street, an easy walk to the Pennsylvania School of Social Work then located in an old house at 1302 Pine Street, and not far by trolley from the building where Jessie Taft was to set up the Seybert School on Poplar Street. From this point on our professional association was close and uninterrupted.

To balance the impression that her letters of 1918 describing the summer school at Smith College convey of the change that was going on in her, the paper which she delivered the following year to the National Conference of Social Work in June, 1919, on the "Qualifications of the Psychiatric Social Worker" is important. It bears witness to the assurance and authority with which she had accepted herself as a "mental hygienist" with responsibility for clarifying the relation between casework and psychiatry and for the development of training for psychiatric social workers. She describes this meeting in a paper written in 1926. Delivered at a meeting of the New York State Conference of Charities and Corrections to honor Clifford Beers and his relation to the mental hygiene movement, it recalls her own association with that movement in vivid autobiographical detail. This paper follows, quoted in full up to the point where she left New York for Philadelphia to work as a mental hygienist with children.

The Relation of Psychiatry to Social Work

IT IS NOT OFTEN that one has the experience of witnessing the birth of an epoch-making movement. One hundred years from now the story of the beginning of mental hygiene will be a vital chapter in the history of our culture.

Like the veteran of a great war, one cannot help feeling childishly important at possessing memories of leaders and critical events. Moreover, there is a fascinating illusion of power in looking back, panoramic fashion, over a bit of history with which one has been sufficiently intimate to be able to follow the pattern unguided. One's sense of belonging to the process and knowing its inner reality is so strong that one begins to feel creatively responsible.

Mr. Beers will forgive me if I begin with mental hygiene when I first knew it, some years after the founding of the first mental hygiene society, when it had begun to show the effect of the combined efforts of psychiatry and social work. At that time it was concerned chiefly with those larger social problems in which psychiatry and social work were equally interested—the aftercare of the mentally ill, the outpatient mental clinic, the relation of mental defect to delinquency, and the allied problems of social

Read at the New York City Conference of Charities and Corrections, May 12, 1926.

56

hygiene, alcoholism, and syphilis. All the early activities centered about institutions—the psychopathic hospital, the hospital for the insane, the school for feebleminded, the prison, the reformatory, the court. This was the day of the eugenics fieldworker with her elaborate charts and her mass of unanalyzed, unassimilated facts, gathered in the hills and backwoods of Dutchess County or some other spot where Jukes and Kallikaks abounded, at great risk of limb and loss of shoeleather. She was perhaps a prehistoric form of what we now call the psychiatric social worker, although she seems to us to have had very little understanding either of psychiatry or social work.

The immediate ancestor of the psychiatric social worker is to be found in a small group of not more than half a dozen persons, among whom I have the honor to be numbered, who were sometimes called mental hygiene workers. They were located in Boston, New York, Baltimore, and Chicago. They worked under psychiatrists in the social supervision of clinic or hospital patients in the community. Miss Jarrett in Boston, Miss Tucker and myself in New York, Miss Thompson in Chicago, are the only ones I am sure of as existing in this dawning period of mental hygiene, but I doubt not that there were one or two others.

There were at this time, about twelve years ago, only three or four centers where psychiatry and social work were undertaking a joint program. In Boston, Dr. E. E. Southard and Miss Mary Jarrett were engaged in a systematic attempt to relate the psychiatric and social factors in the preventive social treatment of borderline mental conditions and the aftercare of more serious cases. Here was built up the most technical, specialized social case-work in connection with psychiatry that appears in this early period, the casework which was largely responsible for the birth of psychiatric social work.

In New York another emphasis was given to the mental hygiene movement by the very different psychiatric view-point which prevailed. Dr. Adolf Meyer and Dr. August Hoch, and later Dr. C. Macfie Campbell and Dr. Thomas Salmon, were among the first to offer vital interpretations of personality and behavior to those who were trying to solve social problems. The Mental Hygiene Committee of the State Charities Aid Association carried on its educa-tional propaganda for mental hygiene, for parole and social service in state hospitals, and for adequate institutions, under the inspiration of this teaching. To Cornell Clinic of Psychopathology, where Dr. Hoch and his staff from the Psychiatric Institute were trying to treat patients in the light of their newer psychology and understanding of mental difficulties, this Committee contributed a social worker as demonstration of the value of social casework in a psychiatric clinic. Miss Katharine Tucker initiated this program, and I was her successor in 1915.

It was inevitable, with the interest in psychological interpretation which animated this group of psychiatrists, that their peculiar contribution to social psychiatry should have been on the side of a dynamic interpretation of be-havior, a method of approach to human beings, applicable to all casework and not confined to the development of a specialized form of social treatment for mental patients. They were interested in relating (rather than in separat-ing normal and abnormal) and therefore conceived of mental health as the concern of every human being. If Boston set the pattern of psychiatric social work, New York put the stamp of its psychiatric thought upon the psychology which was to be the chief tool of the modern caseworker.

From Washington were coming the publications of Dr. White which have so profoundly affected mental hygiene theory and practice; but so far as I know, there was never any overt combination with social work in that city.

In Chicago, Healy had begun, as early as 1909, his investigation of the Individual Delinquent in connection with the Juvenile Court.

Dr. Bernard Glueck was already working within the prison walls to bring psychiatric understanding to bear upon the problems of criminology; and there had been established at Bedford, under Katherine Bement Davis in 1913, one of the first well-rounded attempts to study every aspect of delinquency. The Laboratory of Social Hygiene, as it was called, was a forerunner of the child guidance clinics in its insistence upon a well-rounded diagnostic study. The staff included a psychiatrist, a psychologist, a sociologist, and social workers, or fieldworkers as they were first called. Its failure to develop was due to the failure of the reformatory situation to allow for treatment after diagnosis was complete.

Well do I remember the awe with which we gazed upon Hoch, Meyer, and Salmon when they appeared at Bedford for the first meeting of the Laboratory advisory board, and how we treasured every word of the discussion. Those of you who have always known a human psychology, who have been nurtured on our modern psychiatric viewpoint, will never know the thrill of the first mental hygiene pamphlets to one who had had only academic training. That plain little pamphlet of Hoch's on *The Manageable Causes of Insanity,* bringing mental disease into the realm of the knowable, was the key to an undiscovered country, a promised land indeed to some of us who had been groping in the dust of the academic desert.

Meyer's early paper with its involved title, suggesting the connection between unfavorable personality traits in early life and the later development of a psychosis, was another beacon light. You who are flooded with literature on every phase of mental health cannot imagine how we cherished those early papers. I can remember the first time I ever heard Dr. Salmon speak; and what I carried away from that meeting, a commonplace in our teaching today, was the thrilling realization that every kind of behavior, no matter how bizarre, is an attempt at adjustment.

With those few but pregnant crumbs of a new psychology as a basis, I wrote my first speech on mental hygiene. It was a painful but profound experience. The result was long and labored, and quite unrelated to the needs of the audience, but it had the glow of a religious conversion and the audience responded sympathetically to the sincerity of my emotion.

If you would trace the growth of these beginnings, the gradual but steady deepening of the relation between psychiatry and social work, go to the reports of the National Conference of Social Work. You will be amazed to find how the focus of interest has shifted, how the terminology has changed, how the psychology of social casework has been transformed in the last ten years. In 1914,

1915, and 1916 there were sections on Defectives and The State Care of the Insane and Feebleminded. Mental hygiene was mentioned chiefly with regard to mental defect and there was a beginning of emphasis on prevention of mental disease. Alcoholism, drug addiction, syphilis, social hygiene, and delinquency were in the foreground of discussion. Dr. Healy appeared on a National Conference program in 1914 to tell about his work with young offenders. Meyer, Goddard, Davenport, and Southard appeared in 1915 to talk about the prevention of mental disease and defect, and a program for state care.

It was not until 1917, when the Great War set the problem and the task, that there was such a thing as a Mental Hygiene section at the Conference. The problems of the war absorbed most of the attention of National Conferences for two years. The most significant result of this critical period for social casework was the opening of the first training course for psychiatric social work at Smith College in the summer of 1918. For the first time, thanks to the unwearied efforts of Miss Jarrett and Dr. Southard, psychiatry made a definite attempt to express its contribution to training in a systematic form.

Atlantic City in 1919 was a landslide for mental hygiene: the Conference was swept off its feet. In every section, psychiatrists appeared on the program. The psychiatric social worker was present in person for the first time and violent indeed was the discussion which raged about her devoted head—what should be her training, what her personality, and what the limitations of her province? Should she remain forever different from every other caseworker or should every other caseworker be reborn in her likeness? That was the meeting which burst its bounds and had to be transferred to a church a block away. Dignified psychiatrists and social workers climbed out of windows in order to make sure of a good seat. Was it the emotion engendered by the war, the brilliance of Atlantic City sunshine, or a Boardwalk encounter with a great psychiatrist who dropped a word of encouragement, which makes the Conference of 1919 so radiant in my memory?

Underneath the war fever and the excitement over the advent of the psychiatric social worker, a new note was sounded at Atlantic City, a note prophetic of the next step, the new focus of psychiatric and casework interest on the mental health of the child, the maladjusted schoolchild, the delinquent child, the placed-out child.

Most of us here tonight have no illusions as to the adequacy of our insight into the problems of children, and the sureness of our skill in solving them, but I wonder how many of you have any conception of the depths of ignorance which prevailed in 1917, 1918, and 1919. The family caseworker was aware of children in bunches; she seldom stopped to individualize. The children's worker was beginning to find social history very important, but had little time to get acquainted with the child himself. The visiting teacher perhaps came the nearest to knowing what her young clients were like. As the caseworker began to realize the presence of the psychiatrist and the mental clinic, and as the conviction of the importance of the child's personality grew, she hastened to present the problem child to the psychiatrist, who at that early period was about as much at a loss as she. Do you realize that there were hardly more than two psychiatrists in the country in 1917 who were familiar with children? As far as I know, Campbell and Healy held undisputed possession of the field.

I can remember my own discovery of children, the thought of something young, unformed, unmarred, with whom mental health was as possible of attainment as physical health. What an escape from the intolerable situation of the adult with his fixed ideas and habits! Why spend one's life trying to make over a bad job when children are at hand to be guided into the kingdom of good adjustment? In the inspiration of this new and boundless horizon, I wrote my first paper about mental health for children. Again my own enthusiasm and the ignorance of the audience concealed successfully the pitiful lack of concrete content. Mr. Folks, who read the paper, remarked mildly that I had used a good many words. I knew he was right; I couldn't go behind those words and produce realities, but I felt sure the reality must be there if only I could get to it, and I made up my mind then and there never to give up until those empty words came alive.

PART III

Philadelphia and Children's Work

1918-1934

When Jessie Taft came in the fall of 1918 to the Seybert Institution in Philadelphia to be director of a new Department of Child Study, one of the most important pieces of equipment she had to offer in the eyes of the board and perhaps of the community was her training and experience in psychological testing, acquired in 1917 under the direction of Dr. Mabel Fernald of the Laboratory of Social Hygiene at Bedford Hills, New York. It was at this point that she used her title of "doctor" by which she has been known ever since.

The eagerness of Philadelphia agencies and institutions to use not only this specialized diagnostic technique for its children but all she had to give in understanding of their problems and of mental hygiene, the "new psychology," is evidenced in her many speaking engagements and consultative appointments with agency directors about their problem children. The most immediately pressing problem concerned the children under care of the temporary shelter while awaiting placement by the Children's Bureau. To Dr. Taft, fresh from her experience in seeing the progress made in understanding and helping difficult children in the Farm School she had conducted while at the State Charities Aid Association of New York, a school for these children immediately suggested itself. It would serve three purposes, her report to the Seybert Board states: "First, giving occupation and instruction to children who are being deprived of school by their detention in the shelter; second, furnishing the best possible laboratory for observing the actual conduct of the children under special study; third, offering a place where the difficult child, under careful guidance and understanding, might be straightened out before any attempt should be made to place him."

In spite of the obstacles created by the war and a serious influenza epidemic, a school was opened on December 2, 1918, in the building at 1612 Poplar Street offered by Howard Institution which was closing its service. The fifteen girls then in the institution had to be planned for by Dr. Taft and the Children's Bureau supervisor, and the building had to be made ready for its new uses. In spite of the scarcity of teachers, three teachers were found who were exceptionally fitted for the unusual purposes of this school. A man and his wife were engaged to care for the building, and a secretary for the director was employed. All the staff were chosen for their interest in children and a willingness to make the work fit the needs of the children regardless of conventional standards. Even the bus driver engaged to bring the children to school was a woman whose relation to children made a unique contribution on which the staff as well as the children relied.

The school opened with fifteen children, five girls and ten boys, ranging in age from six to twelve. The children helped unpack and arrange material and enjoyed painting their own desks and chairs. The group shifted constantly, and the shelter was frequently in quarantine, so that it was impossible to plan a school program that had any continuity. For this reason, at the end of a year and a half, in July 1920, the board and Dr. Taft somewhat reluctantly decided that it would be wiser to close the school and develop the mental hygiene service of the clinic of the Children's Bureau. Two hundred and sixty-five children had been studied. In her closing report Dr. Taft says:

> Finally, if we had been impressed by anything in our year's experience it is this: how little anyone really knows about children; how seldom we stop to see them as they are, rather than as objects to be changed by us into something easier to manage; and how pitifully easy it is in the majority of cases to get immediate response and magical transformations as soon as a little understanding and encouragement is provided.

A brief paper published in *Cooperation* in January, 1920, describes "Methods of Observation in the Seybert School"; a longer paper published in *Modern Medicine* in 1920, and abstracted in *Mental Hygiene,* shows pictures of the children in school activities and gives the history of two boys and their change of attitude in the school environment.

A National Conference paper delivered in the Children's Section at Atlantic City in 1919, the same year as her historic speech, "Qualifications of the Psychiatric Social Worker," also makes use of her experience with children in The Seybert School. Her penciled note in the margin of her only copy of this paper entitled, "Relation of Personality Study to Child Placing," reads: "Of historical interest. The first paper of its kind in the Children's Section of the National Conference."

The Department of Child Study which soon became a joint department of the Children's Bureau and the Children's Aid Society, was set up in 1920, with Dr. Taft as director, Dr. Edward Strecker as consulting psychiatrist, and an assistant psychologist. It served not only the children of these two agencies but offered also an extension service to Carson College for Orphan Girls and to Sleighton Farm, and advice and study of problem children to the House of the Holy Child, the Juvenile Aid Society, Presbyterian Orphanage, and other agencies.

There seemed to be no limit to the interest of the director in children or to her willingness to respond to any group that turned to her for help in understanding their problems. Not only social workers but teachers, nurses, and parents were eager for more understanding of children and mental hygiene. Many talks were informal and unpublished, but among those published appeared articles in *Proceedings of the National Conference of Social Work, The Survey, The Family,* and *Mental Hygiene;* papers in other professional magazines such as the *American Journal of Sociology, Modern Medicine, School and Society, Progressive Education,* and the *American Journal of Psychiatry;* and many in popular magazines. There were institutes of several days duration, one in Texas and a two-week summer school at the University of Maine in 1920. She was asked to speak in a symposium on social aspects of mental hygiene given at Yale, and her paper entitled "Mental Hygiene and Social Work" appeared in the volume published by Yale University Press in 1925.

One particularly interesting paper for that period, commissioned by the Bureau of Children of the Pennsylvania

Department of Welfare, "Some Undesirable Habits and Suggestions as to Treatment," had a wide circulation. A 1941-reprint published by *Mental Hygiene* with the "courtesy of the Department of Welfare, Pennsylvania," is marked ninth printing.

The Department of Child Study became increasingly the dynamic center for the growth of the Children's Aid Society of Pennsylvania, and Dr. Taft's influence in that agency itself, on administrative structures and staff workers as well as on children, is apparent in the reports of the department. Her report for the year 1925 described this process:

> The taking over of the entire responsibility for the Child Study Department by the Children's Aid Society came about as the inevitable result of a steady growth in the use of the department by the agency. This growth has taken place not merely in terms of numbers of children going through Child Study but in the quality of casework on every child, in the meaning of Child Study for every function of the agency from reception to placement. Child Study is counted on to take its share in staff training and education, to assist in the problems of home finding, to help out with difficult foster parents as well as difficult children, in short to make its contribution effective in every part of the child-placing process.

The report concludes with:

> The department is gratified with the educational work it has been able to carry out during the year, including nine courses ranging from two to twelve periods, twenty single lectures, and two reprints. The most important step has been the taking on of responsibility for staff

education resulting in a weekly seminar conference with the supervisors, and a weekly class on behavior problems with the visitors. It is more valuable to Children's Aid to have a staff with an adequate understanding of child psychology than to have every child examined in Child Study, and most important of all is that through visitors with such understanding we should reach the foster mothers who make a vital difference in the child's adjustment.

Writing in *Children's Aid News* of September, 1934, on the occasion of Dr. Taft's resignation from the Children's Aid to join the faculty of the School of Social Work, Mr. Edwin Solenberger, then general secretary of the agency, commented: "To fully describe the great contribution made by Dr. Taft during the past fifteen years in the development of our methods and standards would be to write an interpretative history of our growth as an agency during this period."

It speaks of Dr. Taft's trust in this child-placing process, and my own as well, that in 1921 we decided to take a child into our own home, at first on a boarding basis, but looking to adoption if all went well. It was our good friend Sophie Theis, head of the child-placing department in the State Charities Aid Association of New York, veteran child placer, and a genius in fitting unusual homes to extraordinary children, who encouraged us to risk it and who found for us a nine-year-old boy whose circumstances made him difficult to place in the ordinary home with father and mother. Later she found a girl going on six, not free for adoption at that time, and with relatives who wanted to keep in touch with her. To care for the boy we had to have a house, and it was a pure magic of circumstances that there came for sale in Flourtown a house which we were able to finance with the help of friends and "Building and Loan." It lay on an almost uninhabited road, with a coalyard on one side, a church and graveyard in back, a stretch of cornfields across the road, and offered enough ground for a garden. Carson College for Orphan Girls was nearby, as was the house where Elsa Ueland, its President, and Katharine Tucker, Director of the Visiting Nurse Society of Philadelphia, lived with two children, one a boy from the Children's Aid Society who had been placed in this home by Dr. Taft. The children and their relationships to each other and to other children were endlessly absorbing to us. We learned from them while we gave them the best we had of ourselves and our resources. At the same time our stake in our jobs, in the School of Social Work as well as in the Children's Aid Society for Dr. Taft, was deepening with every year. In retrospect I do not know how we managed the demands on our time and attention, and the excitement and concern with which we lived.

There is no doubt that this experience in adopting children contributes to Dr. Taft's paper, "What It Means to Be a Foster Parent," written for *Progressive Education* in 1926, as well as to an article appearing in *The Delineator* of September, 1933, "The Adopted Child," which enunciates her philosophy of growth in one brief paragraph:

> If you ask me finally whether it is really safe to adopt a child, I must answer, "No." It is not safe to adopt and

it is not safe to bear a child. There is no safety which can .
be guaranteed in advance to the fearful parents of own
or adopted children; only the normal, average possibility,
which is all we have the right to expect: that a child
whom we love wisely, and allow to grow freely, will
finally develop away from home ties into independent,
courageous manhood or womanhood.

Side by side with the positive affirmation of her belief
in children, in their individuality and possibilities for
constructive growth with casework help, expressed in the
many papers and speeches of this period, there is evidence
of her struggle to understand what went on in office contacts between a child and herself functioning as mental
hygienist in the child-placing agency. Two papers describe
this problem and affirm the value of the office interview
and the importance of having a person on the agency
staff who can function in this way for the child, "someone
who sits a little apart, . . . someone in whom the bewildered child may find the impersonal security he needs."
These two papers were both National Conference papers,
only three years apart in time, but much further apart
than that in grasp and comprehension of the problem.
The first was written shortly after she had heard Rank
speak to a psychoanalytic meeting in Atlantic City, and
was delivered at the National Conference of Social Work
in Toronto in June, 1924, where Rank also read a paper.
There is no doubt that at this time she was beginning to
consider the possibility of analysis for herself as a way of
learning more about how to use "the transfer" effectively
in her office contacts with children. But it was two years
before she made arrangements for this analytic experience

to begin with Rank in the fall of 1926. The second paper, "The Function of a Mental Hygienist in a Children's Agency," was written in 1927, shortly after her analysis was completed, and delivered to a National Conference in Des Moines in 1927. In it she is subjecting all her training and practice to examination in the light of the revelation that her analysis and contact with Rank's thinking had given her.

Problems of Social Casework
with Children

THIS PAPER will assume casework to mean social treatment of a maladjusted individual involving an attempt to understand his personality, behavior, and social relationships, and to assist him in working out a better social and personal adjustment. Treatment may depend largely upon the obtaining of better environmental conditions, it may center upon bringing about changes in point of view and behavior, or it may involve both in equal degree. In any case the main problem is psychological, in the sense of a practical understanding of the meaning of certain kinds of behavior and the probable effect upon it of the changing of the social situation. Needless to say, successful casework will depend not only on the psychological insight but on the practical knowledge and handling of every available social resource.

Social casework in this sense is applicable to every individual, child or adult, who is not as well adjusted as his own happiness or the welfare of society demands. It has nothing to do with the problem of relief as such. It does not depend primarily upon our economic system and would be as useful to the socialistic as to the capitalistic state. The rich need it quite as much as the poor and the

Paper read at the Mental Hygiene Section of the National Conference of Social Work, New Orleans, April, 1920.

good often quite as much as the delinquent. In short, in the last analysis, the real casework is nothing but the practical application of mental hygiene to individuals who need it, no matter where they may be found. Some of us are sufficiently adjusted, understand ourselves sufficiently well, to need only the help of friends in untangling our difficulties. Others of us need more professional help from the caseworker, who combines with her experience in human psychology the practical ability to make the social resources responsive to our needs. Still others of us are so crippled by a long history of bad adjustment and lack of understanding of our own behavior that the insight and skill of the psychiatrist are required to set us straight before any external adjustment is possible. The work that is done here all along the line is casework. From the normal to the most abnormal client there is no break, only a gradually increasing difficulty and complexity requiring a steadily increasing knowledge and skill to deal with it. The social caseworker thus far has specialized in the manipulation of environmental factors and social resources. She is now realizing that casework is always fundamentally psychological or, if you please, psychiatric, even when it is applied to the so-called normal person, and that environment is never external to the psychology of the client.

Social casework as applied to children is, as yet, rather rare except in a few of the most advanced and highly socialized centers. Treating a child with as much respect and regard for his personality as if he were an adult is a very new attitude in children's work—as new as mental hygiene itself. Yet this is what social casework with children implies.

* * * * * *

Here, [in the dependent group] it seems to me, is the ideal group in which to begin real social casework as applied to children. Every variety of problem is presented, and we set our own social conditions. There could be no more suitable field for studying human behavior and attempting to work out good adjustments between the individual and society in their very beginnings. Moreover, it is in this field that the most intelligent and painstaking casework with children is now being done. It is not to be found except in a few of our most progressive child-placing agencies, but it does exist and where it exists produces most enlightening and satisfactory results which can be used in all children's work. It is upon the field of child placing, therefore, that I have drawn for the material of this discussion on the problems of casework with children.

These problems can be divided into two groups: problems of traditional attitude and inadequate psychology, and problems of practical resources for social treatment. In a sense they are one and the same, for it is the lack of understanding of children, the rigidity of attitude toward them on the part of the home, the foster home, the agency, the institution, and the school that makes the actually available resources of so little help. Moreover a different attitude would of itself tend to create more and better resources, because it would feel the need which is now not recognized even by the more enlightened public. The most difficult problem for the caseworker with children and the one which must be solved and resolved from day to day is, therefore, first, the problem of acquiring a new attitude backed by an elastic psychology which shapes itself through actual concrete experiences with children, and is ever self-critical and open to new material; and second, the problem of getting enough of this attitude and this psychology across to teachers, parents, institutions, and foster parents to be able to carry through the social treatment.

Perhaps our greatest handicap as adults in dealing with children is our proclivity for rationalizing both our own and the child's psychology. That, combined with our conventional morality, works the greatest havoc in child life. We like to think of ourselves as primarily rational, intellectual beings as far removed as possible from impulsive and emotional reactions. We like to think of our conduct as being under rational control, and we deceive ourselves very much on that score. We blind ourselves to the primary importance of the dynamic wish, the will to live, or whatever you choose to call the energic basis of human life. We think of ourselves as acting for the good of society, as choosing this rather than that plan on a purely intellectual basis, as living on the whole the life of reason undisturbed by emotional influences. There are always good explanations for our failures, reasons why we could not be expected to do thus-and-so on that particular occasion. We are late because an unavoidable delay occurred at home, not because we lingered ten minutes too long in a comfortable bed. We missed church because we really felt a cold coming on, and it was a bad day.

Now, while we maintain this theory of conduct for ourselves, we do not as a rule enforce it rigidly. We allow ourselves lapses and we pretty much get the things we want, all on a perfectly rational basis. But, alas! When we turn this attitude on children, unless we have a sense of humor or a vivid imagination, there is nothing to check our rationalization as *we* do not feel the prick of the child's desires and thwarted impulses. We become consistent and make practice conform to theory, as far as we can. We see the child externally, as an object which ought to be trained to behave rationally. Through him we expiate our own human weaknesses. He is the scapegoat. In him our frailties shall be corrected. He shall be trained for virtue, to meet the hard things of life. He shall be punctual, neat, clean, industrious, interested in whatever is put before him, fond of the work the adult gives him, ready to play only at the proper time and prompt to leave that play, however crucial the moment, at the call of bedtime or mealtime. He shall not eat too much or what is not good for him, he shall be taught never to save himself from discomfort by a lie, or gain a coveted object by taking things belonging to other people. He shall be cheerful, obedient, respectful, free from outbursts of temper, jealousy, and selfishness at all times—and above all, regarding that fundamental instinct by which the whole world continues to live, and its particular set of organs in his own body, he shall evince no curiosity. The child, by virtue of his helplessness and natural inferiority, tends to make arbitrary, autocratic rulers of us all. We can do with him what we will and, as adults, are always right. Too often our discipline of the child or interference with his activity is based not on its inherent harmfulness but on its relation to our personal comfort and the ease with which we dominate the situation. *We* can have our way but he can't have his. Too often the controversy between teacher and pupil or housemother and child becomes a

mere contest of wills, with no inherent virtue on either
side, only the deep and rationalistic conviction on the
part of the adult that it is fatal to the child's welfare not
to have the adult come out victorious. We take too lightly
the child's own interests, and the work quality involved
in their pursuit. We do not respect his so-called play, which
we interrupt so often at our own convenience. We ignore
the dynamic force of the child's desires and the inevitability of their finding some form of expression. We do not
recognize his need to gain a sense of power, to experience
success and superiority, and sometimes to be right when
the adult is wrong. The real explanation and understanding of conduct in terms of his wants and feelings will not
be apparent until the child becomes in our eyes a *person*,
worthy of the same respectful consideration which we give
to an adult.

The records of children's agencies are full of this lack
of understanding. Conventional adult morality and adult
interpretation of conduct in external terms, classified and
labeled for all time, is rife in these records. Little Mary
who is five is put down as sexually immoral, because, for-
sooth, led on by an older girl, she became interested in
her own anatomy. Johnny who, strangely enough, has a
taste for sweets and no pecuniary means to gratify it, is
called a thief because the cooky jar and cake box are not
safe from his depredations. Johnny's own mother would
expect him to visit the cooky jar. The foster mother or
the institution matron has a different point of view. There
is no instinctive emotional response here to modify the
rationalistic view of child behavior. Alice, just arrived at
the mature age of six, is damned forever as lazy and a

poor worker because she shows no evidence of enjoying dishwashing or preferring it to playing dolls. When Sammy has done something for which punishment has been promised, Sammy, most surprisingly, will deny it to the bitter end. The truth is not in him. Susie, who is a foundling, is a terrible storyteller. She invents tales of her rich, powerful relatives when everybody knows she was left on a doorstep. And so it goes, page after page, bearing testimony to the impeccable standards of the adult and the inherent sinfulness of the child. The real problem for casework here is to learn how to get records of children that will really contribute to an understanding of them.

In reporting on a child's conduct, the average matron, foster mother, or teacher gives, not a description of a specific behavior but a judgment of the child, a complete classification of his nature, good for all time and predetermining his future conduct. What we have is not an account of Johnny's finding a penny on a mantelpiece the day he especially wanted a certain marble in the corner store, but a labeling of Johnny's inner nature, an identification of Johnny with an abhorrent act. Gradually but inevitably Johnny becomes "the kind of boy who takes things." Thus our records tend to be condemnatory moral judgments rather than scientific descriptions of child behavior.

Why do we have such difficulties in observing and reporting a child's behavior? Isn't it because we fail so often to make understanding the child, rather than the success of our own ideas, our real purpose? Just the genuine acceptance of that purpose and the change of attitude it involves will do more than any other one thing to help us solve our case problems. That which brings out our judgmental attitude, our resentment or disapproval, is conduct on the part of the child that interferes with our purposes. Mrs. Brown has taken Mary into her home, not to help Mary solve her life problems but to have some one to stay with the baby when she is out. Mrs. Brown means well by Mary. She will give her a good home, but when Mary fails to be reliable with the baby, Mrs. Brown's fundamental purpose is thwarted. Condemnation of Mary is inevitable. Mary is reported to the visitor as an unreliable child who is not to be trusted with babies. Miss Jones' job is to teach so much arithmetic in a given time and maintain order in her room. Jimmy is a stumbling block to the carrying out of that program. He interferes seriously with Miss Jones' purposes. Resentment, anger, disapproval of Jimmy is a natural consequence. Even the best-intentioned caseworker sometimes forgets to set her purpose in terms of understanding the child and a working out of the best possible adjustment from his point of view. She has found such a fine home for Mary. There is a big yard, a well-furnished house, considerable culture in the family; there are many educational advantages— but Mary refuses to be happy there. It is human nature to be out of patience with Mary who thus upsets all her carefully laid plans.

There is only one cure for the personal resentment, the emotional reaction, which so often vitiates our observation and treatment of children, and that is really to set up as our purpose something which cannot be interfered with by the child. There is only one purpose which answers this description, the very purpose not to put over something of our own, but to observe and to understand behavior, whether good or bad, and patiently to determine what adjustment, if any, the child is capable of making. To such a purpose Johnny in a tantrum is just as fulfilling as Johnny in an angelic mood. All is grist that comes to our mill. Johnny can no longer hurt us. It is hard to maintain this attitude. Other desires creep in and are thwarted; we react in anger or disappointment. The only salvation for us as professional caseworkers, whether with children or adults, is to represent to ourselves the fundamental object of our work whenever we fall from grace. Only in this way can we free our judgments from the taint of our own emotions and ourselves from the bitterness of disillusion.

The caseworker with dependent children faces a peculiarly difficult situation in that the dependent child by virtue of his very dependency is always potentially a behavior problem. The family background, on which the mental health of every child must largely depend, is in his case inevitably distorted. Thus at the very root of dependency is the soil of potential maladjustment. The normal child develops in strength and confidence on the basis of security and assurance that the mother and father supply. He has the possibility of achieving a wholesome and necessary sense of power because he has this stable foundation to fall back on when his sense of safety is threatened. He can be sure of his home. It will not vanish overnight. Father and mother are all-powerful and can save him from every ill. The family may oversupply the love and backing which the child demands and make a weakling of him, but on the other hand the absence of such an assurance of safety is equally fatal to the growth of normal self-confidence and free outgoing energy.

The child who lacks this fundamental protection becomes at once a prey to fear, uncertainty, and inferiority. He must always be seeking a possible shelter, always hunting a substitute for his natural love-objects, always defending himself from the exposure of his inherent weakness, and comforting himself with dreams and pretenses and substitute activities. Not that the child does these things consciously and deliberately. He can seldom explain what is back of his troublesome behavior. It is for us to re-create continually in imagination the picture of the dependent child's essential insecurity and inferiority, to understand the compensatory factor in his behavior, and work out as best we may a reasonable substitute for the family support he craves. That is why mere excellence of physical conditions is not enough—emotional needs must be met in our placements. The personal equation is more powerful than material good. The reason why Mary in the good home persists in her secretive, sullen ways, the reason why Johnny masturbates, takes things, or runs away, may easily lie just here, and these behavior problems will be solved only when their cause is understood by the worker.

Besides the sense of inadequacy which the dependent child must carry for lack of family safety and normal love, he must also suffer the social inferiority which his status entails among other children. The hunger for importance which a relative lends is pathetically obvious in a dependent group. The child who cannot add to his own glory by stories of the achievements of his relatives is terribly handicapped among his mates. Small wonder that such a child calls an inventive imagination to his aid and supplies his need as best he may with the wild romancing that goes down against him in the agency's record.

Surely nothing more is needed to add to the potential behavior problems of the dependent! And yet, as a matter of fact, two other handicaps are likely to be found in this group: a poor physical equipment due to inheritance or environment, and a leaning toward the dull normal rather than toward the superior in intelligence. This does not mean that there are no superior children among dependents; but that, taking the dependent group as a whole, we find a larger percentage of below-average and a smaller percentage of above-average children than is found in the ordinary public school. That is, the type of family which is broken up and whose children become public charges tend to be of an inferior mental and physical caliber as compared with the general population. All inferiority, family, social, physical, or mental, produces defense reactions. With a group so characterized by all these lacks, we may expect to have the most difficult and prevailing behavior problems which can be dealt with only by workers who understand the psychology involved and endeavor to provide an environment which will supply the needs in a great measure, or reduce the sense of inferiority by lowering the environmental level to meet the ability of the child.

Coming now to the question of practical resources for carrying out the casework plan with the dependent child, if we omit the medical problem, we can group most of our difficulties about two critical situations: case treatment for the problem child with good general ability, and case treatment for the child who is inferior but not defective mentally and is almost inevitably a behavior problem also. The most essential factor in the placement of the first type of child is, it seems to me, the understanding foster home; whereas the second child is more dependent upon the enlightened public school. Such a division is of course only a matter of relative importance. Both home and school are necessary in both cases for satisfactory treatment.

Treatment for the bright but difficult child means the finding of a foster mother who wants to help solve a problem, who is genuinely and objectively interested in children and would like to make her contribution to social welfare in this fashion. The woman who wants a child just to fill up her life and meet her own love needs is not the person we are after. She will resent lack of emotional response in the child, and will be hurt continually by his ingratitude and misconduct. Neither can we use the woman who wants chiefly help in the kitchen or with the children. For the difficult child will only increase her work and thwart her fundamental desire to be assisted in her labor. This too will result in anger and disapproval for the child who needs patience and reassurance. The woman who expects to be paid for her work but will look upon the child as her job, if she has the intelligence and proper personal qualifications, may be just the person we need. There is also the woman with the natural gift for managing children, who will not understand the problem in intellectual terms but will get the results. She is the born mother with the patience of Job, an intuitive understanding of the weaknesses of human nature, and a practical common sense in her methods of correcting them. No foster home will do which does not have in it a woman who will accept the child as a problem and have the patience to work at this problem instinctively or intelligently over as long a period of time as seems necessary.

Can we hope to find such women? They have been found by child-placing agencies doing the best type of work. They are not necessarily found ready-made. Some educational work in a community on the part of the agency may be necessary to uncover such homes, and the caseworker may have to develop the ideal foster mother out of raw but promising material—but that is part of her job. The casework of the child-placing agency must inevitably be done with foster parents as well as with children. The caseworker has to interpret to the home the behavior of the child, has to explain the problem, has to help over the hard places, and show the family the improvement that has already taken place, encouraging them to persist or to try other methods. With the backing of such a family atmosphere, the bright but difficult child may often be adjusted quite satisfactorily in the ordinary public school, as his troubles are not due primarily to lack of ability to do the schoolwork.

With the distinctly inferior child, no amount of home treatment can undo the effect of his inevitable and constant failure to come up to public-school standards. It is here that we get our greatest problems of delinquency, beginning and confirmed. If the case problems presented to me by child-caring agencies in Philadelphia during the past year and a half are any criteria, the crucial situation in all children's work is lack of suitable school opportunities for the dull normal child. In Philadelphia, at least, and I am sure in the vast majority of city public schools still running along conventional academic lines, there is no possibility of obtaining for the dull normal child, who has become a behavior problem because of his sense of inferiority and failure, the treatment that will touch his case, i.e., a school program suited to his abilities. He is not allowed by law to leave the public school when it gets beyond him; yet to face failure, ridicule, and reprimands, day after day, is something which human nature cannot do without efforts to escape from so unbearable a situation. The child will run away either in body or in spirit. He is bound to gain a sense of importance somehow, if not by good conduct by bad. He will take refuge in sullenness, indifference, or in more active, aggressive attempts to counteract the boredom and inferiority of his position. If he cannot shine in school, he can perhaps become the terror of the neighborhood. There is only one possible treatment for this type of child: to offer him legitimate avenues of successful expression. If school or work offers him a chance to act successfully, he will seek social approval just as he apparently sought social disapproval before. All you need to do to prove this statement is to put such a child into a school that gives him work in which he can succeed. He becomes the simplest of case problems. His energy goes over into useful activity and drains off from the unsocial channels. Often he is a new child in so short a time that the change seems almost magical. Let the dull normal child use his hands first and his intellect second, put him with his peers, and not his superiors, and in the majority of cases he will cease to be a problem.

This grouping of children is of course far too simple. There are many children both bright and stupid who find social adjustments so difficult that special attention both at home and at school is necessary. There are children who persist in bad or peculiar behavior even when every requirement seems to have been met in the way of home and school treatment. Casework here is probably wasted until the psychiatrist has gone to the root of the difficulty with the child and relieved the conflicts and repressions that underlie his behavior. The time required for this type of preliminary treatment is so great as to make it impossible at present for any large number of children. The hopeful thing for those of us who work with children is the comparative ease with which many behavior difficulties may be straightened out, when the worker, understanding the defense nature of the child's reactions, is able to provide an environment in which defense is unnecessary.

Case problems with children, as with adults, arise through some blocking of the main trends of life—love and creative work. We have to remember that in the last analysis the success of our treatment depends upon our obtaining for the child at least a minimum of fulfillment in both.

The Social Worker's Opportunity

THE TITLE of this paper should read "The Caseworker's Opportunity," for it is within the field of casework that the greatest widening of outlook and deepening of method

Paper read at the Mental Hygiene Division of the National Conference of Social Work, Providence, June, 1922.

have taken place. At least so it seems to one who is interested in the recent development of a psychology which aims to be a science of human behavior, and its growing influence on casework.

It was only yesterday that the social caseworker needed psychology as the professional advertiser needs it—to add a fine flourish to common sense, to make a tactful approach in the first interview, to get the client to clinic or hospital as painlessly as possible, to reduce the friction incident to the putting over of a well-thought-out, rational plan upon an irrational situation. In those days we could afford to talk about the mental factor, or the psychology of casework, but that was before the advent of "behavior." The static, more-or-less detached and insignificant element which we called the mental side has disappeared in the concept of a life-process, in the course of which the human organism, with a long biological history behind it, in unceasing interaction with other organisms and things, is integrated into that unity of vital forces which we call the personality.

It gives us pause when we stop to realize that it is this living organization of energies which the caseworker has undertaken to direct; energies which will not stand still to be analyzed and spread upon our records, nor cease to be in motion because we have to wait upon our ignorance or find it easier to treat them as separate, fixed units, static traits of character, neatly labeled for all time. Obviously biology, physiology, psychology, and even chemistry and physics are but different laboratory approaches to the understanding of this same life-process, yet no one of them makes any attempt to control the process as it appears in human beings—except in isolated, fragmentary ways.

[There follow details of what these sciences study.]

And yet, with or without conscious psychology, the case-worker alone in all the world is attempting to handle human behavior, undiluted and in its actual setting. Only the caseworker leaves hospital, clinic, office, and laboratory behind and observes the individual in action—at home, at work, in school—playing, loving, toiling, hating, fearing, striving, succeeding, failing—an organic part of a social context. Only the caseworker tries, however ineffectually, to adjust not only the human being but his environment—that play of forces, that interaction between self and group, which constitutes behavior and personality. If she were conscious of the implications of her job, she would know that what she is doing is practicing an experimental psychology such as no laboratory ever dreamed of, she would realize that, theoretically at least, the limit of casework is the limit of what it is possible for the caseworker to know and use about human behavior. She could not apply too great an understanding of people, even in the simplest family situation. One may almost say that how simple any human situation appears depends largely on how little one knows of human psychology.

If this be true of casework with adults, how infinitely more true it is in the casework with children, where habits are not so set or the personality so long formed by social relationships and social heredity. Here the caseworker accepts an almost creative responsibility for the changes that shall occur in the personality and behavior of the child client. Taking the difficult child in a family to the psychologist is no escape for the caseworker. She may obtain an interpretation of the family situation and the child's behavior which is a response to that situation. She may even obtain impractical advice as to practical treatment; however the real problem, the problem of slowly, patiently, persistently bringing about changes in that social situation, so that the child's responses shall inevitably be altered because the stimuli to which he must react are altered, still remains for the caseworker to solve. The psychiatrist in his office may get the child's confidence, he may help to change his attitude and clear up his fears and conflicts; but there inevitably remains the painful process of re-education and social adjustment, which is the only genuine cure for behavior problems, and which must take place in the actual day-by-day living of the patient in the slow building up of new habits and attitudes in the growth of interests.

The visiting teacher or school counselor, while she is concerned with the child in his family relationships, necessarily concentrates on his school adjustments. She has open to her an opportunity in the mental hygiene of childhood such as comes to no other social worker. Here it is not so much the case treatment of the individual child which is important as it is the teaching value of such treatment for the teacher and the school system. The family worker must be satisfied with the slow gains which are made with a child here and a child there. She must get her rewards through the transformations she works with individuals. The school counselor, on the other hand, while she needs to be a skilful caseworker, must be above all a teacher and interpreter of the mental hygiene of childhood in the public school, for only in this way can we ever hope to secure for every child understanding and mental health.

The family worker, or the visiting teacher, while her responsibility is great enough, never experiences quite the terrifying power over human development which comes to the children's worker who snatches her child out of one social situation and drops him down in another, determining, like Fate itself, the influences which shall go into the making of his behavior and his personality. One has only to read the record of a child who has been in several homes and note that there seem to be as many different personalities in that child as there were different social backgrounds, to believe that the placing of a dependent child is to a large extent the determining of his development. There exists no inherited normality or abnormality so fixed and absolute as to relieve the worker of the responsibility for the changes which her placements bring about in the behavior of a child, for the child is never just acting, he is always reacting, and his behavior is inevitably a response to a whole situation. Indeed, it is on this basis that we undertake to readjust difficult children by careful foster-home placement. The frightening thing about it is that it works both ways, and if we do not analyze and understand the subtleties of the interacting social elements in the home we have chosen, good children may become bad as well as bad ones good under our Providential care.

In foster-home placement, then, the caseworker must be responsible for the results. The psychiatrist may interpret the child, but he cannot interpret the home. Placement succeeds by accident unless the caseworker understands enough of human psychology to take the interpretation which the psychiatrist gives and fit it into her own interpretation of the influences present in the family she selects. She is the only one who can get from firsthand observation the picture of what is happening in that home, she is the only one who can bring about changes in the attitudes and practices of the family with relation to the child. Her job is not so much the child itself, but adjusting the social situation so that he may develop favorably in it. She may have to experiment with more than one home, she may have to get help from the psychiatrist to interpret some of the results her placement produces; but it is her experiment, not his, and in the end, within the limits of what is practically possible, it succeeds or fails because of her understanding and skill or lack of it.

What gives the caseworker the right to take on so unlimited a responsibility? The same authority that gives parents and teachers the right to mold children into all kinds of shapes, beautiful and ugly, the authority of necessity and inevitability. Like parent and teacher, the caseworker, if she acts at all, is bound to affect individuals. She experiments with the life-process because she cannot help it. Anything she does is an experiment in human behavior. As long as she does this in ignorance or in terms of doing good to humanity, she manages to escape full responsibility for everything but her intentions. She intends to benefit someone by changing certain obviously bad features of the environment, and for this she has a conscious technique. Incidentally she cannot alter the environment without changing behavior. From this implication she shies, because here her technique grows thin, and she either shuts out the behavior results determinedly or falls back on belief in an intuitive skill developed in the course of experience. Like the parent and the teacher, she tends to narrow the field of her interest by failing to see what is implied in her job beyond what she consciously undertakes, or she falls back on emotional drive and intuitive skill with only a slight development of scientific understanding of the material in which she works.

The caseworker, as a rule, is more self-conscious, more professional, more aware of her real field of action than the average parent or teacher, but she breaks through into conscious appreciation, chiefly in those extreme cases where behavior has become a psychiatric problem. Then she quickly takes her client to the psychiatrist and too often, accepting blindly whatever suggestion she has received for practical treatment, goes ahead trying to carry out mechanically a plan for altering behavior she does not understand. This extreme behavior is too apt to be divorced in her mind from the behavior of all her other clients who, although not pathological, are still worthy of being treated on the basis of the kind of conscious psychology from which the psychiatrist works.

The psychiatrist, too, is in a difficult position. He knows that everything the caseworker does between weekly or monthly visits to the clinic, or perhaps even on the strength of a single visit, is treatment of his case. It is going to affect the behavior of the patient, whether or not the caseworker understands what she is doing. The psychiatrist cannot take over the job. He cannot issue any foolproof scheme for environmental treatment, which the caseworker can carry out automatically as the hospital nurse carries out the orders of the surgeon in an operation. He cannot possibly know the social situation as the caseworker knows it firsthand. He cannot imagine or foresee all the practical contingencies or just what results any particular change will bring about. In short, he cannot, with the best of intentions, absolve the caseworker from the responsibility of working consciously at her job of altering human behavior. Ignorance of how she does it, or innocence of intent with regard to the results produced, cannot blot out the facts. The psychiatrist, in many instances, is doing all he can to get over to the caseworker the psychology of behavior as he sees it; but the caseworker as soon as she senses the full implications of such knowledge is terrified of the responsibility. She does not want all her simpler situations to become psychological, and she would rather leave the obviously difficult ones to the psychiatrist. The psychiatrist too bacomes alarmed when he realizes how much is being left to the caseworker and how little equipped she is scientifically to do the conscious job that psychiatry is putting on her.

The social worker's opportunity lies here. What is she going to do about it? What right has casework to go on experimenting with life itself? Only the right of necessity and a consuming interest. There is as yet no justification in conscious knowledge or technique; but the work is there to be done. There is no other profession ready to do it. Parents and teachers are more likely to follow casework, as the vanguard of experiment in dealing with everyday human behavior, than they are to initiate such experiment. The position of the caseworker is at once the most thrilling and the most terrifying in the whole gamut of scientific or semi-scientific undertakings which seek to gain social control in terms of the behavior of the human organism.

There is no turning back. The choice lies not between doing or not doing, but between doing on a more-or-less sentimental and subjective level, which leaves the results to Providence; or doing as courageously and consciously as possible whatever is done, however inadequate the equipment, struggling for a greater and greater scientific understanding and reduction of the intuitive field to a minimum.

ஃஃ

What It Means to Be a Foster Parent

THERE is a new conception of parenthood abroad in the world today which is going to make a different world tomorrow if it continues to grow at its present rate of speed. I can remember a world thirty years ago when I, a child in that world, found nothing attractive in the traditional picture of a woman's part in life. There was no thrill, no challenge, no promise of recognition and reward. The thought of having children, or bringing them up, or creating a family, far from presenting an alluring possibility of adventure and achievement—a field in which expert skill and knowledge might find expression—loomed before me as a fate to be avoided if possible, the crushing end of all individual development.

This chapter appeared as an article in *Progressive Education,* October-November-December, 1926.

Why we were so easily convinced that working with money, with atoms, with germs, with plants, with bugs, with tools, with books, with paints, clay, sounds or what not, were all obviously more professional, more difficult, more interesting, or more valuable to society than working with children, I'm sure I don't know; unless we did so confuse cooking, scrubbing, sewing, with child care and because our badly organized domestic life has always allowed those occupations to prevent the rearing of children from being the mother's first and most important task. Perhaps too the fact that no bona fide educational institution respected by men included any professional or technical training for this field—not housekeeping, mind you, but child rearing—may have had something to do with it.

It was part and parcel of that world of thirty years ago, which was so blinded to the importance of human behavior as a possible field for scientific research and practical control, and which was so unaware of the place of the child in that field, to look upon the dependent child as an unmitigated burden; the institution as the only tolerable solution of the problem; and to think of all children as somehow owing the parents a debt of gratitude which a lifetime would hardly suffice to repay. Every parent just by virtue of being one, was entitled to love and respect; was always right and if the children failed to respond to his training, could not be held responsible. There were ungrateful children born into the world in those days, children who did not appreciate their parents and who somehow managed to develop most undesirable character and habits in spite of good training. These were the bad children mysteriously born into the world to humiliate and torment good parents. You may see them today sitting in the reception rooms of child guidance clinics waiting to be made over so their parents may have an easier life. At least, that is what the parents have in mind. Whether or not the clinic will be able to do anything with the problem depends largely on whether those parents can reverse their idea of why they came.

Despite the fact that the old ideas and practices still linger in far too many places, those who look back upon the development of the last twenty or thirty years in medicine, public health, social work, education, law, psychology, sociology and psychiatry, may see a new conception of the relations of parents to children slowly taking form. There are many fields today which consider the child, his entrance into life, the way he is trained as an infant, the kind of education he gets, the interests and attitudes he acquires as the very basis and hope of any social control. We have come to realize that one thing is fundamental in any kind of reform: getting at people when they are young.

From these various quarters we see developing a new psychology of the individual and a new conception of what it means to bring up a child. Far from requiring no training and no technique, the job of the parent, particularly the mother, becomes the most difficult and the most important, as well as the most creative and rewarding work the world has to offer, work in which the unprepared, unenlightened, uninterested parent cannot hope to succeed except by accident.

You can see what this means to our whole conception of the dependent child and the basis on which he is placed with a foster parent. Physical birth, flesh and blood connection have ceased to be the important factors in our newer vision of the parent's job. Bringing up a child, not bearing it, is what counts; how much security you can give it, how much stability and confidence, how much physical vigor, how many wholesome attitudes and useful habits, how many creative interests, how much ability to stand on its own feet. Loving a child because he is flesh of your flesh is not all-important, but how effective and intelligent your love is in equipping him for life. Love, ignorant and blind, may hamper his development and ruin his happiness. The test of the value of parental affection lies not in the fact of blood relationship but in the kind of child it rears. By their fruits ye shall know them.

Thus parenthood has been taken out of its conventional setting and lies open to anyone who conceives of it as a job worthy to be done, carrying within it its own rewards, not rewards of assistance with housework or farm, not rewards of support in old age, or obedience and gratitude, but the reward of having some conscious part in the growth of a human being, of adding to your own resources an ever-deepening interest which age cannot dim.

But, you say, surely you do not imply that taking a dependent child from an agency will guarantee the experience of a real parent. My answer is yes, provided you have the right attitude toward children; yes, provided the agency has a professional staff which is expert in the delicate task of selecting a particular child for a particular home; yes, provided you are willing to have yourself and your own situation examined as carefully as the child has been to determine your fitness for each other; and again yes, provided you are open-minded and are willing to be guided at first by someone who understands what it means to adjust foster parent to foster child. There are all kinds of dependent children just as there are all kinds of children who are not dependent and all kinds of homes. You and I might want a child of sensitive makeup with a mind equal to college training, Mr. Smith wants just a good wholesome average kid who will go through high school and be a credit to his father in business, while Mrs. Jones wants a healthy, sensible girl like herself, a steady, practical body who will be satisfied with common school education. Only the trained worker is in a position to know both family and child well enough to combine them.

Provided the agency can supply the suitable child, what are the problems of any foster parent?

First there is one tremendous disadvantage under which many foster parents labor and one great advantage which they often possess over real parents. The disadvantage lies in the fact that any dependent child who has not been in one home from birth has suffered a shock to his confidence in life; he has a basis for fear and for compensatory striving to bolster up his security and make himself feel as safe as possible, which the own child hopefully escapes.

It is essential for any prospective foster parent, especially if he takes an older child, to appreciate this disadvantage so thoroughly that he will wait patiently, as long as it takes, perhaps a year or two, for the basis of confidence, the sense of really belonging, to be established. In the meantime he must be alert to the effect of the lack of security on the child's conduct. Instead of being ready with reproof, criticism, and sharp insistence on immediate change, all of which only reinforce the fundamental fear and increase the need for the unpleasant behavior, he will be ready with encouragement and praise for every sign of progress; and will do all in his power to use only positive means, identifying himself with the child, not holding it off for condemnation, and giving it from the start the realization that they have taken each other for better or worse and must work it out together.

One of the shocks which lie in store for the completely inexperienced foster parent whose ideas about children are theoretical and who has considered his own individual development and comfort without restriction for a good many years, is the discovery that one has to learn to like having children. It is like any other new job, it demands a new technique and new control. He finds himself quite unprepared. All of his habits of living are broken up. These new ways do not come easily. He has to stop and think at every turn. Everything, even the simplest routine of life, has become problematical. Now this is a very disturbing experience. Nobody can enjoy it steadily. There will be periods of exasperation, of wonder at one's folly in giving up a comfortable existence for chaos, periods of hating the strange intruder and wishing he were in Halifax. If only the new foster parent isn't too upset by himself and the fact that far from loving a child he simply despises it, there is hope ahead. Time is the great worker of miracles and nowhere is it more a factor than in this mutual process of adjustment between foster parent and foster child.

The flesh-and-blood parent goes through a similar process but he is held to it by the fact that there is no escape and his tenderness has had a chance to grow slowly to meet the growing complexity of his situation. The foster parent and the foster child know that theirs is a situation from which escape is possible, so they require much more determination and encouragement to live through enough time to come to the period when interest is far greater than desire to be free. Nobody has any idea of this "time" factor unless he has been through it himself or has worked with people who have.

The next prerequisite for the foster parent is the capacity to look objectively at himself and the child and the problems which arise. Here is where the foster parent has a real advantage. The own parent needs to be objective with his child just as much as anyone, but because his own emotions are so much more involved he finds it far more difficult. No one is in the proper frame of mind to be intelligent about a problem if his feelings are so strong he can't think, can't even see what there is to think about, but must get rid of his own joy or his own pain in some impulsive way, however unsuitable or ineffective.

The foster parent, at least for some time, is not so personally identified with the adopted child. From the start his relation to the child has been more voluntary and conscious, subjected more to analysis and thought. His ego is not so immediately hurt when he finds his child unworthy. He is in a position to learn that this is a problem demanding thought rather than emotion, and intelligent experiment rather than punishment. He can easily begin to reap his reward in the interest of the process, even his failures will have a meaning for the next attempt.

The final qualification for the foster parent is that he shall see the necessity of taking at least a second child, after his first is well established, because the fate of the only child is not one to choose voluntarily if it can be avoided, and that he will enlarge his psychology to an appreciation of what it will mean to his first to have a second introduced. All of the insecurity of the first year may be revived on the introduction of a rival. All the tact and patience of that first year will be necessary, not only to establish the newcomer but to re-establish the confidence of the first.

Why should anyone subject himself to such discipline? Because parallel to the difficulty of the problem is the satisfaction of being able to solve it at least partially. It is a never-ending, always-increasing, deepening interest; a source of infinite variety and enrichment of experience, the only stake we have in the life of the next generation, and as a fulfilment of self, worth all that it costs in self-sacrifice.

The Use of the Transfer Within the Limits of the Office Interview

UNDER the general topic "Methods Used by Social Caseworkers in the Development of Personality," I wish to discuss the use of what the psychoanalyst would call the "transfer" within the limits of the office interview. The discussion will be made from the viewpoint of a psy-

Given at the National Conference of Social Work, Division on the Family, Toronto, June 28, 1924.

chologist who is forced to depend upon office contacts almost entirely for any direct treatment; but it is assumed that where an interview proves to be therapeutic in its effect, the processes are the same whether carried on by psychologist or caseworker. The type of interview referred to would exclude technical psychoanalysis, but in my own case would be guided consciously by a psychoanalytic psychology.

A good many people, caseworkers, teachers, and even some psychiatrists dislike very much the thought of an emotional relationship to the client, student, or patient. They often think of this as a sentimental appeal, a use of one's personality to induce the individual to do something which he would naturally evade or resist, an encouragement of crushes, a personal desire for admiration or adulation. People who have this strong aversion to emotional responses in themselves or their clients like to believe that treatment—successful readjustment of families and individuals—comes from practical use of resources, and the education of the individuals concerned through ideas and rational appeals.

While I sympathize with the objection which such people feel for the unprofessional attitude and the lack of insight which often characterizes the personal contacts of the untrained or unadjusted person who bungles on the job because he does not understand himself or the methods he is unconsciously using, I do not think that the existence of bunglers should prevent us from recognizing that the basis of all casework therapy is primarily emotional, not rational or intellectual, and that we who deal with people are responsible for accepting and understanding technically the tools which we have been using more or less consciously and skillfully.

I am using the term *emotional* loosely, to avoid the word *instinctive* and mean by it everything except what we think of as intellectual, rational or ideational; the impulsive, feeling, wishing side of the human being.

The work which a psychologist does in his office presents interesting illustrations of the use of the transfer because the situations are separated from work on the environment and sometimes show rather unusual results even from a single interview. I am far from believing that the interview with the psychiatrist or the psychologist is magic, and I am convinced that for children, certainly, re-education and readjustment must be a continuous process carried out in the home from day to day over a long period; but the office interview gives an opportunity to analyze processes within a well-defined, limited situation where the mechanism is a little more superficial and apparent. . . .

[The paper continues with two case illustrations of adolescent girls who show striking changes in attitude and behavior through office interviews with the Mental Hygienist. In conclusion the paper goes on to state:]

The purpose of this paper is to call to your attention the nature of the underlying forces used consciously by the analyst and unconsciously by the case worker to vitalize ideas and plans. The emotional going over of the client to the caseworker breaks down old fears and inhibitions and provides a safe medium in which the growth of new thoughts, feelings, and habits becomes possible.

The caseworker who has seen to her own adjustment

first, before undertaking to bring about adjustment in other human lives, need have no fear of the transfer but will find in its conscious, skillful, and impersonal use her most valuable tool.

The Function of a Mental Hygienist in a Children's Agency

THE DISCUSSION of this subject is complicated in part by the fact that the position of mental hygienist is not recognized as essential to the work of a children's agency like a reception department or a medical service but is thought of as a luxury, a happy accident, or perhaps as a service better supplied in some other way, as by an outside clinic. It is further complicated by the rapid changes historically, changes which have removed old needs and perhaps created new ones, so that we are no longer sure just what the agency is wanting of a mental hygienist in its midst. Again there is still a confusion partly due to the accident of historical development as to just who the mental hygienist is. What he was, what he is, and what he is going to be may all be different. If we drop the reference to the mental hygienist as a person and think about what we mean by

Given at the National Conference of Social Work, Des Moines, 1927.

mental hygiene in a children's agency, perhaps we shall remove some of the complicating factors sufficiently to get a point of departure.

Most of us would agree that the words "mental hygiene" represent the contribution which modern psychiatry and the analytic psychology have made to social life and social work, particularly to casework with children. By mental hygiene in a children's agency, we mean then the presence of a dynamic psychology by which the personality and behavior of each individual child may be interpreted and on the basis of which the child may be helped to make the best possible social adaptation. That such a vital understanding of children, an understanding which is capable of being expressed in the technique of placement, supervision, or other casework relationships to the child is not only desirable but actually fundamental ideally, no thoughtful person would deny. Practically, we all know how far we are from the attainment of any such goal. The kind of psychology referred to is not yet an organic part of the equipment of the average caseworker today nor of the average agency nor is that anything to be wondered at or ashamed of. As a working technique, it has not been in existence very long. Those of us who can look back over the past ten or fifteen years can remember when mental hygiene was only a theory, a vision, in the minds of one or two great psychiatrists. Hoch, Meyer, Campbell, Salmon, Fernald, Southard, and Healy—those were the men who fifteen years ago began to open up to social work in this country the possibility of a tool adapted to its needs as academic psychology had never been.

*   *   *   *   *   *   *

Just what is the function of a mental hygiene department in a children's agency, as different from casework, after one has discounted medical equipment and mental tests, is a question which a small group of experienced workers (known as the Senior Group) in the Children's Aid Society of Pennsylvania has recently been discussing at some length. In this group there was considerable opposition to giving up difference in specialized knowledge as a legitimate and permanent thing. As we analyzed it, this seemed to be based partly on a realization of how inadequate the average caseworker's preparation has been and how far she is from meeting such a standard; partly on a shrinking from the responsibility which such an interpretation puts on the worker and a desire to retain someone to whom she can turn for reassurance, for moral support, even more than for actual information. Consciously accepting oneself as equal to the mental hygienist in point of view seems to require more confidence in one's own ego than tacitly accepting responsibility by going ahead with the practical job as the caseworker is daily obliged to do.

However, there was no dissent logically from the conclusion that she who does casework lets herself in for understanding theoretically, and facing practically, all that can be known about the behavior with which she deals. Perhaps along with this assumption of superior knowledge upon which the caseworker may lean is an implied superiority in personal adjustment. And indeed, in mental hygiene as in religion, nothing seems more incongruous than a theory which is constantly contradicted in practice. The conclusion that a person who sets out to understand human behavior must be able to understand and handle his own, so that it will at least not interfere with or invalidate the scientific and therapeutic results of his work with other people, seems difficult to escape.

The same obligation to continuous self-analysis and personal adjustment resulting in what we know as grown-up behavior, seems to rest upon the caseworker also. Whether in our present state this means that the mental hygienist in an agency must help to bring about self-understanding in the workers who lack it, would be open to discussion. Surely his teaching ought to be of a kind to contribute to such an outcome. Perhaps we must look to the training schools for a new conception of preparation for social casework—a preparation which shall not be considered adequate unless a comparative objectivity and maturity of emotional attitude be attained. One might even go so far as to question whether it is possible to obtain a vital knowledge of the human emotions and their functioning except via one's own experiences. It is a knowledge which is not gained in intellectual terms. Just how this may be brought about cannot be speculated on here, but the fact remains that neither personal adjustment nor specialized psychological knowledge ought to differentiate caseworker from mental hygienist.

It then became apparent as our thinking progressed that if the mental hygienist had a function different from the caseworker's it must be defined in terms of treatment. Is there something in the office situation, in the mental hygienist's relation to the child, which provides a form of treatment not possible or desirable in the caseworker's contact? We then went back over former ideas about the psychiatrist's interview with the child as having some magic potency. We found ourselves still clinging to that for immediate relief from our casework problems, a desire to believe that in that contact with the mental hygienist something would come to pass, vaguely, mysteriously; something which would make it possible for us to go on with our casework again. Yet we could not analyze what the psychiatrist was actually doing in the office interview.

My own recollection of what I first conceived to be the value of interviewing a problem child is a rather confused idea of gaining information and at the same time producing a therapeutic effect by catharsis. The important thing was to dig deep, to get the child to tell about his own misdeeds. Then there was a period when one searched for mental conflicts. Sex instruction too seemed to give the office interview a *raison d'être*. Yet underneath it all was a groping dissatisfaction, an awareness that nothing in one's report of the treatment interview showed anything which the caseworker with the same insight might not equally well have obtained.

No one who was using the office contact as his medium of treatment seemed to be very clear as to just what were the factors in the psychiatric interview which produced therapeutic results; and, as far as I know, there has never been any attempt to establish a clear-cut theory or technique based on conscious knowledge of the relation of the process to therapy or casework. We all fell back on the superior insight which made the material obtained more relevant and the interpretation of it more significant, but the therapy as far as there was any remained unanalyzed and uncontrolled.

In my own work, I have become more and more aware

that the informational content of the interview matters much less than my attitude and the child's comfort in the relationship temporarily established, and I believe that in that direction lies the clue to the therapeutic function of the mental hygienist as distinct from the therapeutic function of the caseworker. In the field of knowledge or information no dividing line will hold. There is no insight which the caseworker might not and ought not have. There is no information which she might not give the child or obtain from the child under favorable conditions, perhaps more easily than the person in the office.

It seemed to us as we discussed it that what happens to the child in an office interview when it does happen, is in the nature of a releasing emotional experience which is sometimes needed in the treatment process but is often incompatible with the caseworker's function, as it is with that of the parents or foster parents. The child who is thoroughly entangled in his own unconsciously motivated behavior, who in spite of his own better judgment is bringing down upon himself the hostile or fearful reactions of the foster or own family, has to experience what we used to call a "change of heart." Change of mind does no good, talking does no good, promises do no good—only change of feeling will help. To give a child such an experience means to expose him to a situation so safe, so reassuring that none of his defenses are needed and therefore fall away, leaving his underlying fears, loves, and jealousies free to express themselves. The caseworker is too well known to the child ordinarily, too much a real friend or perhaps a threat, too confused with practical issues, to function easily as the symbol of security in this office situation. She has had to understand the foster parents as well as the child, to listen to accusations against him, to try to get him to be a better child, to move him from one home to another. She has perhaps failed him unintentionally in such vital matters as a new suit or a Christmas present, or she has slipped up in a clinic arrangement. She is human and fallible. The more friendly the relationship the more difficult it may be for the child to reveal himself as he is, to run the risk of lessening the worker's esteem by the expression of feelings which he feels she could not approve. The person in the office whose contact with the child is freed from practical issues, and strictly limited and controlled by office conditions, may grant the child a freedom from morality and social obligation which is not easily possible in any other setting. Within the office no resistance need be offered to any attitude however undesirable socially.

The office is a place apart, a place removed from the irritations of reality, from praise and blame, from success and failure. Here the child receives what every human being craves, complete attention and concentration upon himself and his problem. For the time being he has no rival, he possesses the interviewer completely. This the caseworker can seldom do, for there are her other children who come between, there are the interests of the adults concerned, the authority of the agency. Only by great effort can she give the child even temporarily the illusion which he seeks of complete security. And insofar as she is successful, she has perhaps attached the child to her in a dependent relationship which is difficult to separate from reality because of the actual services which she must render,

and impossible to live up to because of her own imperma-
nence in the child's life and the practical impossibility of
continuing to concentrate upon him. This is peculiarly
the case with a child who has never been successfully rooted
in a foster home and looks to the worker for his sense
of stability.

That such intensive personal treatment of child by caseworker is possible and sometimes so skillfully drained off
into other relationships that no unnecessary pain of separation is forced upon the child, one would not deny, but no
worker can carry many cases of this type, nor bring them
to a successful issue without great skill and considerable
nerve strain.

Sometimes when in a children's agency, the child who
becomes a problem is already an organic part of a foster
home and has no personal relation to the visitor, she may
then function exactly as the mental hygienist does—for
the burden of the follow-up work can be carried by the
parents.

The point we wish to emphasize is that what gives the
office interview its therapeutic value is not a rehearsal of
misdeeds or a recounting of old loves or fears, it is rather
an immediate feeling experience produced by the temporary security which the relation to the mental hygienist in
the role of understanding parent affords. . .

Our failure to make of this office contact with the child
the curative agent which it might become is due, it seems
to me, to a failure to sufficiently analyze consciously just
what happens emotionally when talking with a child and to
follow up with a more definite conscious plan the results of
one interview as related to the next, and to the environ-

mental treatment. Therapeutic effects have always followed from interviews at times, but we have not known why it was at one time and not another, and we have been confused as to how to utilize them. We have established no definite technique for producing the therapeutic situation and for refining the process and bringing it under more conscious deliberate control. Our psychology must not only explain the nature of the emotions experienced in the interview but show us how to release them more easily and fruitfully for the child and how to carry over into environmental treatment the insight which we gain, and thus make permanently valuable for the child the otherwise temporary experience of release and satisfaction.

Also the fact that the child's relation to the mental hygienist is emotional calls for complete understanding and objectivity on the part of the caseworker, whose own relation to the child may be temporarily affected thereby, and for a careful working together that one contact may finally flow into the other without undue conflict in the mind of the child.

In the treatment interview—analyzed, refined, and consciously controlled—may lie, it seems to me, the unique function of the mental hygienist of tomorrow. The task will be to bring about such complete understanding between caseworker and mental hygienist that the office interview will never occur as a part of formal routine but as a particular form of treatment which is indicated by the needs of the individual case and is utilized consciously by the worker as an integral part of her plan for the child.

Practically, you are saying, does a children's agency need a mental hygienist, and if it does, how can this be accomplished? The question of an outside clinic versus a person attached to the agency, would need more discussion than this paper permits. However, this much may be said: The work of a children's agency is such that every case constitutes a mental hygiene problem while comparatively few cases are psychiatric or neurological problems. No outside clinic, however valuable, can give all the service needed. That every children's agency should have the services of a psychiatrist is also an impossibility. If the mental hygienist has to be a psychiatrist he will never be available outside of the clinic.

The psychologists are a little more numerous and less expensive, but they are so often not mental hygienists. If one can be found who has had adequate preparation for understanding human behavior as well as giving mental tests, it may be a good way to combine two valuable functions.

The third possibility, which has not been utilized as yet, seems to me to be the hope of the children's agency for whom the psychologist and psychiatrist are out of the question, that is, the caseworker with mental hygiene training. She might or might not be able to contribute a testing technique, but there is no reason why with her equipment she could not function as the office consultant, the person who stays out of the casework and concentrates on analysis, interpretation, and the treatment interview.

If the difference between caseworker and mental hygienist is only a slight difference of function, the super-caseworker of today, with a change of emphasis and a somewhat different technique, may easily become the mental hygienist of tomorrow.

The children's agency will always need someone who sits a little apart, someone less driven by the practical issues, someone who has time, someone who can talk over a case from the point of view of the impartial bystander, someone in whom the bewildered child may find the impersonal security he needs. Why should casework not develop that person out of its own ranks?

Only in this way will the mental hygienist become a reality in every children's agency.

PART IV

Association with Rank

1926-1939

THE ASSOCIATION with Otto Rank which was to prove so influential in the development of Jessie Taft's understanding of helping processes and her skill in therapy and casework needs no introduction beyond what she gives in her biography of Rank,[1] written after her retirement from the faculty of the University of Pennsylvania School of Social Work.

She speaks in that volume of her realization that "for the second time in my life I had met genius," and says of her aim in presenting this biographical study that "it rests upon a deep identification as well as many years of taking back into myself projections that have been gradually withdrawn in the face of age and death." While she would never have used the word *genius* to describe herself, the identification she felt with Rank was based on an immediate, almost intuitive, understanding of his thinking as natural to her, and on an actual likeness apparent to those who saw them together enough to appreciate the extraordinary immediacy and responsiveness in thinking and feeling. I do not know how to describe it except as a spontaneity of feeling, a sensitivity to the other—a rare combination indeed, perhaps the combination that makes the gifted therapist.

[1] Jessie Taft, *Otto Rank, A Biographical Study* (New York: The Julian Press, 1958).

She says of Rank's relation to her:

> His relation to me is quite apparent in the letters. It was based primarily on identification—a genuine likeness in temperament, philosophy, and professional interest, that made communication between us easy and spontaneous, but always on my part with due regard for my own limitations as measured by genius.

The exploration of this identification was to absorb her to the bottom of herself through the years without obscuring the realization of the difference between their separate selves established first of all by his genius but to be discovered in thinking and in practice. For in this quality too they were alike, in a rare sense of individuality in themselves and in a corresponding respect for difference and individuality in another. There was in each, it seemed, a sensitivity to others in direct proportion to the awareness of and respect for the self.

The foreword of her biography of Rank gives her description of the beginning of her relationship with him.

> My first contact with Otto Rank occurred on June 3, 1924, at a meeting of the American Psychoanalytic Association in Atlantic City where he was to give a paper in English on *The Trauma of Birth*, the title of his book recently published in German. As a clinical psychologist from Philadelphia working chiefly with children, I had no official right to participate in a psychoanalytic conference, but I was interested in psychoanalysis as a further training measure for myself in the future, and I wanted to see who these analysts were and what they were like. An acquaintance who had worked in Vienna with both Freud and Rank had told me of something new and

different in Rank's theory as well as in his therapeutic technique that had aroused immediate interest, although I had known nothing of Rank previously except his name and a title, *The Myth of the Birth of the Hero.*

I do not remember how I got to the meeting or what was said there, but I still retain a vivid impression regarding the quality of the several speakers. With one exception all seemed to me unimpressive, if not actually dull, until the slight, boyish figure of Rank appeared beside the speaker's desk. He was the very image of my idea of the scholarly German student, and he spoke so quietly, so directly and simply, without circumlocution or apology, that despite the strong German accent I was able to follow his argument, and I thought to myself, "Here is a man one could trust."

It took two years, with letters and a single interview, before I finally pinned myself down to a definite date for analysis with Rank in New York in the fall of 1926. Meanwhile, I had been saved from myself and my attempt to escape by engaging a substitute analyst, through the latter's untimely death. Later I was able to appreciate what a fateful accident it had been for me, as I remembered the two application interviews with their portent for the future of the analysis. The first man, in spite of his frank doubts of my suitability in terms of age and my limited time allowance, had ended by accepting me, but only after I had remarked, with full awareness of its possible influence on a man who had himself been analyzed by Rank, that Dr. Rank had previously agreed to take me. I left that interview knowing in my heart that I was the stronger of the two and had conquered in the first round.

In contrast, my meeting with Rank had been quiet,

brief, without controversy. No doubts were expressed by him, no fear of my age, no interest in my life history, nor was there any contest regarding my rigid time limit. He did not promise anything. He merely agreed to try, on the basis of the time at my disposal. I can recall only one remark from that interview in response to something I had presented about myself. "Perhaps the problem lies there." And that was all, but on that one sentence I began to make myself over before anyone else should have the chance.

Coming to the point of being willing to subject myself to anything as strange as was psychoanalysis in the United States at this time was not due to any conscious personal need or to lack of professional success, but to the deep awareness of being stopped in professional development. I knew that I had not the basis for helping other people, however deep my desire. Psychological testing of children was useful but, as I knew only too well, it was not therapeutic. Failure with the few neurotic adults who had been referred to me had filled me with guilt and fear. Psychoanalysis seemed to be the only resource, however fearful.

When I finally came to my first hour with Rank, while consciously submissive, afraid, and fully aware of my ignorance of psychoanalysis, my underlying attitude was far from humble. I was, after all, a psychologist. I had some knowledge of myself and my problems. I had achieved a point of view, psychologically. If there was anything in my unconscious in terms of buried memories, I would have to be shown. And so the battle was joined; but I soon found that it was a battle with myself. I was deprived of a foe. It took only two weeks for me to yield to a new kind of relationship, in the experiencing of which the nature of my own therapeutic failures became suddenly clear. No verbal explanation was ever needed: my first experience of taking help for a need that had been denied was enough to give a basis for the years of learning to follow.

At this time I had no idea of Rank's growing difference from Freud or of his alienation from the Vienna group. In cheerful ignorance, I combined with my daily hour a weekly evening lecture given by Rank for the New York School of Social Work, another by Ferenczi for the New School of Social Research, a regular seminar for social work students with a Rankian analyst, and still a third evening lecture course, by whom I do not recall. To this extreme activity on my part Rank offered no objection, but turned my naive daily reports to good account in terms of their meaning for me in the therapeutic process. Never did I sense on Rank's part the bitterness or resentment that he might well have been feeling at a time when Ferenczi, who had but recently been his friend and collaborator, was refusing to speak to him. I did not try to account for the look of pain and constraint that characterized his appearance at the evening lectures, except by recognizing the hardship of reading such difficult material in English to a group no better prepared than myself to understand, and by projecting upon him my own exquisite embarrassment at these revelations of the secrets of the analytic hour.

At the end of an eight- or nine-week period—the time altered just enough to undo my original intent to control it—I returned to Philadelphia overflowing with emotion engendered by a vital experience, at that point quite innocent of theory of any kind, but eager to give to others the kind of help that had been given to me. It was not long before I realized that emotion and intuition were not enough. I had to earn a point of view by my own efforts, had to face Freudian difference, painful as it was, not merely through Rank but in my own thinking, reading, and use of the therapeutic relationship.

Consequently I was grateful for the opportunity to join a Rankian group in New York and gain support for both theory and practice through their weekly evening seminar in the winter and early spring of 1927. This group of fifteen or twenty was made up chiefly of psychiatrists, both men and women, some with previous analytic experience and all with an original Freudian base, who had been in analysis with Rank either in Vienna or New York. They included most of the younger New York psychiatrists of that period, with a few from Boston and one or two other cities, plus an occasional Ph.D. like myself. There were none from the older established institutional group such as Hoch, Meyer, Campbell, White, and Southard, and none from the original Freudian analysts, such as Brill. We were a hardworking group, using as our text Part I of Rank's *Genetische Psychologie*[2] that he had given in the evening lecture course of 1926. Our problems in understanding the text, as well as our common difficulties in applying it therapeutically with no help from Rank, were only too obvious.

When Rank returned to this country in the fall of 1927, he established himself in Philadephia, gave in lec-

---

[2] The lengthy introductory part, with its general discussion of the current problems in psychoanalysis, theoretical and practical, was not used, as far as I can recall.

ture form Part II of *Genetische Psychologie,* and continued the New York seminar with what was now recognized generally as a Rankian group. I was among those who had individual help with practice during that period, as well as the benefit of the discussion of cases in the seminar. Although interrupted by Rank's sudden return to Paris, this seminar was finally completed by him (in the spring of 1928), still utilizing the material from Part I of *Genetische Psychologie,* with emphasis on the relation to the mother as fundamental in the analytic situation and in the difficult problems of end-setting. He was back in 1928–29, meeting with the seminar, and lecturing in New York and Philadelphia.

Thus far, although there must have been increasing awareness of Rank's estrangement from Freud and the Vienna group, heightened by growing opposition on the part of the established Freudian analysts in New York, seminar discussions were still carried on in the familiar Freudian terminology, while Rank's innate authority and rich experience provided the support and guidance needed by these younger analysts, who were far from assured in their own theory and practice.

It was into this uncertain, loosely organized group that, on their first meeting in the winter of 1929–30, Rank, newly returned from Paris and the completion of the second volume of his clearly anti-Freudian *Technik der Psychoanalyse,* launched without previous warning or preparation a new psychology and therapeutic method. I can still recall the sudden shock created by his use of the word "will," so long taboo in academic circles as a remnant of faculty psychology and therapeutically akin to quackery. Only someone with the force and brilliance of a Rank could have carried this medically oriented group through a change so sudden and complete as to have felt like desertion.

The situation was not unlike what happened in the Freudian "Committee" when Rank, their youngest member, suddenly produced without previous consultation *The Trauma of Birth,* but in this case the process is reversed and Rank can use his leadership to hold the group together. The actual course of discussion through the 1930 seminar I have forgotten, and even the minutes that I have preserved do not recall it. There remains only the memory of the initial shock, followed for me by the revelation of the reality of will as a key to my own as well as to my patients' psychology. As I look back I believe that I was perhaps the only one for whom the transition came easily and naturally. I had no medical ties and no stake in Freudian psychology. I had been brought up on pragmatism and the thinking of George Herbert Mead and John Dewey. For me there was nothing to lose.

By external standards the 1930 seminar was a brilliant success, marked by full attendance and interesting material. Several members were benefiting from controlled analyses; there were even plans for a book on Rankian psychology to be made up of contributions from various members. Editorial leadership had been assigned to the Boston contingent, while financing remained with the New York group. The existence of an internal problem was not in evidence until the program of the International Mental Hygiene Association, to be held in the United States for the first time early in May of 1930, came up for discussion. As Rank was scheduled to deliver a paper there, the selection of discussants was important. It became suddenly clear to me that everyone withdrew from the assignment, largely, as I thought, because of the difficulty of commenting on Rank's material. Although at the time I was in a stage of resentful independence, I realized somewhat bitterly that I was the only person in the group who would undertake it; if I did not volunteer, nothing would happen, there would be no friendly discussant from the seminar. Thus I became involved in the first meeting of the International Mental Hygiene Association in Washington that gave Rank the welcome opportunity to declare himself publicly and to face the Freudian opposition openly. Although the majority of the New York seminar was present, no medical adherent stood up to be counted.

This occasion was important in that it marked the end of Rank's leadership with the psychoanalytic group in New York. It also marked the price that would have to be paid by any analyst who separated himself from the medical sanction that remained with Freud. There was no one in the seminar of the caliber to carry on such a fight, no one with sufficiently developed ideological conviction, no one with the requisite therapeutic skill. Thus it was only a matter of time for former adherents and students of Rank gradually to disappear under their protective medical coloring. The projected book was abandoned without explanation. I do not doubt that the many psychiatrists who had been analyzed by Rank between 1924 and 1930 were influenced away from strict Freudian theory and practice, but they failed to proclaim it and, to my knowledge, not a single one understood, much less affirmed, Rank's *will psychology* or the ultimate form of his dynamic therapy. For adherents of Freudian psychoanalysis, Rank's fate was sealed at this point; he was to be treated thereafter as nonexistent.

"The fact that I was not medical and never dependent on medical support for my point of view or practice, together with an innate interest in theory and the conviction engendered by my own experience of Rankian therapy, may account for Rank's acceptance of me at this time as a friend and fellow worker. At all events, from that time until his death, in 1939, I was usually in communication with him by letter or personal contact. It was owing to this friendship and to my understanding of his point of view that, at his death, there came into my possession the papers on which this biographical study has relied, particularly for material preceding 1926. These papers were not willed to me by Rank, for he made no will, but were sent to me by his second wife with the approval of his daughter and her mother as the person to whom he would have entrusted them.

Her analysis with Rank having ended in November after eight or nine weeks in New York, Jessie Taft returned to her home in Flourtown, Pennsylvania, and to her job as supervisor of the Foster Home Department of the Children's Aid Society of Pennsylvania. At the same time she rented an office across from the Social Service Building at 311 S. Juniper Street, Philadelphia, and began to take a few private patients coming to her from the staffs of the social agencies or referred by psychiatrists like Dr. Edward Strecker who knew and trusted her ability as she had demonstrated in the children's agencies of the city. Psychoanalysis was new to Philadelphia at that time, Freud was indistinguishable from Rank, and Dr. Taft as one of the earliest practitioners of analysis was open to the projections of the interested and curious as well as to the criticisms of the fearful and suspicious. She used her own enlivened experience and deepened understanding of psychological and helping problems in lectures and teaching, and students as well as friends and professional associates were drawn irresistibly to seek for themselves a contact with the source of life they felt in her.

In addition to carrying her responsibility as supervisor of the Foster Home Department of the Children's Aid Society and part-time practice in psychotherapy and teaching in the Pennsylvania School of Social Work, she began to work on a translation of Rank's *Technique of Psychoanalysis* in three volumes and his *Genetic Psychology,* Volume III, using evenings and week ends for this purpose. Not only was Rank's thinking difficult, his German technical and involved, but her own German was unused since college days. *Cassell's German Dictionary,* inscribed in pencil with her name and date of December, 1926, had constant usage and barely hangs together now with the help of strips of adhesive tape.

In the translator's preface to *Will Therapy* and *Truth and Reality*[3] she describes her relationship to the material and her work as translator as follows:

My acquaintance with the material dates from 1926 when I began a translation of Volume I. Since that time I have worked more or less steadily on these three volumes, as well as on *Truth and Reality,* not only in

[3] Originally published in two separate volumes: *Will Therapy* and *Truth and Reality* (New York: Alfred A. Knopf, 1936); 2nd ed. in one volume: *Will Therapy and Truth and Reality* (New York: Alfred A. Knopf, 1945).

terms of translation, but through a slow process of assimilation which has finally enabled me to offer this volume *Will Therapy* with a translation of *Truth and Reality* for publication. The translation, on the whole, is faithful to the original, but I have not hesitated when it seemed better in the interest of clarity and good form, to eliminate or reorder certain portions of the text and occasionally to insert explanatory phrases and sentences. . . .

Writing in 1956, she recalls the summer of 1935 in New Hampshire when "using our brief leisure time for writing I was facing the challenge of writing an introduction to my translations of the *Technik,* looking forward to publication. It is one thing to generalize about an authority who is dead, quite another to expose your interpretation of his work to the living author who must know better than you what he meant. I was exhilarated by my own daring and yet full of apprehension. Who can take another's estimate of himself or his work? But I had to do it even if it meant complete rejection."[4]

She sent Rank the material, "regardless of all misgivings and in spite of Rank's repeated expression of lack of interest in the publication of the translation." Rank's letter, which came September 12, 1935, was most reassuring:

I read your Preface and Introduction at once and want to thank you for the excellent job you have done.

There is nothing more to be said about it and nothing to be changed because it stands as a whole and is written in one full stream of expression which is yours and you. I like it very much!

[4] Taft, *Otto Rank, A Biographical Study,* pp. 206–208, 214.

He wrote again on April 2, 1936, when the two volumes appeared, as follows:

> I just read over the week end your introductory chapter to the Technique and want to tell you that I felt this was the justification for the publication.
>
> This is not just a compliment for the excellent presentation—what I mean is that it shows there is somebody who understands it and knows what I mean.
>
> I can see in that way that the fact of your publishing it makes it worthwhile publishing it at all.

Simultaneously with the painstaking, dedicated work of translating Rank which occupied so much time in the years 1926 to 1935, Dr. Taft was developing her own practice and comprehension of therapy. She makes note in a comment recorded among her papers that after 1926 she began to refuse invitations to speak and write, invitations to which she had responded seemingly without limitation in the decade preceding this period of concentration on the therapeutic process. Other developments in the field of social work in Philadelphia and in national organizations supported her decision to limit her own extension activities when the coming of a Child Guidance Clinic to Philadelphia in 1925 and the organization of a national Orthopsychiatric Association in 1926 introduced other resources of knowledge and concern about the problems of children.

With this limitation on outside speaking she concentrated her teaching interest on developing so-called "Personality" courses for the curriculum of the Pennsylvania School of Social Work as she describes in a paper to be quoted later, "The Function of the Personality Course in the Practice Unit," and offered a course in Psychotherapy for Children, in 1934, and again in 1935; the only practice course in psychotherapy ever offered in the School. Her own work with two children in therapy culminated in a book published by Macmillan in 1933, *The Dynamics of Therapy*. This book found a responsive audience among social workers and went into a second printing. Out of print since, it continues to be a valuable book for therapists and counselors for the careful records it presents of her therapeutic work with two children.

Included in this present volume are the brief speech which she gave in discussion of Rank's paper on "The Development of the Emotional Life" at the first International Congress on Mental Hygiene held in Washington, D.C. in May, 1930, and "Living and Feeling," a paper written in 1933 for *Child Study*. Included also from *The Dynamics of Therapy* are the "Foreword," "Conclusion," and the chapter entitled "The Time Element in Therapy," in my judgment among the most characteristic and significant expressions of her philosophy.

Discussion
of a
Paper Delivered by Dr. Otto Rank

IT WOULD BE FUTILE and presumptuous to attempt to discuss briefly a paper so profound and far reaching in its implications as Dr. Rank's "The Development of the Emotional Life." For psychology, it offers the beginning of a new analysis and evaluation of feeling based on a type of observation and experience which thus far no laboratory technique has been able to attain, and without which it seems impossible to understand the functioning of the emotions in relation to behavior and consciousness.

Behavioristic psychology and the qualitative methods of the laboratory have produced thus far nothing but caricatures of emotional reality as human beings know it: a description of glandular reactions which may be physiologically and chemically correct, but has no meaning for psychological experience as such; a scientifically accurate account of an infant's overt behavior, whose claim to be

A discussion of a paper delivered by Dr. Otto Rank: "The Development of the Emotional Life." Delivered at the First International Congress for Mental Hygiene, Washington, May, 1930.

For her discussion of this occasion, see Jessie Taft's *Otto Rank, A Biographical Study* (New York: The Julian Press, 1958), pp. 146–152.

called emotional has never been established; or the report of adult responses under conditions so artificial and meaningless that only the zeal of the experimenter could confuse them with emotion as it actually operates in daily life. The approach of Gestalt psychology with its recognition of direct experience and the total situation gives a greater promise for a fruitful study of emotions, but thus far experiments seem to have been confined rather to perception, memory, learning, and the like.

It is from the field of psychoanalysis, where alone profound emotional reactions are open to direct observation, that one would expect a description and analysis of emotions that might correspond in some degree with the complexity and richness of our conscious experience. To my knowledge, however, this is the first time that we have been offered anything approaching a psychological analysis of living emotions as they operate in the immediate present.

What concerns us here, however, is not so much Dr. Rank's contribution to psychology as the implications of his position for our more practical mental hygiene interests. It is quite possible to deduce pessimistic conclusions from the premises before us, but in the brief time which is allotted, I choose rather to point out two corollaries which in my opinion are optimistic in their application.

A theory of emotions which not only recognizes but embraces their inevitability, which is not trying to escape them, to reduce them to conditioned reflexes, or infantile patterns which ought to be abandoned, gives us a new basis for self-respect, a new standard of values, and a very different concept of growth and maturity. As long as emotions are feared and condemned, as long as we struggle to attain the lifeless ideal of a maturity which is not subject to the negative separating affects, so long are we bound to a standard which already spells defeat, or success at the price of self-deception and a deadening of all feeling.

The social worker has long since come face to face with this doctrine of perfection under the guise of maturity or adjustment. It reduces to an absurdity the attempts which have been made from time to time to describe the personal qualifications for social casework. It is soon apparent that what is being required for the professional helping of others is nothing less than the righteousness demanded of the priest, with this difference, that very little stress is laid upon external behavior; *goodness* has been transferred to the inner realm of motives and feelings; has become in fact, emotional adjustment as nearly complete as possible; *badness* is now failure to adjust.

It soon becomes evident that what is actually meant by adjustment, is a condition in which one is not subject to the disturbing affects so characteristic of ordinary people. This expectation of perfection is never more in evidence than in the attitude of the professional and personal friends of the newly analyzed. It takes courage and conviction for one just out of the analytic experience to admit even to himself that pain, depression, anger, jealousy, and physical illness are still realities for him. Perhaps even the analyst himself is not quite free from the illusion of a static cure. It should be a relief, then, not only to the young social worker who has despaired of attaining this emasculated maturity or has rebelled against its coldness, but also to the parents and teachers whom we have tried to convert to an impossible objectivity in their relations to children, to find a theory of emotions which permits us to have them.

From this viewpoint the problem of maladjustment is seen to depend not on the existence of negative feelings but on the inability of the particular individual to accept and endure experience in feeling-terms; to face, not an environmental but an emotional reality, on which love has not greater hold than hate, joy no better claim than despair. The parent is hereby freed from a mental hygiene which seemed to demand a hardness and a disinterestedness incompatible with parental love, as well as an immunity to fear and irritation conceivable only in cases where personal relationship is nonexistent. The teacher too is to be allowed to be human, provided only she permits the child the same privilege. When we stop to realize the defense which human beings have put up against the acceptance of an inner world subject to guilt and fear as well as love and tenderness, it may seem that Dr. Rank has set us a task even more difficult than the work of eradicating evil from its natural habitat, the human soul. There is, however, this to be said for Dr. Rank's position: because it offers no final solution, sets up no static goal, it is capable of being used in a relativistic world. A morality which has to be achieved by denial, a maturity which would obviously bring all growth to an end, are certainly open to doubt and suspicion as to their fitness for use in a life which more and more we are coming to accept intellectually and scientifically as process.

The second deduction which seems to me hopeful for mental hygiene concerns Dr. Rank's concept of emotions in its relation to behavior. From this viewpoint the refuge from socially undesirable impulsive or compulsive action, would seem to lie, not in a denial or repression of emotions but in the cultivation of greater tolerance for emotional tension. It is interesting in this connection that psychoanalysis is often feared and criticized because it is supposed to stand for a releasing of impulses which may be far from valuable to society. Yet actually the tendency and effort of analysis should be to make the denied impulse emotionally conscious, so that the expression achieved will be an expression not of the impulse itself, but of the emotion which measures the full value of its voluntary inhibition in the analytic relationship. From this standpoint, analysis offers a training in the inhibition of impulse in favor of emotion, and insofar as it is therapeutically successful, increases the individual's tolerance for all emotions, thereby reducing the necessity of so much blind, uncontrolled, and frequently antisocial behavior. This is to say, that in bringing the hidden impulses to conscious realization, we allow emotion to take the place of the unconsidered isolated impulse, and bring it into relation with conscious will and intelligence.

For social caseworkers this theory indicates the value of being able to release negative as well as positive feelings within the casework relationship, rather than striving to keep what we call a good contact at all costs, thus forcing into impulsive unrecognized behavior, attitudes which might have been worked out in conscious emotion verbally and harmlessly expressed. For parents, Dr. Rank's understanding of emotion, might well provide a new basis for guidance and a great relief in the realization that ability to feel is not only a necessary evil but the only guarantee of behavior which is capable of becoming truly social.

Living and Feeling
"As a man thinketh in his heart, so is he."

THERE is no factor of personality which is so expressive of individuality as emotion, none so antagonistic to generalization. It is by the emotional quality or pattern of the total personality that in the last analysis we differentiate one person from another, friend from foe, average from superior, foolish from wise. Think of your friends and the respects in which you find any two of them essentially unlike. Perhaps you will say one is less able than the other, or one is more beautiful to look upon, or one is more generous, but if you really pin yourself down to a discriminating analysis of the basis of your judgment, I think you will find that the difference lies in the quality, depth, completeness, and spontaneity of the emotional life, not fundamentally in the appearance, the behavior, or the intellect. An able mind can bore us, exemplary behavior

An article published in *Child Study*, January, 1933.

leave us cold, beauty lose its charm, if not dynamically related to the emotions which are at the core of integrated, conscious personality and give it the essential quality or coloring to which we respond, not only with recognition but with an implicit acceptance or rejection.

We can always find reasons for loving this person and for disliking another apparently equally worthy individual. But the reasons are not causes; they merely support immediate response, which for us is the emotional truth about these particular persons. Therefore, while there are generalizations about emotion which are true for all children, actually the emotional sphere is the most untouchable aspect of any particular child, least subject to coercion, influence or leveling. It is the intensely personal, highly individualized, and conscious quality of emotion which has made it so unprofitable a field for scientific research and has driven its investigators to the physiological interpretations and the purely behavioristic descriptions with which much of our modern psychology rests content. Only with the rise of the psychoanalytic approach to the individual and the increasing interest of social casework and mental hygiene in prevention or adjustment has emotion come into its own. Out of this recognition of emotion, as somehow the center of all problems of personal and social adjustment, have arisen two methods of attack which may seem more different than they really are.

One is the attempt to discover types and set standards for normality, to list desirable and undesirable emotions, and to suggest programs for promoting the socially valuable and discouraging the socially destructive. Some psychologists harbor grave doubts about the desirability of any emotions for civilized men. They are phenomena to be borne as part of our animal heritage, but only as an inevitable burden on intelligent, controlled living. Fear, for instance, is quite generally condemned and treated as an unnecessary by-product to be avoided as far as possible by controlled conditioning of the earliest experiences. Jealousy, hatred, and rage are to be placed under the ban and tolerated only until they can be stamped out or brought under perfect control. The positive emotions are little understood and only roughly differentiated. Often we can find no accepted terms to describe the infinite variety and shades of difference which characterize a rich emotional life. Emotion that falls in the positive field quickly becomes literary description—even in a psychology test. If we seek for emotional truths, we turn to the great creative personalities, who have affirmed their own emotions fearlessly. We can learn little from the scientist.

The second approach to the problem of emotion is that of the psychiatrist, the psychoanalyst, and the social caseworker. It has a certain advantage over the scientific method in that the emotions it deals with are real, not manufactured in the laboratory, and it admits from the start the unique and individual character of any particular emotional problem. However, it often loses this vantage ground for the study of emotion, because it assumes that it is necessary to cure or reform the individual in terms of an accepted norm; this is as vitiating to the individual as the scientist's averages. Since both the scientific and the mental hygiene approach leave something to be desired, we must turn elsewhere for further light.

Perhaps the truth is that we fear emotions, fear their

uniqueness and their nonconformity, fear them in ourselves since they proclaim our difference, and fear them in others since we cannot control them. Perhaps scientist and therapist, like the rest of us, are blocked in their efforts to understand any given emotional state as it actually is, because to them too the underlying impulse, however restrained, is to check it, divert it, or mold it into something else.

In these fearful or repressive attitudes toward emotion the layman joins wholeheartedly. He, too, is always on guard against emotion, which betrays him to himself and to others as he really is, and often exposes him to more reality in the other person than he is ready to face. For the adult, as for the child, emotion spells danger. If you ask a patient in analysis why he objects to being angry, he may say that he is afraid of what his anger will bring out in retaliation, but more often he will confess that it hurts his pride to be vulnerable. Anger admits that he has been touched, that he has a weak spot. Jealousy and hate also are admissions of weakness, of negative attachment or bondage to another. Love itself, in its simplest form as a felt and admitted need, is usually violently resisted unless some affectional hold on its object is assured; for love too would put us at the mercy of another. Men traditionally scorn emotion, women have been branded as emotional with this same underlying implication of weakness. On the other hand strong spirits of all ages, men and women alike, have proclaimed their emotions vigorously and without apology. There must be a reason why the emotional life, which the creative individual affirms, is so often denied, feared, or condemned by the scientist as well as by the layman.

The usual answer is that there are good emotions and bad ones, emotions that are useful and those that are useless if not harmful. It is right to cultivate joy, love, tenderness, sympathy, pity, and to root out fear, anger, hate, guilt, and jealousy. The average parent works along these lines on an apparently sound, rational basis. It may trouble him perhaps, if he stops to think, that he minds so much these manifestations of fear or rage in his child, that they should call out such immediate powerful responses in himself. On the other hand, he may pride himself on his imperturbability, while his child batters away at him in a fierce passion of desire to disturb this inhuman calm. The mental hygiene and child guidance influence has increased the self-consciousness of the enlightened parent and often the result has been an even greater shame for emotional upset in the family life, and still sterner efforts to remain as impartial and passionless as the ideal therapist is supposed to be.

In my opinion this attitude rests upon a complete misunderstanding of emotion and its role in living. It simply reflects the fear of life which is attached primarily to emotions as indices of vital response and with which every human being must cope in greater or lesser degree. It is useless to regard emotions as something which we can tolerate, cultivate, or eliminate at will. They are as inherent in living as in thinking. They measure the degree of self-consciousness, the delay, or modification and organization which the developed individual is able to institute between raw impulses and final behavior; and they are therefore an inevitable accompaniment of the problem-solving intelligence and the organized will. Emotions are indices of felt values, both positive and negative, which become conscious only when there is a break, voluntary or enforced, between the will and its realization, a separation between desire and its object.

If the self is negatively involved, if its impulses are checked, or its purposes interfered with, the value of these inhibited tendencies to action and their meaning to the whole self is measured by the degree of feeling which is stirred up by their being blocked. If the source of the interference is located outside of the self, and is felt as utterly alien and unreasonable, then the result is registered in feelings of irritation, anger, rage, or blame. If the obstacle seems overpowering, perhaps fear, despair, or dull depression will come to the fore.

Often, however, the period of delay is a result of choice, of determination which holds in check the impatient urges to immediate satisfaction for the sake of the deeper purposes of the total self. Then emotion becomes positive. The pain or fear of waiting is borne more or less willingly, and the delayed or surrendered end may be represented in feelings of love, longing, tenderness, joy, impatience, excitement, or the like, since final satisfaction—the union with the object or achievement of the desired end—is postponed or inhibited voluntarily, not blocked by a separating, external force.

As soon as some kind of effective action becomes possible, whether it be in the direction of successful accomplishment, emotional expression, or escape from the insoluble problem, emotion ordinarily subsides. It is clear that the greatest awareness of self and "object" is at the point of the greatest blocking, where the will stands out as quite separate and unable to relate itself to the outside reality. As soon as the will can flow freely into action, either direct or symbolic, it loses this intense consciousness of difference and isolation, and becomes one with the outer world in which it functions smoothly once more. To decry emotions then, even the unpleasant and separating, is to quarrel with self-consciousness itself. To insist that the child get rid of hate, anger, fear and jealousy, or even to deny them wholly from the start, is to put a penalty on becoming a conscious self. It is hard enough for the child to admit that outside forces are stronger and can defeat his will; but if the pain, fear, and rage which such interference causes are not to be felt, what measure has he of the will's value to itself? Father and mother are among the defeating, thwarting objects to which the child must both oppose himself and yield. If he can bear to feel the hate which his parents' more powerful wills arouse, and they can bear to let him, he will also be capable of feeling the joy of resting upon their strength, instead of fighting against it blindly or yielding in abject submission.

The price one pays for success in denying negative feelings is a lessening of the ability to feel positively. Feeling is one. It goes with whatever the self admits as vitally important. To be able to feel, one must be willing to care. And to care is to expose oneself to loss or injury or defeat as well as to fulfillment and success. The goodness or badness of an emotion is determined, then, not by its pleasantness or unpleasantness, not by its positive or negative, uniting or separating character, but by the extent to which the individual accepts it as a part of himself, a necessary reflection of his own evaluation of living, instead of projecting it completely upon an external cause.

In the child or the undeveloped adult, positive feelings are hardly more social and lovable than negative; love in its first form has no more genuine regard for the object than hate. The child hates the mother when she refuses a request; the fault is in her. He sees, not himself hating, but his mother as a hateful person. When the mother is ill he realizes dimly the need he has for her and there may be a sudden sense of tenderness, a wish to do something for her, a painful longing for her ministrations, or at last, if the illness continues too long, resentment at her failure to meet his need or fear of total loss in death. In all of this you have a picture of emotions in embryo, undeveloped, unaccepted, unrealized. Only in the moment of tenderness does the child approach the point of love which sees the other as a separate person.

And how rare it is to see or to experience love for the other as he is, rather than love for the other as we need him to be for our own fulfillment. The mother herself has the same problem. She has to battle with her own need of the child, and the frustration which his growth and welfare imposes upon her use of him. We say a certain woman loves her child too much. We mean that she is not able to love him because she cannot control her own use of him for the sake of his growing self and its needs; that she cannot be herself or let her child become himself, but loses herself in him. Love, as far as it exists as a developed emotion, is a measure of one's acceptance of separation and separateness. It is an esteem for the object in itself and a recognition of one's own self as inevitably different, which is possible only when the desire to possess in reality is voluntarily surrendered as incompatible with living. The impulse to possess need not be denied or rejected, but its expression can be controlled in favor of a deeper will to be free, if one is willing to feel his love and act his freedom.

The difference between developed emotion and simple emotion is like that between organized, responsible will and crude impulse. The impulse slips over into action with little consciousness, it is neither accepted nor rejected by the self; it just happens; and it is on that level that little children begin. The anger of the little child is normally momentary, has not much body, and goes over quickly from the sense of being thwarted into explosive, irrelevant action: a scream, a kick, a blow. The little child does not think of himself as angry but of the object as bad. Unless he is allowed to be angry, even though he is not allowed to hurt someone else, he will never learn where the feeling belongs. The task of the parent is not to stop the emotion, but to help the child to be responsible for it, to bear it. The parent has no right to deny the reality of the child's fear, his hate, or his rage, since the child, if he is true to himself, has to feel what he feels and cannot change his feelings to order. The parent has a right, however, if not an obligation, to check destructive acts unless they are confined to comparatively harmless emotional expression. The child may hit the dog in lieu of the parent, may call names, or make faces. These are natural and necessary outlets for the violent feeling which has to go somewhere and which no child and few adults can keep inside completely. But the child may not kill the cat or stick pins in his baby sister however much he would like to. And if you, as a parent, can bear to admit and help him to admit what and how he feels without too much denial, he will require far less checking in actual behavior.

It is safer to feel hate than to act out the unconsciously murderous impulse. The murderer in cold blood is he who cannot bear within his own soul the tension of his fear and hate, but must project them blindly upon another person as if he would rid himself of death and destruction within by setting it up outside of himself. This is action catharsis which works too finally and too really to be remedial for the self or safe for the other. Emotional expression is tempered, it is not raw impulse, but impulse which has come through the medium of the conscious self as far as there is one.[1]

Emotion then is a safeguard against destructive behavior when the self can grow to the point where it is able to feel its own contradictory impulses consciously and accept of its own will the burden of responsibility which they impose. The child as a beginning, undeveloped self will tend to impulsive, inconsistent, unrecognized action, rather than to emotion and emotional expression, and to the negative rather than to the positive emotions. Activity of any kind is the simplest and most effective escape from feeling, particularly from fear; while anger and rage as

[1] Otto Rank, *Modern Education: A Critique of Its Fundamental Ideas* (New York: Alfred A. Knopf, 1932), Chap. 3.

the most easily felt and expressed emotions provide the quickest emotional relief. It is interesting to note how easily and naturally the child interprets any emotional disturbance as anger or aversion. Many children will not admit fear, although dislike is easily expressed; this is astonishingly true of adults also, despite the fact that fear is an omnipresent reality for anyone who lets himself know it. Strong positive emotion is almost equally unbearable.

Thus we have a five-year-old reiterating her grief for the death of a dearly loved parent in an explosive "I'm so mad, my father died."

Often after a painful absence a child rejects on first meeting his most beloved friend or possession. Parents are frequently hurt at this apparent lack of appreciation or positive feeling, when it is the pain of feeling at all which the child does not know how to handle, or his embarrassment at the flood of feeling let loose upon him by the parent which drowns out his own lesser response.

If by denial, reproof, or overwhelming counterfeeling, the parent discourages too effectively his beginning efforts to meet experience with emotional recognition of its value, the child will take care of his feeling reactions in one of several ways. He may turn them back to the physiological level where they do not humiliate him by referring to the real object of his reaction, but are just sensations in his own body—experienced perhaps as nausea, headache, or constipation, which no one can deny or blame him for. Or he may utilize them in habits which he seems unable to control even when he tries, but which are nevertheless very effective in conquering the parent. He may express them more directly in aggressive behavior or hyperactivity. Or perhaps he may try to deny all feeling in spells of lethargy and indifference which resemble depression. You will find that each individual has a typical way of dealing with what he is unwilling or unable to feel, but no one outlet is chosen to the exclusion of all others. Physiological functions, activity, symptomatic behavior, are all utilized in some degree by everyone to drain off potentially painful or fearful emotions.

It is clear then that to discuss norms and averages in the emotional life is difficult if not impossible. Behavior we may limit rightfully in terms of social necessity, but who can decide what anyone ought to feel or what he will actually feel? And if we could decide, how could we enforce it? That people differ in emotional capacity as well as in emotional development seems to me as true as that people differ in intellectual equipment and development. There certainly are individuals who are superior, or at least very different from the average person in their emotional sensitivity, depth and spontaneity, as well as in their capacity to sustain emotional tension over long periods for creative expression. There also seem to be individuals who have potential emotional superiority, but who are caught in an insoluble conflict with life and do not develop their powers; just as some persons never seem able to utilize to the full their natural endowments in the intellectual field.

With the emotions, as with health and intellect, we have the problem of original equipment as against the results produced by the actual experience of the individual in interaction with life as he finds it. This will differ for every child. Hence we can no more set a standard for what is emotionally normal, in the sense of desirable, for a particular child, than we can determine by norm what he as an individual ought to become. We can, however, help to free the particular child to become himself in his own terms at least emotionally, if we can divorce our rejection of his specific behavior from a rejection of the child himself. Yet that is the way it feels to the child when the emotions which constitute his intensest sense of self are condemned.

You ask how this can be done. Certainly by no cut and dried formula of child training. Emotion responds only to emotion; the self goes out and expands only in the presence of a respect and acceptance which it can feel. The child has a right to experience not only his own feelings but the emotional reactions which he arouses in the parents, to feel his own power over them as well as theirs over him, to know their momentary hates, fears, and rages, as well as their supporting love and tenderness. This is not destructive unless the parent, by projecting his emotion too completely, forces the child to carry an impossible burden, or perhaps monopolizes the field so that the child's less powerful and confident feelings are given no opportunity for expression.

In other words, if the parent respects his own emotions and is willing to feel in the presence of the child the anger as well as the love which the child is, or should be, able to arouse in him, then the child too will find it not so hard to express the hurt or the fear or the sense of injustice which otherwise he would tend to hide even from himself. I do not mean to imply here that the parent should let anger govern his treatment of the child or permit his love to smother him or rule him; but that he should be able, without guilt, to admit and bear as feeling this relation to his child which, by its very depth and reality, exposes him to periods of pain and defeat. If this seems to give the child too great an advantage, since it lets him feel immediately the human weakness and limitation of the parent, remember that the only way the child can learn to bear the strength and weakness which belong to man and are the source of his deepest conflict, is through his experience with adults who have accepted both. What the child needs in his parents is not the perfect understanding and unmoved calm of the therapist, but contact with living, responsive, changing persons who are not afraid to feel in relation to him or to each other. We need not worry that our child feels more strongly or differently from ourselves or other children. Nor is there need to fear any norm or label which science or psychiatry can suggest. But that he should fail to experience as deeply as he might is certainly a cause not only for the study of the child's problem but for a heart-searching examination of our own capacity for meeting life without too great denial of its positive or negative values. For if the parents are living their own emotional lives with a fair degree of responsibility and acceptance, the child too will learn in time to feel what he feels when he feels it, and thus gain the courage of himself. For to feel is to live, but to reject feeling through fear is to reject the life process itself.

The Dynamics of Therapy
in a Controlled Relationship

IN THIS VOLUME I have combined results of work and
thought written at different times during the past three
years as experience crystallized, and therefore without the
unity of a book conceived and brought forth as a whole.
There is, nevertheless, the integration of a consistent
interest and viewpoint, together with the continuity which
characterizes any record of developing experience in which
a conscious psychology and philosophy are interacting
with immediate, yet controlled contacts.

Therapy as it relates to the balance of forces in the
organization of personality has always been of prime importance to me, but my concept of what such therapy involves has undergone a complete revolution in the past
twenty-five years. It has developed from the notion of a
reform of the "other" through superior knowledge of life
and psychology, a concept closely allied to that of scientific
control in the field of emotions and behavior, to my present
acceptance of therapy as presented in this volume; a
therapy which is purely individual, nonmoral, nonsci-
entific, nonintellectual, which can take place only when
divorced from all hint of control, unless it be the therapist's
control of himself in the therapeutic situation.

While many words could be written in the abstract about

This chapter appears as the "Foreword" in Jessie Taft's *The
Dynamics of Therapy in a Controlled Relationship* (New York:
The Macmillan Company, 1933).

what I mean by therapy as growth, and the therapeutic relationship as dynamic, it seemed to me that only a verbatim or nearly verbatim recording of the content and interchange in such a relationship could give meaning and life to my explanations. I have used two records therefore, not to prove anything, but to give my abstractions a chance to come alive for those who want to understand emotionally. I have chosen records of contacts with two children; first, because they are brief enough and simple enough to serve as immediate experience for the reader without entangling him in symptoms and interpretation and second, because therapeutic contacts with children were new enough and problematic enough for me, to sharpen every theoretical issue and to challenge whatever I might possess of technical skill. My own uncertainties regarding the nature of the therapeutic relationship seem to have been lodged in children, and there only was I able to settle them; which is not to say that I think of direct therapy for children as nonproblematic, or frequently indicated; but merely that in these experiences I have satisfied myself and answered my own doubts as to the possibility of setting up the therapeutic relationship with a child without detriment to him, regardless of its effectiveness or desirability as a method for solving environmental problems. I am not, therefore, advocating analysis of children or any other form of direct treatment for their behavior and personality problems, I am merely using the therapeutic relationship with two particular children to illustrate my conception of therapy.

It is necessary to make one more explanation in terms of my own peculiar experience since for me psychological therapy, as a profession, includes not only the various forms of psychoanalysis but the direct treatment undertaken by social casework in which, justifiably or not, the client's relation to the caseworker is utilized more or less consciously and responsibly for the amelioration of emotional and behavior difficulties. This assumption of responsibility by social casework for healing as well as practical aid has developed rapidly in the eastern part of the United States, stimulated by the growth of mental hygiene and child guidance clinics. It has come to a climax in so-called "psychiatric social work" where the function of the caseworker is usually recognized as primarily therapeutic. The efforts of social agencies organized for a particular function such as relief, health, child placing, to keep step with this growing emphasis on psychological understanding, interpretation, and treatment have resulted in the confusion to which I refer in the first chapter between social work as therapy and social work with some other practical goal. Although, technically speaking, I am a psychologist, I have always been associated with social agencies and have never divorced my interest in therapy from its application to casework where the problem is even more compelling because it is undefined theoretically, complicated practically, and seems to imply a discipline as exacting as that which psychoanalysis requires. The first chapter, "The Time Element in Therapy," was written at the close of the second case, and represents from one aspect, the net result of my thinking about the relation of this type of therapy to the casework of the two social agencies with which the children were connected. In both of these agencies, but particularly in the second, time is important not only theoretically and philosophically but actually, as a vital factor, determining the possibilities of any treatment.

The term "relationship therapy" is used to differentiate therapy as I have experienced and practiced it, from psychoanalysis or any process in which either the analytic or the intellectual aspect is stressed or the immediacy of the experience denied or confused with history. It was only gradually that I became sufficiently confident of my own difference to want to give it a label, but it now seems necessary to use some name to designate a philosophy and technique which have little in common with psychoanalysis as generally understood, but are, on the contrary, antipathetic to the Freudian psychology and practice. My quarrel with casework, however, is not that it is psychoanalytic, but that it undertakes therapy under the guise of practical help, without becoming responsible for it overtly, or it fails, for lack of understanding, to be therapeutic incidentally within the limits of a concrete function.

The Time Element in Therapy

THE WORD "THERAPY" is used instead of "treatment" because in its derivation and in my own feeling about the word, there is not so much implication of manipulation of

Paper read at the National Conference of Social Work, Philadelphia, May, 1932. Reprinted as Part 1 of Jessie Taft's *The Dynamics of Therapy in a Controlled Relationship* (New York: The Macmillan Company, 1933).

one person by another. To treat, according to the dictionary, is to apply a process to someone or something. The word "therapy" has no verb in English, for which I am grateful; it cannot do anything to anybody, hence can better represent a process going on, observed perhaps, understood perhaps, assisted perhaps, but not applied. The Greek noun from which therapy is derived means "a servant," the verb means "to wait." I wish to use the English word "therapy" with the full force of its derivation, to cover a process which we recognize as somehow and somewhat curative but which, if we are honest enough and brave enough, we must admit to be beyond our control. In fact if it were not so, life would be intolerable. No one wants another to apply any process to the inmost self, however desirable a change in personality and behavior may seem objectively. We may be willing to let the physician cure a bodily ill, although even that is not so sure, but the self is defended against every encroachment, even the most benevolent. Resistance to cure, however, is not necessarily open, conscious, or violent. The most docile patient is often best able to demonstrate the worthlessness of the remedy and the helplessness of the doctor. In the face of my own personal realization of the impotence of the other to help me unless I let him, in fact of my necessity to keep him impotent lest he use his interest in my welfare to interfere with me, I am forced to accept the full limitation which this recognition implies in my own power to help others. I know in advance that no one is going to experience change, call it growth or progress if you have the courage, because I think it would be good for society, good for his family and friends, or even good for himself. I know equally well that no one is going to take help from me because someone else thinks it desirable. The anxious parent, the angry school teacher, the despairing wife or husband, must bear their own burdens, solve their own problems. I can help them only in and for themselves, if they are able to use me. I cannot perform a magic upon the bad child, the inattentive pupil, the faithless partner, because they want him made over in their own terms.

This means not only a limit put upon those seeking help but a genuine limitation in myself, an impotence which I am forced to accept even when it is painful, as it frequently is. There is a beloved child to be saved, a family unity to be preserved, an important teacher to be enlightened. Before all these problems in which one's reputation, one's pleasure in utilizing professional skill, as well as one's real feeling for the person in distress are perhaps painfully involved, one must accept one's final limitation and the right of the other, perhaps his necessity, to refuse help or to take help in his own terms, not as therapist, friends, or society might choose. My knowledge and my skill avail nothing, unless they are accepted and used by the other. Over that acceptance and possible use, I have no control beyond the genuineness of my understanding of the difficulty with which anyone takes or seeks help, my respect for the strength of the patient, however negatively expressed, and the reality of my acceptance of my function as helper not ruler. If my conviction is real, born of emotional experience too deep to be shaken, then at least I am not an obstacle to the person who needs help but fears domination. He can now approach me without the added fear and resistance which active designs for his cure could surely produce and can find within the limitation which I accept thus sincerely, a safety which permits him to utilize and me to exercise all the professional skill and wisdom at my command. On the other hand, the person who seeks the domination of another in order to project his conflict and avoid himself and his own development by resisting the effort of the other to save him, is finally brought to a realization of the futility of his striving, as he cannot force upon me a goal which I have long since recognized to be outside my province and power. Whether such a person will ultimately succeed in taking over his own problem, since I cannot relieve him of it, can be determined only by what actually happens. There are those who are unwilling or unable to go further, an outcome every therapist must stand ready to admit and respect, no matter how much his professional ego is hurt or his therapeutic or economic aim defeated. This is in no sense to be designated as passivity in treatment. As I conceive it, the therapeutic function involves the most intense activity, but it is an activity of attention, of identification and understanding, of adaptation to the individual's need and pattern, combined with an unflagging preservation of one's own limitation and difference. With this preliminary explanation of the choice of the word "therapy" in preference to treatment—because of its original connection with serving or waiting upon, not in the moral or religious sense, but in the realization of a psychological fact of limitation which must be accepted before therapy is possible at all—I am ready to discuss time in relation to the therapeutic process. It might have been discreet to limit my title to therapy as exemplified in social casework since I intend to consider it for the most part in that connection, but what I have to say about time is true, as I see it, for all therapy.

It is the type of work found in the child guidance clinic which comes nearest to what I mean by casework as individual therapy, and it is this kind of casework which I wish to consider in its relation to time. Here where there is no practical barrier, where the agency is set up to offer therapy, we are faced with the full responsibility for the time factor, on the one hand the problem of unlimited time, on the other equally, the danger of cutting off too soon something that might have eventuated in therapy if only the worker had held on a little longer. In the therapeutic casework with which I am acquainted it seems to me that the caseworker has finally accepted, at least intellectually, the fact that she can be of no use unless the client wants something, is willing to take her help, and actively seeks it; but she is not yet rid of her feeling of responsibility for his improvement. Why go on week after week if nothing happens to indicate progress; how justify herself for this piling up of time; how recognize when there has been enough therapy except by results. Yet for results she cannot be responsible without putting pressure on the client. As soon as she decides what ought to happen must she not take command and decide, however tactfully, that the client should come longer, or has come long enough? Responsibility without control is the dilemma of therapeutic casework as now practiced. Then there is the worker who has given up responsibility for the client's behavior in the world, for any final shaping of his personality, but who still cannot free herself of responsibility for the interview in which she takes part. How can she go into it blindly and passively? She may be willing to be silent, to be very slow and patient, but is she not there to somehow guide the process to a result which will be therapeutic? If the whole affair is to be left to the client where does she come in? It is no wonder she clings to history and the value of catharsis. If she cannot show the patient how to live, if she cannot give him moral, religious, or ethical instruction, at least she can see to it that he empties himself of his past, and even that he learns to interpret in ways he never thought of. In other words she can use the hour or two of the weekly conferences to bring out material.

That this preconceived idea of what the interview should sooner or later bring forth, tends just as much to the control and domination of the client as if she had tried to re-form his habits or his morals, very few caseworkers ever realize because if they did they would be greatly at a loss as to what function remains for them. Moreover, the re-living or rehearsing of the past plus the worker's interpretation of it, seems to offer some kind of rational limit to an otherwise unlimited affair. If it is dangerous to use the disappearance of symptoms as a criterion, then what can be used? Perhaps the fact that all the material from the past seems to have been brought out and understood, will provide a natural ending. But, as I know only too well from my own earlier efforts, it is a very baffling experience to see your patient with his past apparently clear to him and you, all his involved relations to his parents finally revealed and neatly interpreted, but his problem of living as unsolved as ever. "Yes, I understand," he says, "But what can I do about it? I don't find it any easier to live." If you decide that he should continue to come what happens next? There is

always something, there always will be something to be discovered in his past that he has not brought out before.
There is really no limit to the past with this approach, and
the client may well go on until he rebels or you grow too
weary to bear it, and end the struggle with or without
therapy.

The futility of this type of relationship to the client has
led certain caseworkers to the recognition of two other
factors which may be determinative of therapy and perhaps
contain an inherent time limit or criterion for ending. The
one recognizes the relation between worker and client as
dynamic and present, the other recognizes time as a qualitative as well as a quantitative affair, valuable in and for
itself when it is actually utilized in the passing moment
without dependence on a next time. The first factor, the
recognition of the reality of the relationship between
worker and client and its dynamic changing quality has
been quite completely accepted, at least verbally, among
the more radical group of caseworkers. But the cloven hoof
remains, in my opinion, in the fact that the dynamics of
the immediate relationship is often obscured by the concept of living out, reliving, or solving past relationships
on the worker. According to this concept, the worker is
being used in the present, but only as a lay figure on which
to project experiences and feelings from the client's past.
An utter confusion results, a practical denial of the reality
of the present which is functioning for the sake of the past.
Once more the worker is effectively hidden behind the
screen of father, mother, brother, sister, while all the time
her value for the client is that she is none of these and he
knows it. He may be using patterns which were developed

by him in birth, nursing, weaning, toilet training, Oedipus situation, and what not, but he is using them now, with all the changes wrought by years of living, using them afresh as they are in the present hours, in immediate reaction to someone who behaves as no one has ever behaved to him before; someone who understands and permits a use of herself, which determines for the client a new experience valuable, if at all, in and for itself. He does not want a father or a mother, but he does want someone who will permit him ultimately to find himself apart from parent identifications without interference or domination; someone who will not be fooled, someone strong enough not to retaliate. The client may feel toward the worker attitudes which recall his earlier ties to mother or father as they developed biologically, but the moment the worker confuses her own relation to the client with his relation to anyone else past or present, that moment she has again entangled herself with history, with external fact, with the static goal of definite material, and also has escaped her own responsibility for the present. The relation may be dynamic, but the client is unable to avail himself fully of its therapeutic possibilities because it is predetermined, set in advance, without creative opportunity.

According to this doctrine, which I am criticizing, the client is not really "cured" or through, until he has lived out all the faulty biological and sociological relationships. If he has apparently exhausted his use of the worker as a mother, he is not safe to go until the father relation has been lived through also, and so on. How long it should take before one can be sure that everything essential has been re-experienced consciously is as uncertain as material and relationships from the past are unlimited. Once more therapy is defeated by the setting up of an external norm or purpose for which the caseworker must assume responsibility willy-nilly, but which, unfortunately, again contains no inherent time limit.

Driven into a blind alley by this limitless possibility in longtime treatment, certain groups have taken refuge in what has come to be known as "the short contact." Here, for the first time in the history of casework as far as I know, a few caseworkers are struggling with the fundamental problem of therapy. It is interesting to see that they have been able to come to grips with the real issue only when they have set up for themselves an arbitrary limit in time. What happens, they ask themselves, to make a single or short contact meaningful, as it often is, for client and worker even if they never meet again. The fascination which the study of the short contact holds indicates that somehow it contains the whole problem of therapy, if only it can be mastered. I find the significance of this concentration on the short contact by individuals who represent the experimental emphasis in casework to be threefold. First, it indicates a self-confidence which has freed itself to the point of taking responsibility for its own part in a process. Second, it points to a growth and achievement in casework which can afford to admit a limitation. Third, it is a recognition of the fact that whatever takes place between worker and client of a therapeutic nature must be present in some degree in the single contact if it is ever to be there. If there is no therapeutic understanding and use of one interview, many interviews equally barren will not help. In the single interview, if that is all I allow myself to count upon, if I am willing to take that one hour in and for itself, there is no time to hide behind material, no time to explore the past or future. I myself am the remedy at this moment if there is any, and I can no longer escape my responsibility, not for the client but for myself and my role in the situation. Here is just one hour to be lived through as it goes, one hour of present, immediate relationship, however limited, with another human being who has brought himself to the point of asking for help. If somehow this single contact proves to have value for the applicant, how does it happen? What in the nature of my functioning permits this hour to be called therapeutic at least qualitatively?

Perhaps one reason we find it difficult to analyze what takes place in the short contact, is that here we are brought face to face with a present from which it is hard to escape and which in consequence carries symbolically and really our own personal pattern as it relates to time and the self-limitation which is involved in its acceptance. Not only is the client limited by this brief period of time, not only is he facing the possibility of being turned out too soon or kept on after he is ready to go, but I also am forced to admit my limited function as therapist, dependent as I am upon his right to go when he must or to deprive me of a second opportunity no matter how willing I may be to continue the contact, no matter how much he may need the help I have to give from an objective standpoint. My only control, which is not easy to exercise, is my control over myself in the present hour if I can bring myself to the point of a reasonable degree of acceptance of that hour with all of its shortcomings. The fact that our personal reaction to time gives a clear picture of the real nature of our resistance of taking full responsibility for therapeutic casework, makes it necessary at this point to consider time and its relation to therapy more philosophically.

Time represents more vividly than any other category the necessity of accepting limitation as well as the inability to do so, and symbolizes therefore the whole problem of living. The reaction of each individual to limited or unlimited time betrays his deepest and most fundamental life pattern, his relation to the growth process itself, to beginnings and endings, to being born and to dying. As a child I remember struggling with the horror of infinite space, but the passing of time was even more unbearable. I can remember my gratitude for Christmas, because at least presents remained, something lasted beyond the moment. There was deep depression in adolescence over the realization of this flow of time. Why go to a party since tomorrow it will be over and done with? Why experience at all, since nothing can be held? On the other hand, there is equal fear of being permanently caught in any state or process. Fear of being bored is perhaps its most intellectualized form, panic in the face of a physical trap or snare its most overwhelming and instinctive expression. As living beings we are geared to movement and growth, to achieving something new, leaving the outworn behind and going on to a next stage. Hence we do not like a goal that can never be reached nor yet a goal that is final, a goal beyond which we cannot go. In terms of this primary double fear of the static and of the endlessly moving, the individual is always trying to maintain a balance, and frequently fails because of too great fear either of changing or of never being able to change again. To put it very simply, perhaps the human problem is no more than this: If one cannot live forever is it worth while to live at all?

We see this problem and this double fear reflected in every slightest human experience from birth to death and consequently also in the caseworker's as well as the client's attitude toward the long or the short contact. Whether or not she can face the reality of either, depends on whether life to her can be accepted on the terms under which it can be obtained, that is, as a changing, finite, limited affair, to be seized at the moment if at all. The basis for believing that life can be thus accepted, beyond the fact that all of us do more or less accept it if we continue to exist, lies in this: that we are, after all, part and parcel of the life process; that we do naturally abhor not only ending but also never ending, that we not only fear change but the unchanging. Time and change, dying and being born, are inner as well as outer realities if fear of external violence or compulsion does not play too great a part. Life is ambivalent but so are we, "born and bred in the briar patch," And on this fact rests the whole possibility of therapy. We cannot change the fundamental biological and psychological conditions of living for others, or for ourselves, but somewhere within each individual is this same life process which can go on for and of itself, if the fear which has become excessive primarily in birth and the earlier experiences can be decreased in quantity sufficiently to permit the inherent normal ambivalence to function and hence to provide its own checks and balances. Time in itself is a purely arbitrary category of man's invention, but since it is a projection of his innermost being, it represents so truly his inherent psychological conflict, that to be able to accept it, to learn to admit its likeness to one's very self, its perfect adaptation to one's deepest and most contradictory impulses, is already to be healed, as far as healing is possible or applicable, since in accepting time, one accepts the self and life with their inevitable defects and limitations. This does not mean a passive resignation, but a willingness to live, work, and create as mortals within the confines of the finite.

I know of no more poignant presentation of the release which comes from yielding to life as it is, with its inevitable endings, than is given in an article by Gertrude Carver, "Early Holiday," in the October, 1931, *Atlantic Monthly* which gives the experience of one who faces death from a fatal disease with ample time for realization and no sustaining belief in immortality to blur the immediacy. "In this literal acceptance of death," she says:

> I now find the only authentic preface to living. . . . I should have expected to share in the face of death the panorama of life that proverbially presents itself to a drowning man, but the scroll of the years refused to unfurl. The hidden record betrayed them, however, by burdening the present moments with an anonymous significance. Repeatedly I was made aware that every impression, every contact had incorporated itself into myself by a law of mysterious but complete assimilation, until my previous selves with their contemporary experience had endowed my present self with dimension. They were myself but so unified, so drawn into the present, that there could be no separation of episode. Time, necessary as an impulse and chart to memory, did not exist. There-

fore, not only was my future, by the imminence of death removed, but in a strangely satisfying way my past no longer existed, except in the expanded vitality of the present. With the future denied, and with the past automatically denying itself, it was as though the moment, transient and ephemeral in the laws of time, challenged those very laws and reaching out across boundaries dissolved by the removal of past and future, became reality, infinite and precious. A concentrated urgency impelled each second into aeons and frustrated time. In a present so powerfully weighted, where was there room for even a thin thread of concern about immortality?

I have never come across anything in literature which so perfectly explains the use of a time limit in therapy. Since death is so much more final and compelling than any time limit man can set and difficult to take into the self, so complete an experience is seldom granted, but the principle is the same and however strange it may seem, all endings, all partings being more or less shadowed with the fear of death, become important and fearful out of all proportion because their value is symbolic. Perhaps the ending of a longtime therapeutic relationship, agreed to by the patient from the beginning, takes on more of this compelling quality than any other situation where threat of death is entirely absent; hence its therapeutic worth, which consists primarily in this fear-reducing heightening of the value of the present and the releasing discovery that an ending willed or accepted by the individual himself is birth no less than death, creation no less than annihilation.

So literally true even in the slightest situations is this description of our relation to time and particularly to a

time limit that in any therapeutic interview where in coming the individual admits a need for assistance, it is possible
to see the operation of this person's paticular pattern, his
own way of reacting to time or if you like to the life problem itself. This one is at your door fifteen minutes too
soon, the other keeps you waiting, or perhaps fails to turn
up at all. The very one who makes you wait at the beginning of the hour may be equally loath to go at the end and
leaves you to be responsible for getting him out. The other
who comes before you are ready is on edge to be gone before the time you have allotted to him is up. Neither can
bear the hour as it is, with limits set by the other, even
though he has agreed to them beforehand. The one makes
you bear the burden of his lateness, the other tries to bear
too much, both his own responsibility and yours, depriving
himself of what is his, and you of the chance to contribute
what you have already assigned for his use in terms of time.
And so it goes, for every individual a slightly different
pattern, but with the same motivation which is so deeply
symptomatic of the individual's problem that one might
fairly define relationship therapy as a process in which the
individual finally learns to utilize the allotted hour from
beginning to end without undue fear, resistance, resentment, or greediness. When he can take it and also leave it
without denying its value, without trying to escape it completely or keep it forever because of this very value; insofar he has learned to live, to accept this fragment of
time in and for itself, and strange as it may seem, if he
can live this hour he has in his grasp the secret of all hours;
he has conquered life and time for the moment and in
principle.

Here then in the simplest of terms is a real criterion for therapy, an inner norm which can operate from the moment the person enters your office to the moment at which he departs more or less finally, whether he comes once or a hundred times. It is a goal which is always relative, which will never be completely attained, yet is solved in every single hour to some degree however slight if the client really wants help and I offer a contact in which limitation is accepted and acted upon, at least for myself. If I believe that one hour has value, even if no other follows; if I admit the client's right to go as well as to come, and see his efforts and resistances in both directions even when he cannot; if I maintain at the same time my own rights in time as well as my responsibility and limitations and respect his necessity to work out his own way of meeting a limit even when it involves opposition to mine as it must, then I have provided the essentials of a therapeutic situation. If with this personal readiness, I combine self-conscious skill and ability to utilize the elements which make for therapy, the client may if he chooses, in greater or lesser degree, learn to bear this limited situation which, as he finally comes to realize, is imposed by himself as truly as by me; by his own human nature, no less than mine; or, if you like, by the nature of the life process itself.

I have often heard discouraged caseworkers with much—perhaps too much—psychoanalytic information, question the value of casework, since only psychoanalysis seems to offer real therapy. The problem, as I see it, lies not so much in the caseworker's lack of equipment for carrying on psychoanalytic treatment with her clients as in her failure to comprehend the nature of therapy and what she undertakes when she sets out to help other people, either practically or personally and psychologically. There is no question in my mind as to the value of casework once it learns to utilize within the limits of a practical function the psychological insight to be gained from an understanding of the therapeutic process. Therapy is a matter of degree, of depth, and may be present anywhere, but the quantitative element must be controlled in terms of the ostensible function otherwise it becomes either a waste or a detriment. In my opinion the basis of therapy lies in the therapist himself, in his capacity to permit the use of self, which the therapeutic relationship implies, as well as his psychological insight and technical skill. If this is true, therapy is potentially present wherever the therapeutic attitude is maintained, whether the contacts be one or many, and whether the vehicle be casework or some form of professional therapy. However, to offer individual therapy directly and frankly involves a training, personal discipline, and responsibility for self, as well as a willingness to take payment which the majority of caseworkers have not achieved.[1] Yet they are being forced into a kind of long-time, intensive casework which seems to be nothing unless it is professional therapy in disguise; relationship deliberately set up with therapy as its goal, carried as far as the caseworker knows or dares under conditions involving practical responsibility for the patient which no professional therapist would accept. Few caseworkers are willing to be entirely responsible for this type of work. Either

[1] The fact that it seems not only possible but natural that the social worker should receive no compensation from the client for the therapy derived from the relationship implies that the client has no responsibility, and the "will to health" is largely the will of the worker directed toward the client's improvement.

they do not let themselves know what they do or they rely upon a supervisor or psychiatrist to soften the responsibility which they are not able to carry. The alternatives seem quite clear to me. Either the caseworker should prepare herself to do individual therapy responsibly and proclaim it as a function to the client or she should learn to differentiate social casework with a practical goal from casework with a therapeutic function and to value it for itself.

Relationship therapy as a technical process dependent upon repeated contacts as well as a conscious control of the dynamic thus set up, with a definite beginning and ending in time, is a highly specialized discipline which the caseworker has no more right to practice than any lay person unless she has prepared herself adequately.[2] But she has a right, nay more, an obligation to understand the interplay of forces in a helping relationship, so that the mere repetition of interviews will not precipitate her into a process that she cannot stop but cannot utilize, or the shortness of the contact deprive it of the therapeutic quality which the acceptance of its functional limitation would ensure.

While the topic of this paper is Time, I end as I began, not so much with concern for limiting treatment in time, although that is one of the most valuable single tools ever introduced into therapy, but with the necessity for accepting deeply, not merely intellectually, but emotionally and organically in our daily living, the reality of personal as

---

[2] It is difficult to say what constitutes preparation for practicing relationship therapy; certainly one requirement is that the would-be therapist should first have experienced in himself what it means to take help, to be a patient.

well as functional limitation. A time limit is a purely external, meaningless, and even destructive device if used
by someone who has not accepted limitation in and for
himself. It becomes then merely a weapon turned on the
other, or a salvation to be realized through and by the
other. In order to use time as a major element in therapy
one must first have come to grips with it in oneself, otherwise the limitations which it introduces as a therapeutic
agent are unbearable and what the therapist cannot bear in
and for himself, the patient cannot learn to bear either, at
least if he does, he succeeds in spite of, not because of the
therapist.

In the last analysis, therapy as a qualitative affair must
depend upon the personal development of the therapist
and his ability to use consciously for the benefit of his
client, the insight and self-discipline which he has achieved
in his own struggle to accept self, life, and time as limited
and to be experienced fully only at the cost of fear, pain,
and loss. I do not mean that knowledge is not necessary,
that technical skill is not necessary; they are, but they are
of no value therapeutically without the person. To make
casework therapeutic, incidentally or deliberately, one
must *be* a therapist and only to the extent that this is true
are the relationships one sets up therapeutic, regardless of
the label, the number of visits or the interpretation recorded in the dictation.

We do not think of the physician as conceited or ego-
tistic because he admits his ability to heal the sick. In
fact, we would consider him reprehensible if he did not
offer conscious skill and power to those depending upon
his professional ability. When it comes to a therapy which
is internal and rests upon strength of will, freedom to feel,

and an ability to lend oneself to the use of the other, we shrink from the position into which we are put by admitting that we are able to offer these things in addition to knowledge and skill. Apparently we cannot face this degree of self-assertion easily or if we can, perhaps we are not justified, but are merely determined to do what interests us even if we have no real understanding of the therapeutic process into which we plunge so recklessly. The caseworker who accepts her therapeutic function, as it were surreptitiously, is actually denying responsibility, refusing to develop or accept the self which is required by her job, a self with real strength to be utilized therapeutically by the client. On the other hand, the caseworker who must help, who plunges into involved relationships from which she can hardly be extricated because the case is so interesting she cannot resist it, is not really accepting responsibility any more than the one who plays safe. She is only pursuing her own reflection, seeking the solution of her own problem by trying to force salvation upon someone who seems to exemplify her unrecognized, unassimilated, emotionally unaccepted conflict. The one denies strength, the other weakness, while to be any use as therapists each must admit and become responsible for both, not in the client, but in herself.

The social worker who makes no claim to therapeutic casework, but sticks to a concrete function other than individual therapy, certainly runs less danger of being destructive when she refuses the self-conscious responsibility which therapeutic casework demands; but the fact remains that she can never realize the full possibility even of the practical goal, can never attain to conscious guidance of the relationships with which she deals, can seldom contribute therapy except by the happy accident of personality, unless she brings to her task an understanding of therapy through relationship which enables her to avoid it, to limit herself in terms of her agency function and the best interest of her clients. The next step for casework, as I see it, is not to become more psychological but rather to become responsible for therapy, for practicing it overtly or for refraining deliberately, but in any case, for knowing and bearing its strength as well as its weakness, in other words, for accepting itself.

Since my own experience does not provide firsthand material for analysis of the casework situation, I must content myself with a presentation and discussion of the long-time, overt therapeutic relationship as exemplified in the two records of children which follow, where the effect of limitation in time, in space, and in practical possibility is clearly indicated both in its immediate thwarting of child and therapist and in its ultimate value for the growth process.

The Forces That Make for Therapy

ON THE BASIS of these concrete pictures of relationship therapy, I should like to present in conclusion, briefly,

Originally published as "Conclusion" in Jessie Taft's *The Dynamics of Therapy in a Controlled Relationship* (New York: The Macmillan Company, 1933).

what seem to me to be the sources of the therapy to be derived in these contacts.[1] Therapy is a process in which a person who has been unable to go on with living with more fear or guilt than he is willing or able to bear, somehow gains courage to live again, to face life positively instead of negatively. How is this possible? If one thinks of an exact scientific answer to the question, I must confess that I do not know; that, at bottom, therapy of this kind is a mystery, a magic, something one may know beyond a doubt through repeated experiences, but which in the last analysis is only observed and interpreted after the fact never comprehended in itself or controlled scientifically any more than the life process is comprehended and controlled. Yet it is possible to describe it theoretically in philosophic or psychological terms although one realizes that the description will be of no therapeutic value to any patient and of no immediate avail to any therapist who must play his part at the moment without rehearsal or prompting.

From the point of view here presented, the source of failure in living lies primarily in fear as a quantitative factor, and the effect of this fear upon the balance which is required to accept and maintain the conflict inherent in the life process on a comparatively constructive basis, at least sufficiently so for growth to go on. Fear is a necessary part of all experiencing, a consequence not so much of immediate external danger as of the inherent ambivalence of the human being who must always be pulled in. two directions, must always long for and avoid the problematic situation, must fear stagnation even while he resists

[1] See Otto Rank, *Genetische Psychologie,* Vol. II.

his own impulse to growth. In other words fear is inherent in individuation and self-consciousness, in the necessity to be both part and whole.[2]

That the growth process is never wholly pleasant is self-evident. Because we do not control it, it always involves some reluctance to let go what has been, some fear of the unknown that is to come. Change of any kind, be it organic or purely external, partakes of the same dual value; holds within it the possibility not only of desirable acquisition but of loss. At bottom, all growth or change like the birth process[3] which is its prototype, is seen to contain the elements of death as well as life. As a rule the death aspect is only partial and is more than compensated for by the new life created thereby. Yet always there is the lurking possibility of total loss, of the final passing out of this particular individualized form of life which, in truth, is its ultimate fate. However speculative it may sound and however differently it may express itself in any particular case, the fact remains that always, at bottom, every serious blocking in a human life is the expression of an unsolved or rather unaccepted conflict between the will to become more and more individualized, to develop one's own quantum of life, and the reluctance to pursue wholeheartedly a course which is beyond control by the individual will and which inevitably leads to the annihilation of this dearly brought individuality.

The possibility of healing for those who are caught in the fear of living, because of undue violence, interference

[2] See Otto Rank, *Technik der Psychoanalyse* (Leipzig: Deuticke, 1931), III.

[3] See Otto Rank, *Das Trauma der Geburt* (Leipzig, 1924).

with, or difficulty in, the earliest growth experiences, perhaps even before birth, experiences which are somehow not outweighed or compensated for by later successes and satisfactions, lies primarily in the fact that to live with enough satisfaction to want to keep on, is natural. We are after all living creatures, part and parcel of this so strange and ambivalent process called life. Somewhere in each and every human are the very impulses and needs which make duality of aim and direction exactly right, the only reality for which we are fitted or which we could accept. We fail to recognize this inherent fitness when the quantity of fear aroused by the fate of initial strivings is so extreme that paralysis or overcompensation occurs. The balance between self and other, part and whole, life and death, becomes too one-sided and the individual is thrown too far into a denial of the impulse to move or an overinsistence upon movement, into a self-depreciation or over-assertion, into rejection or overestimation of his fellows.

Fear, which is attached to a too prolonged static condition as well as to whatever breaks up or threatens a cherished wholeness, whether it be an external danger, a flaw in the solution of a problem, a fateful person or an inner unrest, is a necessary accompaniment of living. Only when it is so great that it chains the individual to one or the other aspect of the process, to the exclusion or attempted exclusion of the other, does it become pathological. If the human being cannot enjoy the experience of completion and wholeness either for fear he will stick in it forever or for fear that he will not be able to keep it, then he needs help, not to root out fear but to reduce it to reasonable proportions so that it may function effectively as part of the life process, to spur or to check as the situation demands, instead of acting as an irrational block to living. The antidote for fear is successful experiencing. The fear of being caught in wholeness, in union with the other, can be reduced only when the impulse to unite completely is lived through deeply enough to convince the individual that since it has not, it need not destroy him. The fear of moving, of breaking away from the warmth and safety of a wholeness thus attained, is lessened only when release from external interference permits the impulse to movement, to development, to become dominant, so that the individual discovers in himself the possibility of a wholeness of his own making which is even more satisfying than the wholeness of union and frees him from a too binding dependence on the other.

To conquer the problem of living then, insofar as this is possible, is to learn to accept it as process, to achieve a freedom and a balance which permits the shattering of any particular wholeness, without mistaking it for total disruption and finds in the breakup of the old, not merely loss but the material for new creation. The person who has finally achieved a balance between the claims of self and reality so flexible and responsive that it can no longer be seriously disturbed by living, has perhaps carried through his impulse to individuation to a fulfillment which permits of dying as a final expression of the as yet not-fully realized impulse to unite, to lose the self as a part in the larger whole. That such a completeness of living is only a theoretical goal goes without saying, nevertheless, individuals differ unbelievably in the degree to which they approximate it. Is it not possible that much of what we call the fear of dying is largely the guilt for not having lived? Death, which is present in every moment of living from conception to the grave, must surely be a natural process too if not imposed from without.

It is this getting away from the sense of external violence and imposition to a convincing realization of inner forces which are not fearful and alien but belong to the own self as well as to external reality that is necessary for healing. The neurotic is caught in life as in a trap. Fear will not permit him to recognize his own creative power or to admit the destructiveness which he shares with the rest of life. He must be everything or nothing, all powerful or consumed with fear of a reality which is stronger than he, perfect or condemned to an intolerable imperfection. What he needs is to learn to flow with life, not against it; to submit willingly, to let himself be carried by its strength without giving up responsibility for being that particular part of the current which is uniquely himself, yet like enough to the rest to take the same direction, to be moved by similar forces. That he can be destroyed by life is true, and that, when threatened by destruction from without, he feels life as alien and fearful is true also, but it is equally true that even this life which can turn against him is like him, is bone of his bone and flesh of his flesh. Somewhere within him is the capacity to accept it, to go with it, to know on the one hand the joy and responsibility of the individual creative will in its wholeness, and on the other the need to submit as a creature, a part, to the domination of the all-powerful but sustaining whole. Otherwise there is no therapy.

Relationship therapy, then, is nothing but an opportunity to experience more completely than is ordinarily possible the direction, depth, and ambivalence of the impulses which relate the self to the other, to outer reality, and to discover firsthand the possibility of their organization into an autonomous, creative will. There are two, and only two sources of the feeling of wholeness to which we attach our sense of security in living, and which enable us to bear the anxiety that change and disruption occasion. One is the peace which the individual feels as part of a whole when he is sustained by a sense of organic union with the other, as the child is sustained in the mother's body, not annihilated, but held in a sufficiency of strength which is felt as its own. The second is the security and power which are painfully acquired by individual striving in the face of fear and partiality, through the slow growth and organization of the self, the creative will, whose strength partakes of and contributes to the great underlying forces of life. Love, sex union, religion, philosophy, the group, provide the natural substitutes for the primal sense of security which is derived from the beneficent aspects of the maternal strength before the disillusioning shock of birth, where the individual's share in producing so great a change is often wiped out or obscured by the impression of external attack and compulsion. Even sex may fail as a natural therapy for fear, if the grim organic memory of that first too forced and violent introduction to autonomous living has not been softened by the tenderness and restoration of union at the mother's breast, followed by some sense of ego achievement in the weaning and early habit training. On the other hand the education of children, creative work, art, science, mechanics, are expressions of the organized individual will which has attained in itself and its own creativeness a wholeness that enables it to bear the fear of individuation and the separation from the whole.

The reason why these experiences in relationship which I have called therapeutic, work healingly for the individual, is that there is present always in every human being underneath the fear, a powerful, more or less denied, unsatisfied impulse to abandon the ego defenses and let the too solid organization of the self break up and melt away in a sense of organic union with a personality strong enough to bear it and willing to play the part of supporting whole. The therapist, who agrees to live for this limited time in the interest of the patient, who gives up temporarily the projection of personal needs and impulses in order to allow the patient to work through his own unmolested, provides an opportunity which is unique and irresistible in that it permits a realization of wholeness and security as part of a protecting supporting medium like nothing in human experience unless it be the intrauterine existence. Many patients realize in this relationship for the first time a kind of cosmic ecstasy far beyond the sexual, like that which the mystics describe, a oneness with life, an harmonious flowing into reality. That such an intense emotional realization of one human impulse should arouse equally intense fear goes without saying. It is the final overcoming of fear, fear of loss of the self, and fear of the loss of the other, to the point of taking the experience regardless of consequences, that constitutes the first victory for therapy.

With children, the struggle against yielding, in terms of

a projected will conflict is evident enough, but the child is less capable of emotional awareness than the adult, and expresses the positive joy of an accepted impulse to union very shyly and indirectly. Rather he acts out his regression in infantile behavior and real dependence on the therapist, while the adult with help is able to reach his fulfillment emotionally, with the relief of verbal expression. The yielding and submission which mark the climax of the initial clash of wills between patient and therapist, are tolerable only because, as the patient finally comes to see, they are an expression of his own nature which he has been fighting as if it were being imposed upon him by the therapist. To accept defeat then is really to conquer, to overcome fear sufficiently to be able to yield to the impulsive self and the sweep of the life forces.

The success of this half of the therapeutic experience depends on two factors: one, the degree of fear which the patient has to overcome; and second, the ability of the therapist to keep from interfering, to exert no compulsion beyond that needed to maintain his own integrity in the situation, and to be able to accept without fear, denial or sense of personal involvement, the full value of the love experience for the patient. The patient does not need to be warded off, except as he demands response in kind or carries his impulses into unacceptable action. He will not cling forever unless he meets counterresistance in the therapist. His own will to selfhood which has been held in abeyance during this phase of domination by the love forces, will now of its own accord begin to restore the balance and initiate the movement which leads to separation. The therapist has only to recognize it, to admit its rightness and reality when the patient is too confused by guilt to confess it openly.

There remains, then, one further experience to be gained from the therapeutic relationship, without which it becomes a trap as truly as the previous life experiences of the patient, and that is a constructive, creative leaving of the therapist and the therapeutic situation which will diminish the fear of individuation; since to leave convincingly is to find that one can bear both the pain and the fear of withdrawal from a depth of union never risked since birth or weaning, and to discover within the self a substitute for the lost wholeness. No particular therapeutic relationship presents such a clear positive picture, since it always has in it all the uniqueness, unexpectedness, and ambivalence of real experience which is lost the second it is abstracted. The interaction between the will to unite and the will to separate is continuous from the first moment to the last. In every hour there will be minor yieldings and minor withdrawals. Underneath these shorter surface movements the patient as well as the therapist feels a deeper current which flows with a different time-span but with the same interplay of conflicting tendencies. The week has its own ebb and flow just like the hour and yet there is a general trend in terms of a still longer span, which carries the love impulse to its climax of acceptance and brings the ego strivings to the final point of rejection of the supporting relationship and assertion of the independent self. The hours and weeks which are dominated by the growing power of the transference emotion are never without resistances and rejections on the part of the ego, nevertheless as this is lessened, the total character of the separate parts changes also. The twentieth hour does not feel like the fifth or the tenth. The union which has been attained through hours and weeks of minor destructions and re-creations is fairly strong and elastic enough to contain considerable difference without shattering. Therefore when the sense of wholeness in the transference emotion is most complete, it is also most able to bear the already included and tolerated impulses to separation. It is at this point of greatest security, that the second trend in the relationship can begin to make itself felt; and gradually as the ending becomes a reality which is more and more accepted in terms of the need of the patient to be free, to exercise his own strength, the hours and weeks take on a different coloring under the now frankly enjoyed assertion of the growing ego, which by living through the therapeutic relationship, has come into possession of its own strength as well as its weakness.

Time, then, as arbitrarily utilized to limit the therapeutic situation, is nothing more than the external symbol, the tangible carrier, of the inevitable limitation in all relationship, which becomes tolerable here for the first time, only because the patient is allowed to discover it one-sidedly, in himself, in terms of his own will and nature. This discovery, which he makes and accepts in greater or lesser degree within a comparatively brief period, has no more final, fixed, guaranteed quality than any other growth experience. No therapeutic relationship, however valuable, can make up for years of refusal to live. The more the individual has been able to accept life before he comes to the therapist, the deeper and richer will be his experience in this particular relationship and the more effectively will he be able to connect it with the reality outside. The individual whom extreme fear and unfavorable circumstance have estranged from his fellows and deprived of the deeper human entanglements, may experience what for him at the level where he is, is a miracle of fulfillment and release, yet find himself with a long and painful period of living to be gone through slowly, by himself, in reality before he is able to utilize to any marked degree the potentialities of the therapeutic awakening.

There should be no sense of failure, no critical attitude, either toward therapist or patient, if the patient comes a second or a third time, for a single contact or for a series of contacts in order to realize, at a point where his own development permits, the fullness of the experience which he was unable to bear at first; to yield himself once more to the feared love forces in order to separate more completely than he had been able to do at first. In fact, I am ready to affirm the increased value of the therapeutic relation which is not cut off violently in complete separation, but rather carries over into reality, so that the growth process may be a gradual freeing, as it is biologically, with successive swings toward union and independence, until the individual naturally attains the balance which permits the therapist to drop out of his life, in favor of less one-sided relationships. To insist that the patient shall leave forever and never be heard from again, or even to imply that virtue lies in such a course, is to arouse the negative will conflict, and endanger at the last moment the therapeutic possibilities in what has gone before. The patient must not only be free to return as he is to go, but in certain cases may even need encouragement and some suggestion that it is better not to spend all of his strength in trying not to come; a second denial which might be almost as disastrous as the original blocking. The patient, like the rest of mankind, can learn to bear life only gradually. It is therefore no crime, but a sign of growth, that he is able to return in the face of fear, to experience more deeply and fully the life forces which he knows he has not yet accepted to the limit of his capacity and thus to acknowledge in turning to the therapist once more, not only his need for help but the new strength which enables him to take it.

In order to act upon this philosophy therapeutically, the therapist himself must be sufficiently free of guilt and the pressure of self-interest to be able to distinguish between the patient who returns merely to assure himself that there is nothing here that he wants and the patient who is trying to summon courage for a deeper experience. Only if the therapist is as ready to help the patient to get away as he is to show him his need to come back, can he bear calmly the accusations which both the public and the patient himself are quick to make, imputing ulterior personal or economic motives which can be settled only by his own conscience or, in the last analysis, by the efficacy of his method for the patient.

Relationship therapy, inasmuch as it is only an intensified, condensed growth experience, induced by specific conditions which combine unique freedom with unique limitation, can never exhaust itself within the brief period of actual contact, but on the contrary releases growth capacity which continues to effect changes in the person, more conspicuously and consciously of course in the years immediately following the experience. This does not imply an alteration in the fundamental pattern that characterizes the individual ego. The nature of that pattern, its peculiar form of response to life, is the essence of individuality and could not change materially without destroying the person as such. But the balance in the relation of the forces which constitute the self can shift in the constructive giving up of a therapeutic relationship; the too extreme swing or the too one-sided expression of ambivalent impulses will be modified gradually to permit a functioning which, for the individual, is release to be himself, not a transformation in terms of an alien standard. For relationship therapy, like life, utilizes the forces already within the human being and therefore, insofar as it is effective, is never finished while the individual survives, but continues to develop in time, the inevitable medium in which man creates, no less than the symbol of his final limitation.

PART V

Functional Casework and Teaching
1934-1950

essie Taft's father, Charles Chester
Taft (b. 1855).

Her mother, Amanda May Farwell
(b. 1849).

Aunt Amanda Farwell Jarrett (b.
1833), who lived with the Tafts.

Jessie Taft, one year old (1883).   Jessie at the age of five (1887).

Jessie at fifteen (1897).

left: Jessie Taft in 1912 or 1913.

right: Virginia Robinson around 1910, when she first met Jessie Taft.

Jessie Taft after having received her Ph.D. from the University of Chicago in June, 1913.

Dr. Taft in Bedford Hills, New York, where she worked from 1913 to 1915 as assistant superintendent at the New York State Reformatory for Women—her first job in social work.

"The Pocket," the house on East Mill Road in Flourtown, Pennsylvania.

Sophie Theis, head of the child-placement department of the State Charities Aid Association in New York, bringing a girl to "the Pocket." *Left to right:* Miss Theis, Martha, Bobby Ueland, Everett Taft, Jessie Taft.

Summer in New Hampshire, 1923: Everett and Martha Taft, Jessie Taft, and Virginia Robinson.

opposite: Jessie Taft around the time of the publication of *The Dynamics of Therapy* in 1933.

Jessie Taft and Virginia Robinson in Vermont in the summer of 1959.

THE BULLETIN of the Alumni Association of the Pennsylvania School of Social Work for May, 1934, begins as follows: "It is a red-letter day when we welcome Dr. Taft as a full-time member of the faculty. We are all richer for her influence on social work; to most of us she is an old friend coming into a new relationship to us. At our request she has written this, sharing her thinking with the Alumni:

Why am I leaving the children's field for teaching? Perhaps you might better ask why I have taken so long to come to the Pennsylvania School. The Children's Aid has been detaining me for sixteen years, with a hold so appealing that my gradual entrance into teaching has hardly been evident even to myself. It is only as I look back that I can see the entering wedge fifteen years ago, in my first extension course in psychology. I can still remember how thrilling and terrifying an experience that was, in a dark little classroom at 13th and Pine. I wonder how many of you Alumni remember the School in that location? I began to come then and I have been on my way ever since. For years I was not allowed to give anything but extension courses. They did not satisfy because in an extension course the teacher does the work and perhaps gets the response. At any rate, there is not much opportunity to see students progress, or to be responsible for the effect of one's methods, when the members of the class are not working for credit and can be held to no standard of accomplishment.

Meantime the school increased by leaps and bounds, the second year was evolved, and with it the need for teachers grew. I saw my chance to become a member of the teaching staff and begged for a class of regular students. My prayer was granted. In 1929 I began to teach Personality IV and V to the vocational students and for the first time took on real responsibility for teaching. No class was ever more respectfully regarded by a teacher than my first group of regulars. No class was ever more beloved. Then came renewed interest through the training of students in Children's Aid, and I became ever more closely identified with teaching and the school.

Meantime my experience with psychological treatment of children and adults was constantly deepening and finally, after seven years of continuous practice, it came to a saturation point and I felt that I had to teach, not merely Personality IV and V, but a technical course which I had found to be reliable and extremely useful practically even in a large child-placing agency. It was lucky for me that my own call to teach therapy came at a point when the Pennsylvania School was on the verge of developing a program for a third and fourth year of work. Perhaps we came to it together. At any rate, for the first time since I came to Philadelphia, I was able to see myself leaving the children's field. It is not that I am tired of planning placements for dependent children. I can conceive of no occupation more absorbing, more completely satisfying in its sense of reality—of social justification for living. I leave it because it has become almost an indulgence, because I love it too much and do it with too little struggle. Teaching is for me the unconquered, undeveloped territory, where I may experience whatever personal growth remains to be experienced, and make a more definitely technical contribution to social work before I leave it. It is perhaps a giving up of the joys of practical immediate living for the sake of handing on one's values to others; making them, at least, more permanent.

As Dr. Taft tells in the letter quoted above, at this time, when she was ready to leave the Children's Aid Society of Pennsylvania and was asking Kenneth L. M. Pray, Dean of the Pennsylvania School of Social Work, for a full-time position on his faculty, the School was ready to initiate an advanced curriculum, the first in the country. Dr. Taft's experience in therapy and her interest in distinguishing casework from therapy were preeminently suited to the development of such a program, and her thinking and teaching stimulated and guided this program from 1934 until her retirement in 1950. The announcement of an advanced curriculum attracted former graduates of the School to work for the master's degree, offered by the University of Pennsylvania for the first time in 1936, as well as graduates of other schools curious about the teachings of the Pennsylvania School.

Dr. Taft interviewed the applicants for this program, planned the field-work placements, and taught the basic course in social casework practice and a course which she called "The Helping Process." When supervisors and executives who wished to remain as responsible workers in their own agencies began to apply and it became apparent that we could not get adequate supervision for them in their agencies, Dr. Taft offered an opportunity for a supervisor or an administrator to come into this program and work individually on any problem that concerned them in their own professional performance. As the need and demand for this individual help increased and other members of the faculty became interested in offering this service, Dr. Taft helped them to take on the new kind of responsibility involved. So her teaching position in the School became a focus for new development in the faculty and for a deepened understanding of fundamental helping processes.[1]

A new understanding of teaching and learning as process that could not be described by content or intellectual requirements alone was beginning to act as a ferment throughout the entire organization of the School and its curriculum planning.

In a series of courses[2] offered on an extension basis to experienced workers in the evenings, Dr. Taft brought distinguished speakers from professional and scientific fields who responded to the idea and content that informed these courses as she described them under such titles as "Theories of Personality Development" (1935), "The Organization of the Self" (1936), "Growth, Learn-

[1] The development of supervision as a training process is described in: Virginia P. Robinson, *Supervision in Social Casework: a Problem in Professional Education* (Chapel Hill: University of North Carolina Press, 1936; "Introduction" and "Meaning of Skill" in *Training for Skill in Social Casework* (Social Work Process Series, Philadelphia: University of Pennsylvania Press, 1942); and *The Dynamics of Supervision Under Functional Controls: a Professional Process in Social Casework* (Philadelphia: University of Pennsylvania Press, 1949).

[2] A detailed account of these courses and of Rank's relation to them is given in Jessie Taft's *Otto Rank, A Biographical Study* (New York: The Julian Press, 1958), pp. 204–205, 211, 223–224, 228, 246.

ing, and Change in the Development of the Individual"
(1937). Rank gave a major part of the 1937 lecture series
and followed this in 1938 with an entire course which he
called "Symbols of Government," using Thurman Arnold's
book of that title for discussions. These lectures of Rank's,
following the series he had given in the late twenties, and
Dr. Taft's translations of *Will Therapy* and *Truth and
Reality* "constituted a body of philosophical and psychological thought which the faculty found inexhaustible in
the depth of understanding of the self in its growth and
relationship processes."[3]

One particular course offered in the advanced curriculum in 1934 and 1935 made direct use of Dr. Taft's technical skill in therapy and gave her the opportunity to
experiment in teaching therapy for children. Offered as
a practice course for workers who were currently carrying
a child in a therapeutic process and who were willing to
use their records in conference with Dr. Taft, it limited
itself by this requirement to a small group of caseworkers in the Philadelphia Child Guidance Clinic, the Children's Aid Society, the White-Williams Foundation, and
the faculty of the Pennsylvania School of Social Work.
This course made its contribution to the development of
the Child Guidance Clinic practice but it was soon evident to Dr. Taft that a practice course in therapy was not
functionally sound in the curriculum of a school of social
work, and it was dropped after 1936.

[3] See Virginia P. Robinson, "University of Pennsylvania School
of Social Work in Perspective: 1909–1959," paper delivered at the
Alumni Colloquium in June, 1959, and published in the *Journal of
Social Work Process*, XI (1960), 10–29.

The discovery of the use of function[4] in helping processes, the most significant and influential concept in the development of theory and practice in the Pennsylvania School of Social Work, remains Dr. Taft's most significant and enduring contribution to theory and practice in social casework. Her conception which rests upon a profound psychological understanding of self and other and of the responsibility assumed by the helper in a relationship process is as valid today as when it was formulated. Extensively as it has been used in the field of social casework both constructively and controversially, its full implications have not been exhausted.

The first formulation of the functional point of view appeared in the *Journal of Social Work Process,* described in its announcement as a technical journal to be published occasionally. Volume I, Number 1 (1937) of this *Journal* carries Dr. Taft's definitive statement of the relation of function to process and illustrates the responsibility she carried as editor for the selection of articles chosen from theses of advanced students or from super-

[4] In *Otto Rank, A Biographical Study,* pp. 228–229, Dr. Taft quotes Rank's reaction against the use of "function" when he writes: "I get more and more suspicious of words (or terms)." She goes on to say: "Rank was the last person to understand function as used by the social agency, for he himself had never been in the position of representing any agency. The only function he knew was a professional one, but in his case self-oriented and self-maintained. Its importance as a support for the social worker was hard for him to realize or to conceive of as allowing for a truly helpful relation to the client. At any rate Rank should not be held responsible for the functional approach in social work, which has been a bone of contention in social work discussions and often identified with the Rankian influence on the Pennsylvania School."

visors or executives who were working with her in exploration of the problems illuminated by this understanding of function. The entire volume bears her imprint.

From this point on Dr. Taft assumed responsibility for stimulating writing and for editing and publication of journals and pamphlets focused on different points of current problems in the development of functional casework practice.

A second paper which carried this concept of function into other social work processes was delivered at an annual meeting of the American Association of Psychiatric Social Workers held during the National Conference of Social Work in June, 1939, and published in the *News-Letter* of this association (1939).

In 1939 Dr. Taft organized a third journal around problems in the field of child placing dedicated, as she says in her "Introduction," to "the underlying imponderable problems of social work with children."

She welcomed the invitation from the *Annals* of the American Academy of Political and Social Science to write an article on foster-home care for children, as an opportunity to describe to an audience reaching beyond social workers "the steady growth in technical skill in the relatively small area devoted to the placement of children in foster homes" the area of her own casework experience and competence. In this article she gives the history of the development of a professional practice related "not so much to a particular psychology of behavior as to a new understanding of growth as a living process which can and must be utilized psychologically as well as physiologically in any effort to help human beings, particularly children—a new theory of helping in which the human will is accepted as a potentially creative force capable of overcoming and even of utilizing for growth the external and internal forces with which it must struggle."

The point of view of growth basic to her understanding of all child-placing processes was highly controversial when these articles on child placing were written in 1939 and 1940. Dr. Taft examined this controversy in her classes at the School, and in an article published in 1943 as a conclusion to a pamphlet which she edited, *The Role of the Baby in the Placement Process,* she discusses this difference in viewpoint, using as illustration of the point of view with which she found herself in fundamental disagreement several articles by Dr. Florence Clothier, at that time intimately connected with the work of the New England Home for Little Wanderers.

That the same difference in a basic point of view of growth persists in the field of child placement today is evident in current literature from the field.

The problems of the application of the concept of function in the field of family casework constituted a source of conflict to students and a challenge to the faculty during the decade of 1930–1940. It was not until the summer institute in 1943, however, that the School undertook to examine these problems publicly. From the discussions and papers presented in classes and seminars in that institute, a journal, *A Functional Approach to Family Case Work,* was prepared and edited by Dr. Taft. In a "Foreword," Mr. Pray described this journal as "the first organized presentation of the functional approach to family casework." The publication of this first journal in the family field was followed by a second: *Counseling and Protective Service as Family Casework: A Functional Approach,* in 1946, and in 1948 by a third: *Family Casework and Counseling: A Functional Approach.* Dr. Taft's introduction to the 1944 journal was reprinted in the 1948 journal. Her discussion of the cases utilized in the journal gives clear and definitive statement of her point of view on counseling and of the problems that are current and controversial today wherever counseling is done. These questions include the place of counseling in a social agency, the responsibility carried by the counselor, the form and structure of a counseling process, the meaning and value of the use of fee, of a time limit, the use of the present moment in the process, the influence of reality factors, the difference between the one-to-one relationship in a therapeutic process, and the three dimensional world in a counseling situation.

Throughout all of Dr. Taft's writing on casework, her interest in theory, in the underlying philosophic basis, is always present along with her realistic technical interest in the casework. When Rank raised a question about "the real self" in his letter responding to her article of 1937, "The Relation of Function to Process," she affirmed her genuine interest in the technical. His letter of November 18, 1957, reads in part:

> I read your article in the Journal—good stuff and clear but uneven. That is, where you are your real self you are philosophic (deep—too deep for them) and where you talk on their level you are not yourself. I guess that can't be helped and social work lies somewhere between.

To this she appends a footnote to say:

> Rank was mistaken in thinking I was not myself where
> he says I talk "on their level." My interest in the tech-
> nical, practical problems of the help-giving processes of
> the social agency was as great as my interest in theory,
> as later issues of the *Journal of Social Work Process* on
> family counseling, child placing, etc., bear witness.[5]

Contrasting her "technical" interest in the case with
my own interest and the interest of many other teachers
of casework, I recognize a unique quality in what Dr.
Taft gave to a casework problem and to any casework
discussion. In the minds of students she became associated
with the so-called Personality class, particularly the second-
year class in which she made use of the biographies of
William Ellery Leonard, Gamaliel Bradford, Mabel Dodge
Luhan, John Middleton Murry and Katherine Mansfield,
and D. H. Lawrence. But it was the casework class which
challenged her skill most fully and happily. She would
never let herself "work" on a student's case in advance of
the class session preferring to wait for the participation
of the students, valuing the freshness and spontaneity of
the discussion. "The important points," she would say,
"the points I did not see in a first reading always came
out in class." There is no material to illustrate this freedom and spontaneity in casework discussions. In contrast
one can find many illustrations of her critical ability in
the carefully prepared, thorough, logical analysis of a
point of view of casework different from her own. It delighted her to get hold of an article criticizing the functional point of view and stating a different approach on

[5] Taft, *Otto Rank, A Biographical Study*, p. 241.

which she could use her mind freely and fully. The journals contain several illustrations of her handling of a different point of view, for instance, her examination of Dr. Florence Clothier's[6] opposition to the practice of functional child-placing agencies in placing babies, or her discussion[7] of the use of time limits, in which she contrasts her own point of view with that of Alexander and French as described in their book, *Psychoanalytic Therapy.*

In response to a book entitled *Social Casework in Practice,* by Florence Hollis, published by the Family Welfare Association of America in 1939, she sends detailed "comments" to *The Family,* beginning:

> There is nothing for which a teacher of casework should be more grateful than for the appearance of a new book in the area of practice, especially a book that is sufficiently objective, substantial, and workmanlike, to command respect and permit of clear-cut, detailed disagreement.

When in June, 1941, Gordon Hamilton devoted a major National Conference paper, "The Underlying Philosophy of Social Casework," to a criticism of the functional point of view, Dr. Taft responded with a "comment" prepared for *The Family,* but which for some reason she did not send to the magazine for publication.

[6] Dr. Clothier, no longer associated with the field of child placing, but now Assistant to the President of Vassar College, has been good enough to read this material and consent to its use.

[7] Jessie Taft, "Discussion" of M. Robert Gomberg's "The Gold Case, a Marital Problem," in *Family Casework and Counseling, A Functional Approach,* ed. Jessie Taft (Philadelphia: University of Pennsylvania Press, 1948).

Her casework gift was perhaps best known to a few mature able students or graduates of the School who had the courage to bring a problem to her at the point of developing a new service in an agency or hospital. Here she could work creatively and brilliantly with full recognition of all the factors involved. More than this, when she had made her contribution, had looked at the situation round and about and given her thinking freely, she could leave it with the worker for the development of the service in the reality situation. This much insight was not always easy to take, but for those who could stand up to it her contribution often became the solid ground on which a new and difficult service was established.

She was not averse to extending this kind of casework thinking outside of her field of influence when it was asked for sincerely. From London, a case was sent to her by Miss Marjorie Cosens, an English psychiatric social worker who had audited several courses at the Pennsylvania School of Social Work, with record reading and conferences at the Child Guidance Clinic, requesting that she comment on the casework for publication. Under the title "The Dane Case," several pages of Dr. Taft's comments appeared in the magazine, *Social Work, a Quarterly Review of Family Casework* (July 1949). The same number contained a review by Miss Cosens of *Training for Skill* and *Family Casework and Counseling*.

The selection of papers from casework practice would not be complete without reference to her interest in the public school and its possibilities for greater helpfulness in the child's development. Many early speeches and papers were addressed to teachers' meetings and organizations and to school counselors. A National Conference paper delivered in Washington in 1923, "The Relation of the School to the Mental Health of the Average Child," expresses this interest. Among her most recent papers is one addressed to the counseling personnel of the Division of Pupil Personnel and Counseling of the Philadelphia School District at their meeting on January 8, 1947. In this paper she states her belief that school counseling is directly related to the kind of professional helping that is called functional helping and describes her own relation to the development of this point of view. Finally she describes the function of a counselor in the public school as she conceives it and the problem of becoming a representative to the child of the whole school with full appreciation of how hard it is for the counselor who has been a teacher to find and support this new helping function. The paper is interesting also for the discussion of her difference in point of view from that of Carl Rogers who had addressed the group in a previous meeting. This paper in mimeographed form is still in active use by the department.

This account of her relation to casework practice and teaching must be put in perspective by an account of her relation to the content and teaching of the personality courses without which the practice courses would have lacked balance. In a long paper written for the *Journal of Social Work Process* she describes the development of the personality course and its relation to practice in the student's training. It carries an autobiographical account of her relation to the development of the curriculum of the School which is important for this volume.

The Relation of Function to Process
in Social Casework

❦ IN THE NINE ARTICLES which compose the first number of this *Journal*, with all their variety of agency background, professional experience, and personal viewpoint, one common factor stands clear, and that is a degree of accepted understanding and use of "helping" as a technical process basic to the exercise of every social work function. The taking and giving of help are seen as two opposite but complementary currents in a single complex process on which social work must base whatever it hopes to achieve in the way of effective understanding of the client and conscious control over its own procedures.

There is a universal tendency in all human development to progress by extreme swings from object to subject, from the external, the physical, and the social, to the internal, the psychological, and the individualistic. This is evidenced in religion, in ethics, in art, in philosophy, and in social theory as well as in psychology and all our ways of working. At one moment we place all truth in the outside world where we try to analyze the object as a separate entity; again we turn upon the self, the doer, and study him in all his subjectivity. Either

"Introduction" to the *Journal of Social Work Process*, I, No. 1 (November, 1937).

concentration destroys or ignores the reality that lies only in the living relationship between the two.

Social casework has naturally not escaped this inevitable swing from outer to inner and back again. One trend follows the client as an external social problem, approaching him at first punitively, then benevolently but reformingly, and finally reaches the level of social planning and mental hygiene. The other trend is seen in the history of boards and social agencies, from individual indulgence in charity, to responsible private organization for helping on a more or less professional level, and finally to helping as a legitimate function of government; from the lady bountiful, through the pioneer reformer to the sociological social worker, and finally to the psychoanalytic, psychiatric, highly trained professional of today who finds his own psychology even more important than the client's. At the moment, this dichotomy is evidenced in social work in several directions and is in a state of transition from one emphasis to the other. The intensely psychiatric, psychological, subjective phase of interest in both clients and workers seems to be passing, along with the shift from intensive, indeterminate casework by the private agency to the highly functionalized administration of public money by governmental relief and assistance boards.

Even within the area of so-called intensive casework, interest is being diverted from hereditary factors and individual social histories confined largely to family relationships, to the larger area of economic and cultural influences. The caseworker is still subject to her personality handicap or her emotional problems, and may resort to psychoanalysis as a last step in professional training, but she is also being held to a more objective requirement in knowledge of economic and social conditions as well as psychological understanding of her client.

Yet neither of these shifts from inner to outer, from the more subjective and personal to the more objective and social, holds the solution for a social work that intends to arrive at a technical grasp of its own practice. It is necessary to know and appreciate the economic, the cultural, the immediate social setting of those who constitute our clientele, it is essential to understand and accept tolerantly but without evasion, the human psychology that is common to worker and client in our culture, but this is only the beginning. There is one area and only one, in which outer and inner, worker and client, agency and social need can come together effectively, only one area that offers to social workers the possibility of development into a profession and that is the area of the helping process itself.

Social casework has fallen into the no man's land that lies between the scientific and the professional, between knowledge and skill. It has not succeeded as yet in developing enough of either to command the complete respect of other groups or to establish its own self-confidence. That social work cannot become a science is taken for granted by virtue of its practical basis. To establish truth, or to engage in scientifically valid research can never be its aim, since, always, whatever it does is vitiated for science by its avowed purpose, which is to help. Where helping human beings comes first, interest in furthering scientific observation must be sacrificed, for the one destroys the other. No man can serve two masters at the same time. This is as true for social work as it is for therapy. Even in the medical field, where research and practice are always encroaching upon each other, we know only too well, that the good research worker does not make the physician.

Does it follow, then, that social work must remain blind, haphazard, well-intentioned, and fumbling? Is there no professional skill possible, no assured knowledge of what one does or how to do it? I think, on the whole, it has been like that. I think the bewilderment of the student in his first year of approach to the practice of social work as he finds it, is an index, not only to the inherent difficulty of disciplining the self in terms of a professional standard, but to the actual confusion as to what casework really is, in the minds of his teachers and supervisors. Too often we have to admit we know not what to do. Is this confusion, this uncertainty, this lack of conscious skill, necessary because of the nature of the medium in which we work, or is it that we are not yet ready to grasp the solution, to face the implications of the way out of chaos? This seems to me to be the crucial problem of social work today: Do we know or can we know what we do and how and why we do it? To solve this problem will not make social work scientific, but it will put it on the level of a profession that can be taught, learned, and practiced by those possessing the ability and the will to undergo its discipline.

I believe that there is a way out of our dilemma and that the papers in this beginning number of the *Journal of Social Work Process,* have found the clue and have begun to move in a fruitful direction. They are all characterized by two attitudes: an ignoring of the static, the analytic, and a concentration on the dynamic, on the immediate interaction between the two participants in the activity of asking and offering help. This shift from the tendency to an even deeper and more futile analysis of either side, subject or object, client or worker, to an attempt to grasp the nature of the process itself in all its relativity and immediacy, is as important for the advancement of our understanding of human psychology as it is for social work. It parallels in importance the transformation that physics experienced when it turned from a static analysis of substance to bodies in motion and from the understanding of matter in general to the discovery of the laws of particular moving bodies in their relativity. "What is now important to the investigation of dynamics is not to abstract from the situation, but to hunt out those situations in which the determinative factors of the total dynamic structure are most clearly, distinctly, and purely to be discerned. Instead of a reference to the abstract average of as many historically given cases as possible, there is a reference to the full concreteness of the particular situations."[1]

Academic psychology is too removed from human need to feel the immediate responsibility of social work or to be subject in the same degree to the human resistance and refusal that determine the truth or falsity of the social worker's psychology so promptly and so pragmatically. Even the medical profession, with all its responsibility for

[1] Kurt Lewin, "The Conflict Between Aristotelian and Galilean Modes of Thought in Contemporary Psychology," in *A Dynamic Theory of Personality* (New York: McGraw-Hill Book Company, 1935), p. 31.

human life, is protected in part from the consequences of its psychological, as well as its medical failures, by recognized professional authority and legal sanction. Social work, on the other hand, with no authority and less sanction, must work in the full light of its own ignorance continually exposed, as it is, by the practical results or lack of them. That it has succeeded in getting by thus far despite its slow blundering advance, is due, not only to the fact that there was no better way of meeting the human needs it serves, but also to the fortunate circumstance that it has not been a money-making, but a money-spending enterprise; and that it has served chiefly the poor and ignorant who had often neither the wisdom nor the power to reject a service they could not pay for. But now that the state has gone into an area that social work claims as its own, now that vast administrative and economic problems are involved and huge expenditures of public money are at stake, social work will have to meet competition from other groups who want to fill the big jobs, to handle the large sums, and even to grapple with the interesting complexities of the situations now facing us. Unless social work knows something about dealing with people that no other professional group has discovered, unless social work can really bring to bear a skill that outweighs its lack of administrative and business experience, it will not survive the tremendous demands and the public scrutiny involved in meeting the large-scale social need of today. There is no escape, therefore, from facing the necessity to establish ourselves firmly, not merely on the basis of social need, but on a foundation of professional skill.

In my opinion, we already have that basis if only we

can relinquish our too great sense of responsibility for the client and his need in order to concentrate on a defining of what we can do and a refining of our knowledge and skill in relation to the carrying out of each specific and accepted function. This may seem to be nothing more than an argument on the practical question of single versus multiple function which has arisen as an immediate and momentary issue owing to the introduction of public relief and assistance and the consequent struggle of private agencies whose functions have been undermined, to find a legitimate *raison d'être*. In my opinion, the present situation has merely pointed up a difference in approach and psychological understanding that is absolutely vital and determinative of professional development. Nor is this question confined to social work. It is fundamental to all human advancement, scientific as well as practical. In the most general terms, the problem reduces itself to this: On what aspects of living can man work fruitfully with his will and his intellect, and in what respect and in what areas must he accept limitation, the limitation of his own partiality and finitude?

Something must be admitted as *given,* something with which he starts and on the basis of which he is free to construct and create to the limits of his human capacity. But always, what he does consciously and intentionally with his mind and his will, has to do with meeting a problem set by nature, the *given* element in life equation; set, it is true, because man himself puts out a need and must discover some way to make nature supply it. The human mind, as all psychology agrees, develops only in conflict, in necessity to defend the organism or to fend for it, to find an answer to need outside or in. The human will, likewise, gets its organization and increase of power through continuous meeting of internal and external obstacles. It, too, is dependent on struggle, is primarily negative in origin.[2] But need itself, the impulsive, involuntary energies that keep man breathing and eating, mating and reproducing, struggling to satisfy and maintain himself alive, are not within the area on which man is fitted to work consciously or to exercise a too complete and willful control. They are the *given* internally, the basic limiting forces within which, if he can submit to them, he yet has freedom to create, to organize, to develop, to refine, and to expand—indefinitely.

Needs and impulses are part, then, of the positive, creative forces found in the universe of our experience and are the energies through which we are enabled to work, to think, to fight, to control, but they themselves are not subject to complete human determination in the self or in the other, any more than are the basic physical forces of the universe. Inside and out, man may pit his strength only *against* or *with* them; he cannot use his will or intellect alone for positive creation. Without the element of submission to the positive, the *given,* in himself as in nature and other men, he becomes sterile, no matter what his effort or his intent. To take upon oneself responsibility for complete determination of any life force in its expression, is to court failure or self-destruction.

This may seem a far cry from the practical problems of the social worker, yet its truth if understood with con-

[2] For the development of this conception of will, see Otto Rank, *Truth and Reality* (New York: Alfred A. Knopf, 1937), Chap. 4.

viction, would transform much of our present practice,
as science was transformed when it learned to put its effort
on understanding the law of the process in a particular
situation, not on objects as separate entities. The approach
to social work via the needs of the individual applicant
is an approach that leads to inevitable failure and confusion, since it focuses attention and effort on something
that can never be known exactly or worked on directly.
Even the client, himself, can only discover what his need
really is by finding out what he does in the helping situation. If, however, we limit our study of needs, to the
generally recognized categories as they emerge out of the
larger social problems, and leave to the individual the
freedom, as well as the responsibility, of testing out his
peculiar needs against the relatively stable function of a
particular agency, there remains to us a large and comparatively unexplored area for future development; an
area in which to learn how to maintain our functions intelligently and skillfully and how to isolate whatever can
be isolated from the particular situation, in terms of the
law, the nature, or the general pattern of the helping
process. This knowledge, however, can never be applied
to the control of the client, neither of his needs nor of
his behavior, for they are always changing, but only to
ourselves, to refine and reform our professional selves as
well as to increase professional skill.

In science, the hypothesis, the problem, the experiment,
the controlled situation, are only various forms of putting
up a manmade limitation to nature, to see what will
happen and what characterizes the process. In social work,
the limitation with which we operate is necessarily the

function. Certainly function is never completely static or inflexible, certainly it alters over a period of time in terms of changing social conditions or should alter; but relatively, it is the known factor, the comparatively stable, fixed point about which client and worker may move without becoming lost in the movement. Every helping situation is an experiment for the worker and for the client. The worker sets up the conditions as found in his agency function and procedure; the client, representing the unknown natural forces, reacts to the limitation as well as to the possible fulfillment inherent in the function, over a period of testing it out. He tries to accept, to reject, to attempt to control, or to modify that function until he finally comes to terms with it enough to define or discover what he wants, if anything, from this situation.

The social worker, like the scientist, must be able to accept the results of the experiment, whether or not they go against his natural human desire to help or refuse to help. He must respect the process and the limitations inherent in work with other people whose needs and impulses are as "given" and as "unpredictable" as his own. He, too, must stick to the supporting function and the area in which he has a right to act, as a professional person. For both worker and client, the function is a protecting as well as a limiting influence. By it each is defended against the tendency to encroach upon, or try to influence, ignore, or control the other. Through it, each is strengthened as well as curtailed. Without it, there is no fixed point, no focus, no spot from which to measure or to understand, however relatively, the very process on which social work is based.

Why do we find this road so hard to follow, so difficult to admit as the only one? It seems to me the answer lies in a common human weakness and natural resistance, not only to any limitation but to admitting the inevitable negative at the basis of all manmade progress. We like to think of social work as a purely positive, benevolent, constructive, influence in the community. As human beings full of kindness and the positive impulse to help, we approach the client on the basis of identification with his need. We would like to make our function over to fit it if necessary. We are there to give, not to refuse, to fulfill, not to thwart. The client, then, is left with all the negative elements on his side—and negative elements there must be in any reality situation. He is forced to ungrateful, ungracious doubt, to refusal, to hesitation, to escape or evasion, or to a disguised struggle with the very help he sought.

There can be no professional development out of such a purely human contact. For the professional situation, there must be one side at least, able to meet the forces in a helping equation objectively and without the necessity to give or to refuse; one person who understands that the negative aspect of function is necessary and releases the client to the possibility of something positive and constructive; one person who can define himself in terms of what he is there to do and leave the other free not to know but to discover whether this is an answer to his need. Such a conception of helping, with the acceptance of the negative elements involved and the knowledge and skill to utilize them, makes of social work a potential profession. It *is* possible to know a function, to work on a function, to alter a function; it is also possible to learn to understand the helping process and to control helping situations in terms of function, and to train and develop the professional worker on the basis of accepted function. On the other hand, it is not possible now or ever to know a client as he is in himself—or, for that matter, a worker either—except as part of a process in which, with one relatively fixed or known quantity, the other may be defined in terms of what it does; for "the ego itself is fundamentally temporal, it is not a time-independent state. It is always going somewhere and the stability of the ego must, therefore, always be seen in relation to the direction in which it is moving.[3]

The ego of the worker is stabilized into a professional self through identification with a function which is "given," "known," so that we do know of the professional person on his job what we cannot presume to know of him personally, the general direction in which he is going. The client, however, is first, last, and always a private person, unless he has become a professional asker for help, with a knowledge and skill of his own. The direction in which his ego is moving we can know only relatively and momentarily, in terms of his impact with the worker's direction, embodied in the function he represents. Unless we have the conviction and the strength to endure that impact and learn to utilize its negative, fearful, unpleasant, elements, we admit at the outset that no professional action is possible. The help that occurs, if any, must be left

[3] Kurt Koffka, *Principles of Gestalt Psychology* (New York: Harcourt, Brace, 1935), p. 332. For the further development of this conception of ego organization, see the remainder of Chap. 8.

entirely, instead of partially, to chance, or at least to the
area of the unknown and the unpredictable. To wish to
set up a function individually to suit each particular need
is to throw the helping process into an activity in which
nothing can be used as a point of reference, into a complete relativity. The application of function is open to all
degrees of skill and creativity in terms of a particular situation but unless one expects the client's need to remain
fixed and stable, the only access to the helping process as
a profession is through the utilization of a relatively fixed
function with all its personal and professional limitation
of the individual worker.

It seems to me that casework has been thrown into confusion by its inability to find its place between pure
therapy and public relief. The worker in the private agency
has tended to identify himself with the therapist in a freedom to respond to individual need on an individual basis
in contradistinction to the public-relief worker who responds to a category of need with a categorically rigid
function. The worker in the field of relief on the other
hand is struggling with the dilemma of whether he should
insist that relief is casework or whether he should repudiate casework affiliation and perhaps put the carrying-out
of the relief function on a business basis. In teaching casework classes, I have found that the student in the public
agency, despite his desire to learn how to do casework,
uses his function and the mass quality of his job to defend
himself against what seems like an impossible responsibility for seeing the individual, in the exercise of a function involving so many people in a working day. To him,
any talk about a *helping process* going on in all the rush

and turmoil of a relief application desk, seems mystical or theoretical or, at least, out of his reach. Such fine points are for private agencies and child guidance workers who have time. According to his nature, he wavers between scorn of such petty "fiddling while Rome burns," and despair of his own impotence to do likewise, or perhaps a grim determination to find out sometime, somewhere, just what this casework helping really is.

I believe that the problem evidenced in student reactions is real, is serious, and demands of us who pretend to know what casework is, the clearest and most courageous thinking of which we are capable. Casework is not a magic. It is a process that can and does go on under conditions that remain human, but it cannot operate when the mass to be handled gets beyond a certain point. The worker who really understands this process of helping and who has back of him a clear-cut sustaining function can exercise it for a surprising number of clients in a day, but there is a limit. He, too, is human, and there is no machine to go on making the product accurately, when he gets too weary to see another person or to care whether the client or himself, lives or dies. The law of diminishing returns begins to be felt very promptly in all professions that depend on the quality and strength of the helping person to sustain himself as a helper in feeling and interest as well as in determination or compulsion. The psychologist who has to turn out a dozen or more routine psychometric examinations a day, will soon be little better than a machine. After he has responded with keen insight and warmth to five or six children, the others begin to matter less and less. This is inevitable—the psychologist's only recourse is to rebel, to refuse to become an automaton and this refusal cannot be merely to save himself, but to save himself from his client, as a real psychologist. The same is true for the psychotherapist. He can help only as many patients as leave him enough time to remain a human being, with interest and kindness and strength—enough and to spare—for the other's use.

Therefore, the student who trains in relief, unless he has a highly protected load, is right when he presents the problem of his own exhausted self. It may be that the relief field, except when specially set up for training, does not permit the worker to experience the reality of the helping process unless he has already learned to be a professional caseworker elsewhere. But the more serious problem remains as to whether mass relief can be handled individually or on a casework basis even by a trained caseworker who accepts the philosophy of helping here presented and is skillful in practice. This, I think, is a real question, to be determined only by experiment—but there is no doubt in my mind that public relief on a large scale represents the extreme limit of the function that can be exercised by social casework on a helping level.

Therapy as usually practiced and in popular belief, represents the opposite extreme from public relief with relation to casework and is often reacted to by caseworkers with a similar scorn, repudiation, envy, or identification. There are caseworkers who feel themselves to be primarily therapists, just as there are those who feel inferior because they cannot lay claim to therapy, or those who would scorn to relate themselves to it. It is at this point, that the basis of differentiation changes from a difference in pressure of numbers to a difference in the desirability or inherent worth of the function itself. The therapist's function is assumed to require better training, greater skill, more responsibility, than the caseworker's and is so far removed from public relief as almost to defy comparison. It is undoubtedly true that therapy, at its best, *is* more highly professionalized than casework. It *does* demand a longer training and preparation and a greater discipline. The therapist *is* required to take an individual responsibility for what he does, that the caseworker never knows and cannot know without ceasing to be a caseworker. There are therapists, it is true, who rest upon institutional protection or belong to a sustaining group as a caseworker rests upon his agency, but in the last analysis a therapist cannot be protected from his patient and his own individual responsibility for what he does in the relationship. The caseworker's responsibility, on the other hand, real as it is, must first of all be to the agency and its function; only as agency, does he meet his client professionally.

However, for the caseworker, the real differentiation between therapy, social casework, and public relief at the opposite extreme, seems to me to lie not primarily in numbers or training or responsibility, but in what is conceived to be a more satisfying function as regards the relation to the client. The therapeutic situation is regarded as one in which the patient is given whatever he needs, without stint or refusal. It is a function the therapist can afford to identify with since, in such a view, it separates him hardly at all, or at least not for long, from an equally satisfactory identification with the needs of the patient. In other words, it seems to be largely a harmonious unity of purpose—the therapist's to give, the patient's to want and to take exactly what is to be obtained. Of course, a little scrutiny would soon arouse the social conscience of any intelligent relief worker who would see this as an overweighting of the individual's rights and privileges at the expense of the common good. But the aspect which social casework needs to realize is quite other than this superficial criticism; it is the fact that actually, therapy, from one viewpoint, might be thought of as the most niggardly and depriving of all the helping functions, since no matter what happens, the wise therapist refuses to give tangible aid, even to the point of refraining from practical advice or helping in any way with the reality problems of the patient. The patient asks and thinks he wants, every kind of reality response. He is kindly but firmly and consistently refused. The function of the therapist, then, requires him to maintain himself as a truly separate person who takes no material responsibility for the other and accepts no unfair treatment of himself, despite his understanding and tolerance of the consequent reactions.

The only thing a therapist gives to the patient is a deeper experience of self. He does this by refusing to inject his own personal interests, by constantly seeing, responding to, and accepting the self of the patient insofar as the latter learns to admit it and carry it responsibly; but at the same time—and this is the negative side of therapy—he continually resists and thwarts the patient's attempts to put the fearful or unwanted impulses upon him, in the form of blame, suspicion, hostility, or even of love and dependence. Despite—or shall we say because of—the hardhearted aspects of such a helping relationship, there is no situation that requires greater discipline of the professional person; and none that seems to the patient to give so completely, to the point that he knows he cannot pay for what he gets but must accept that he has taken help. To the lay person, who thinks of giving in positive terms, the therapist would seem to be an inhuman monster since he has utilized to the full the negative aspects of helping to develop professional skill. Even to the untrained relief worker, one would have difficulty in explaining why and how such a limiting experience could be therapeutic; it would seem to him almost as depriving as his own function.

There is only one answer to this apparent paradox, and that is that the limitations of therapy if skillfully maintained are ultimately discovered by the patient to be human limitations, inherent in his very nature. Although he forces the therapist to uphold them while he rebels and accuses or tries to escape, ultimately it may be possible for him to experience them as belonging to his own makeup, although usually obscured and softened by their projection upon other persons and things. The therapist does not interfere with his patient in reality, neither to give nor to deprive; that is, the purely therapeutic relationship contains a minimum of outside reality; it is confined as much as possible to one person, the patient. The problem for the patient lies partly in this very fact. He gets too much of himself for once, and has to find himself again in real life, in relation to other people whose rights are as his own and who do not live for him, even for an hour a day.

The difficulty with relief, on the other hand, aside from the administrative problems of any large-scale operation, lies in the inherent resistance to its function on the part of both worker and client. The power to give, to refuse, to limit, the actual means of subsistence for other adult human beings who have been deprived through no fault of their own of the opportunity to maintain themselves, is a function that cannot be accepted as right or good by any thoughtful person. At best it can only be tolerated as necessary. For a young worker to learn to bear professionally the punishment he must take in sustaining such a function, is no simple achievement. First of all he has to accept it for himself as, under the present conditions, the best the country can do. He does not have to approve it or want it to continue. But if he cannot decide to represent it as his agency function consistently and with self-respect, no matter what his sympathy with the client, he has no right to remain on the payroll. This is necessary not merely because it is fatal to do and keep on doing what one believes to be wrong, but also because the only chance a relief applicant has of getting something other than his check out of the experience, lies in the relief worker's capacity to meet this impossible helping situation with the courage of his function and the understanding of the problem it creates for the recipient. As I have already pointed out, how possible it is for an untrained beginner to learn what helping means on such a function and with the added burden of great numbers, is problematic. The disciplined worker can exercise even a relief function with understanding, but whether such a worker could or would continue to struggle with mounting numbers and a thankless function indefinitely, is even more problematic. That there is a place for whatever social casework understands about how to help and what the need to take help does to people, in setting up policies and procedures all through the public relief and assistance programs, there is no doubt.

It is evident that if the therapeutic situation is too unreal, public relief is too real, too actually depriving and controlling, for casework, as here defined, to operate to the best advantage. Social casework lies somewhere between these two extremes, always in the world of social and human reality, and consequently always with the not-too-great limitation of some kind of defined, restraining function. To maintain its professional integrity it requires an area in which some choice remains to the client, in which refusal is possible without destroying the individual. The social casework agency meets real need, but the need it supplies is not absolute, is not the only one, and permits of more than one possibility of fulfillment. The relief applicant, theoretically, may choose to reject the allowance to which he is entitled if he cannot or will not accept the attendant conditions, but the caseworker can hardly feel that a decision to starve, to beg, or to become a hobo in preference, is a valuable experience although actually it may be so. Such life and death limitations, deprivation, and control, tend to go beyond the boundaries of the humanly acceptable situations on which all helping professions are primarily based. However, with all that can be said against relief as a casework medium, tribute must be paid to the miracles of helping that can and do take place within these forbidding and inhuman limits when the caseworker brings to his task a sincere belief that his function, however hard, is worthy of his support and that the applicant has a right to the attitudes and emotions such a function necessarily arouses, and has the courage and kindness to see the process through on a professional level.

The material in this volume is confined to those functions that not only permit but require professional skill and knowledge of the helping process for their effective exercise. They are characterized by moderate reality, if one may use the phrase. The function, however important, is permissive, not obligatory. The client may choose to meet its limitations or find another way out. Neither client nor worker is exposed to such a complete involvement and individual responsibility as in the therapeutic relationship. The worker's responsibility is mediated by the agency and what it can and cannot do. The client's risk is lessened by the fact that he is not putting out a life and death need but only a partial want, something he can work to obtain in more than one way, or even do without, if necessary. The importance of what can be done to utilize the dynamics of these partial and human helping situations when they are met on the level of professional understanding and skill is indicated in the papers that follow, but only indicated. As social casework learns to accept its own limited area of usefulness and concentrates on the process to which it has given its purpose and determination, its capacity for growth will widen and deepen to the extent of human ability to give and to take help constructively.

Social Casework with Children

IN ATTEMPTING to account for the lag in the development of casework theory and practice in the field of child care as

"Introduction" to the *Journal of Social Work Process*, III, No. 1 (December, 1939).

evidenced in the meager published material, in comparison with the rich casework literature coming from the psychiatric and family fields, one must take into account the extent of the child welfare field on the one hand, and on the other, the inherent difficulty of its central function, child placement. Child welfare is as broad as the field of social work itself. It coincides with the specialized fields of family, medical, and psychiatric social work at every point where service to the child is involved; it includes recreational and educational opportunities developed by group-work agencies, institutional care and foster-home placement for dependent children, and the wide range of services in behalf of the delinquent child. Moreover, a sound program of child welfare is inextricably bound up with a health program for children in which the professional contribution comes from medicine, dentistry, and nursing and may be administered by these professions rather than by social work. In this bewildering range of child welfare services, the child-placing function alone stands out as the one professional task which is distinctive and unique for this field.

It is not easy to supply a theory for removing a child from its parents, or yet to turn the practical exigencies of such removal into a smooth exposition of conscious, controlled practice. Nor is it a simple matter to describe technically the experience of helping a foster-home placement to work out over years of slow development. To wrest awareness of process and professional skill out of long-time realistic human relationships, carrying a responsibility for the actual living of many children, is a slow, uneven, baffling struggle. No wonder that, while the human purpose and belief in the value of the function have been expressed frequently in the literature by leaders of the child

welfare movement, practitioners have seldom emerged
from the welter of manifold obligations to the foster homes
and foster children in their caseloads to formulate or
justify their own day to day procedures.

It is without apology, therefore, that this number of the
Journal, while it includes contributions from the highly
specialized and developed functions of child guidance and
school counseling, as well as a paper from the field of
medical social casework with children, is frankly devoted
to a clearer formulation and exposition of what is implied
in the professionally conscious placement of the dependent
child in a foster home and the relation of this form of care
to the community that supports it. All of the papers that
follow regardless of the age and length of experience of
the writer or of the particular function discussed are
characterized by a central theme, which seems to me to go
to the root of the inherent difficulty in casework with
children, particularly dependent children; that is, the
kind and degree of responsibility that is to be assumed professionally and the relation of that responsibility to the
growth process going on in the child himself, to the adults
on whom he depends immediately, and to the community
that supports him. The therapeutic, the medical, the
counseling responsibilities of the social work practitioner,
to the child and to the related adults are sufficiently grave
to call out the last degree of skill and understanding, but
they do not seem to me to be comparable to the courage
and conviction required to help a parent and child to
separate temporarily or permanently; to carry out that
psychological decision in the realistic terms of placing an
actual child in an actual foster home whose concrete needs

and limitations must also be taken into full consideration; and finally, to sustain that placement responsibility in relation to the community as a whole. How can any human being know enough to make such decisions; how can any practitioner find the courage or belief to move flesh and blood children into relatively unknown homes, or to fill these anxious homes with comparatively unknown children? Obviously, no one could presume to such omniscience if this is the kind and degree of responsibility involved. Certainly there is no theoretical basis, no reliable diagnostic scheme available to justify such an undertaking. Yet, the truth is, that where children are concerned, the temptation of the adult, or one might say his conscientious compulsion, is to take too much responsibility or none at all.

In undertaking the function of child placement, then, every practitioner is brought face to face with this adult dilemma in regard to children, which must be dealt with personally before it can be handled professionally. In a long experience with the training of students placed in a children's agency for their field practice, we have found that each student has to struggle with his own relation to the problem of desertion or forced separation, a problem which faces him in one form or another in every parent and every child the agency undertakes to help. At one extreme is the student who can never accept the rightness of taking a child from its home, who cannot identify with the agency's function, who cannot admit that a child must sometimes leave his own people and that a foster home offers a constructive possibility; at the other, is the student who denies, because he cannot bear it, the pain and inevitable trauma inherent even in the most thoughtful considerate taking over of a child from his own parents and in the most fortunate foster-home adjustment. Between these extremes lie all varieties of natural identification or failure to identify with the child or the parent or the agency, and every stage of individual growth and independence in relation to own parents and own home. The very function of child placement, then, strikes at the root of the student's personal development and forces him to come to grips with its meaning for him in order to carry it sincerely and responsibly with the client. Four student theses have been included in this number of the *Journal* because of the vivid picture they present of the discipline the student undergoes in learning to carry the process professionally, and of his capacity to translate this discipline slowly, it is true, but reliably into authentic insight and skill.

While the practitioner's personal relation to the function is undoubtedly one of the basic difficulties in child placement, there is an equally serious and inevitable handicap in the ambiguous character of the child, as a growing though not grown, a partly dependent yet increasingly independent organism, with potential as well as immediate value for himself and for society. How can the practitioner arrive at and maintain the delicate, ever moving balance between the responsibility he *must* carry and the responsibility that belongs to the child, a responsibility the latter may be slow to admit or shoulder, but which he will not fail to defend however negatively, if the worker usurps it? As if this aspect of the division of responsibility were not enough, there remains the complication of the child's dependent relation to adults. How does the practitioner's responsibility

for his function correlate with that of the teacher, the doctor, the adults who are responsible in the family setting,
natural or acquired, and finally with the right of the community to be considered? All of the papers on foster care,
especially the group of student theses, express in their
descriptions of the actual process of placement with individual children their awareness of what is involved and
their efforts to keep the balance between legitimate responsibility for the child in the community and an assumption
of helplessness that leaves him no room for self-determina-
tion and individual growth. There is also a new conception
of continuing relationship and joint but clearly differentiated responsibilities on the part of own parents and
foster parents to be maintained on a fluid developing basis
as long as the foster child remains in care.

Two final articles examine questions of financial support
for a child care program and point to the urgent need for
the development of state and county structures backed by
citizen interest and responsibility to make possible for
dependent and neglected children the protection that is
essential for them. There are grounds for belief that, in
spite of certain critical conditions in the present, sound
social planning for children will make progress, but it is
well to keep in mind that no degree of planning can lessen
the inherent dualism of the role which the child must play
and the inevitable dilemma of the adult in relation to it.
It is to these underlying imponderable problems of social
work with children that this volume is dedicated.

❧❧❧

Foster Home Care for Children

WITHIN THE ALL-INCLUSIVE FIELD of child welfare, the relatively small area devoted to the placement of children in foster homes becomes increasingly important to professional work, because it is the one area in a wilderness of possibilities and scattered effort where there has been a steady growth in technical skill based on understanding of the meaning and values of so-called child placement to parents, child, and foster parents.

To take a child from the home he has known and set him down in the midst of another family, there to find a place for himself if he can, has been viewed through the years, despite increasing use of rapidly changing psychological theory, as a series of necessary but comparatively unrelated events culminating in the child's arrival in a home where hopefully he will remain. Acceptance and utilization of the continuity and living character of this removal-placement experience, shared by own parent, child, worker, agency, and foster parent, constitute something new in social work and in child welfare.

In the Philadelphia area, the past decade has witnessed a realization of psychological insight in terms of actual, day-to-day practice that was not dreamed of in 1930. I shall

Paper published in the *Annals of the American Academy of Political and Social Science: Children in a Depression Decade,* November, 1940.

base my presentation on this practice, with which I have firsthand experience, because I believe that it has great significance as the high point of achievement for this period and the basis for assured progress.

The viewpoint that underlies this advance in practice is not related so much to a particular psychology of behahior as to a new understanding of growth as a living process which can and must be utilized psychologically as well as physiologically in any effort to help human beings, particularly children. This brilliant insight was first realized consciously in therapy with adults by Otto Rank, whose single-minded devotion to the welfare of the patient, regardless of the classical tenets of psychoanalysis, led him not only to a new therapeutic method, but to a new theory of helping, applicable in any field in which the human will is accepted as a potentially creative force capable of overcoming and even of utilizing for growth the external and internal forces with which it must struggle.[1]

It has taken more than ten years for this theory and method, first introduced to Philadelphia social workers by Dr. Rank himself in 1927–28, to eventuate in practice that is authentic for the tasks which belong to social casework, clearly differentiated from therapy as such.

The Philadelphia Child Guidance Clinic, under the leadership of Dr. Frederick Allen and Miss Almena Dawley, has provided the medium through which this new understanding of growth as a process that may be brought within the confines of clinical control has gradually been

[1] Otto Rank, *Will Therapy*, trans. Jessie Taft (New York: Alfred A. Knopf, 1936).

translated into concrete form. We have seen unhappy, destructive, shut-in, or delinquent children and their parents using a few weeks or months of contact with a therapist and a social worker to grow into a new relation to each other and eventually to the remaining social environment. This has happened not sporadically, but with increasing uniformity through the years.

To accomplish this result the clinic therapists and caseworkers have acted on their belief in the importance of choice, of self-initiated movement, of struggle, of negative as well as positive self-expression, and of continuous separation from the outworn psychological past as vital to natural growth. In the interest of what Miss Dawley has designated "the interrelated movement of parent and child," the organization of the clinic provides an artificial medium for a concentrated, intensified growth process experienced by the child as therapy, by the parent as casework, but brought together in a final leaving which becomes at once a dynamic for better social relationships and for increased freedom as individuals.[2]

To translate this conception of growth as applied to children in their own homes into a comprehension that would vitalize and unify the complicated traumatic steps incident to child placement, where child and parent go their separate ways, perhaps forever, has been the contribution of Miss Irene Liggett of the Children's Aid Society of Pennsylvania, who within the past five years has worked out through her staff and agency structure a practice that

[2] Almena Dawley, "The Interrelated Movement of Parent and Child in Therapy with Children," *American Journal of Orthopsychiatry*, IV, No. 4 (October, 1939), 737; Frederick H. Allen, "Participation in Therapy," *ibid.*, p. 748.

makes of child placement a coherent and professional, yet humanly controlled process.[3]

At no time in the history of child placement has the importance of growth been overlooked, but until recently it has been externally conceived, in historical, cultural, medical, therapeutic, physiological, or educational terms, with little comprehension of the child's immediate control over his own development and his capacity to use or refuse the well-considered plan of the placement agency.[4]

In addition to the child, there is the parent (one or both), not necessarily dead or out of the picture, and equally organized in relation to the agency which he has approached with the inevitable fear, guilt, determination, or doubt involved in "putting a child away."

In the very recent past and in many instances in the present, the removal of a child from his home has been thought of as depending on a decision reached, not by parents but by a social agency or perhaps by more than one agency after mature deliberation and investigation, or perhaps even after prolonged efforts on the part of a family agency to rehabilitate the home. That the parent himself must initiate and be responsible for accepting and actually taking the steps in a placement process in order to give the agency a sound basis for placing the child is a new concept in child care.

[3] While Miss Liggett is responsible for the insight that translated theory into practice in the field of foster-home placement, other agencies in and near Philadelphia have been quick to utilize her pioneering, each in its own distinctive fashion, particularly the Children's Bureau and the Juvenile Aid Society of Philadelphia.
[4] Irene Liggett, "Agency and Child in the Placement Process," *Journal of Social Work Process*, I, No. 1 (November, 1937), 54.

In this view the movement toward placement starts with the parent who applies to an agency for help in making a plan for his child. The agency enters into an exploratory process with him, so that he may move step by step, if this is possible at all, into the beginning experience of giving his child into care and relinquishing to a foster home many of the responsibilities that he has previously carried.[5] The use of the temporary boarding home as the testing ground for agency, parent, and child, in trying out the beginning actualities of foster-home placement, constitutes perhaps the most brilliant and important discovery in the utilization of the principles of growth by the placement agency.

There is no longer any attempt to deny the inherent trauma of a too early and forced separation of the child from his natural home. No placement agency believes that foster-home care at its best can be more than a substitute for what every child craves—his own parents, even those parents whom we might classify as undesirable. Nevertheless, the new practice rests on the conviction that the child's impulse toward growth is so powerful that, other things being equal, he will seize upon whatever he can find for his own development. The problem of the placement agency is how to make it possible for the child himself to choose placement, at least to the extent that he will utilize instead of resisting it.[6]

[5] Norma Philbrick, "The Interrelation of Parents and Agency in Child Placement," *Journal of Social Work Process*, III, No. 1 (December, 1939), 17.

[6] Marian R. Gennaria, "Helping the Very Young Child to Participate in Placement," *Journal of Social Work Process*, III, No. 1 (December, 1939), 29.

To accomplish this end, the placing agency, not unlike the Child Guidance Clinic, sets up a structure that allows the parent to work through this problem of "putting away" with a supervisor, while the child is carried by a case-worker.[7] Thus parent and child together, with the help of casework, move through a separating experience which, however painful, is at least shared, and, if not chosen primarily by the child, can be accepted by him as something his parent finds necessary. The parent, unless he gives his child up for adoption, usually remains in the picture, but his former relation to his child must give place to a new pattern, modified more or less continuously through the years if placement is on a longtime basis, but never without its vital part in the placement configuration. This process, however painful, can, with the help of the agency and its workers, constitute development for parent and growth for the child.

There is in this practice an underlying assumption about psychological growth which should be explicitly stated at this point. While the potentiality for growth is inherent in the living organism, the human being has the power to interfere with it by refusing the new or clinging to the past. Movement ahead, to be as fruitful and developing as it can be for a child, must be willed, accepted, or chosen in some degree. Otherwise, the natural growth process can be distorted, repressed, or refused in manifold ways, with a stubborn strength that is hardly credible. Even a baby in arms can refuse to be nourished

[7] Helen Baum, "Function as the Integrating Force in Child Placement," *Journal of Social Work Process*, I, No. 1 (November, 1937), 41.

by a situation which for some reason he does not or cannot accept; witness the problem of own parents with the baby whose will is negatively engaged.

With this conception of growth, and the admitted necessity of engaging the will of the child in any plan made for him, it is evident that no agency can psychologically place a child who refuses to be placed, even though he remains in a foster home physically. It is therefore essential for an agency that acts on this comprehension to do whatever it does with the child's participation. If, after every effort has been made to give him his full responsibility for the share in placement, he is unable to use a foster home constructively, the agency must have the courage to give up the struggle and refuse to be responsible for his continued placement in a foster home.

For the child, as for the parent, the initial experience of foster-home care in the temporary home provides a concentrated period for trying out, with the help of the caseworker, many of the aspects of this new way of living. The worker who has a vital understanding of what her task is at this point will stand by and under the child as he reacts with struggle, pain, fear, temper, or misbehavior to the day-by-day experience of foster home, clinics, and agency procedures. When this child, backed by his parent and sustained by his temporary foster mother and the agency visitor, finally comes to the point of moving into a permanent-boarding foster home, chosen for him and waiting to receive not just any child but this particular one, he may go with trepidation and uncertainty, but he goes also with an underlying eagerness and anticipation toward something that has become in part his own undertaking. He moves forward through the medium of a process that he has shared actively from the start, to the degree that his age and experience have permitted.[8]

Not only lay persons but many professional social workers as well are repelled by what seems to them a too spartan procedure that allows the child to face thus openly the stern reality of separation from his own home. This is a natural enough reaction, and no worker who has gone through the process just described will deny that it takes all the courage and conviction that she and her agency possess. But the fact remains that the placement situation is essentially painful, unnatural, and undesirable. Our problem is how to make of unavoidable trauma an opportunity for individual overcoming in terms of psychological growth. Since no child can face separation as a whole, in its full emotional value, without being annihilated, it falls to the child-placing agency to use its structure and routine to make of foster-home placement a homely, day-by-day procedure, broken up into little experiences that the child can grapple with, resist, and overcome.

In such a humanized process, made up of bits of daily living that have purpose and direction which the child can comprehend and accept in the little without complete refusal or complete acceptance of something too large to grasp, both child and parent can often find in foster-home placement, with its continuing agency responsibility, something that does not replace the original home, it is true,

[8] Mary N. Taylor, "The Temporary Home as an Integral Part of Adoption Procedure," *Journal of Social Work Process*, I, No. 1 (November, 1937), 67.

but nevertheless can create a new and bearable living situation secure enough to be used as a basis for genuine development.

This entering into placement on the part of parent, child, and agency is no simple matter in itself, but it constitutes only the beginning of longtime, complex relationships and responsibilities that must be consistently carried over the years, until the child either returns to his natural guardians, enters the working-world on his own, or is taken over by the foster home so really that at adolescence he is already a natural part of the family and the community in which he has been brought up.

For the successful accomplishment of its service, the child placement agency must depend ultimately on its foster homes, both temporary and permanent. The finding of such homes constitutes another skilled and delicate process, which, even when it eventuates in uncovering a usable home, is only the barest beginning of the understanding, the effort, and the patient skill that must be expended in maintaining it as an actively cooperative foster home through the years of its usefulness to children. Into this home-finding procedure that has baffled social work from the beginning because of the uncertainty of the agency relation to the foster home applicant,[9] where the need of the client seemed no greater than the need of the agency, has come like a revelation the new clarity and direction that functional casework permits.

As long as the child is the focus, it is not too difficult

[9] Alice Laden, "The Prospective Foster Parent as Client," *Journal of Social Work Process.* III, No. 1 (December, 1939).

to conceive of the placement agency as beginning with the need of the child, and trying in every way to meet, from the outside, that need as seen by the agency.[10] While this leaves both child and parent as participators in the casework process, at least they are the center of the plan which the agency arrives at in its study of the needs to be met. With the foster-home applicant, however, the need basis is obviously confusing and conflicting. Every person who comes to an agency asking for a child, even though it be only a child to board, has some kind of need or needs, related to what he asks for, and the board money in itself is seldom sufficient to account for his interest. There are other forms of boarding much more remunerative. The significant fact is that he asks for a child or children, and is seldom deterred even when it is proved to him that the board barely covers the child's living in the home, and that this is not a gainful occupation from any point of view.

Once the foster home applicant is recognized as a person who is seeking to have a need satisfied, what is the role of the agency committed to the need of the child? How far can it make this prospective foster parent's need the focus of its activity? It seems clear to me that only the function of

[10] The "client's need," in current casework theory, is opposed to the agency function or service as the proper focus of casework treatment or process. The two words "treatment" and "process" contain in themselves the difference in the operation of the two views. The one operates on, the other with the client. For an exposition of the former, see Fern Lowry, *Differential Approach in Casework Treatment*, Pamphlet, Family Welfare Association of America, 1935; and Deborah F. Rosenblum, "The Clarification and Meeting of the Client's Needs," *News-Letter*, American Association of Psychiatric Social Workers, Vol. IV, No. 1.

the agency as the focus of any relation into which it enters professionally can save the situation from complete confusion. The needs of the prospective foster parent may be as vital and worthy of being met as those of the child, but the two sets of needs may also conflict. To help the foster-home applicant in terms of his need may be to neglect completely the need of the child to be placed with him. Nothing but a definition of function and a willingness to stick to it can save the placement agency from irreconcilable conflict in the basis of its approach to home finding and child placing, both of which are essential to its operation.

For functional casework, these two activities constitute no problem as far as focus is concerned. The processes, while inherently difficult, are basically alike except for the differences introduced by the function itself.[11] The placement agency is not organized to meet the needs of prospective foster parents, but to place children constructively. True, it does need homes for its children, but it does not need any particular home to the point of having to accept as foster parent someone whose need for a child is such as to defeat the very purpose for which it has been created. The home-finding branch of the agency must meet the need of the applicant, it is true, or the home would never work out; but that need must be such as to fit in with the fundamental purpose of the agency, and only the capacity to keep that purpose constantly in view will enable the home finder to steer a path through potential confusion.

[11] For this point of view see Jessie Taft, "The Relation of Function to Process in Social Casework," *Journal of Social Work Process*, I, No. 1 (November, 1937), Introduction.

Home finding, too, as an expression of casework skill, has come into its own with the new understanding of participation in a process on the part of applicant and caseworker, so that a decision to use or even to reject an applicant for children to board becomes in the majority of cases a joint result. The agency's needs in the concrete are presented step by step as the realities against which the applicant can try out his particular interests, in a mutual testing process which will determine whether or not there is a sufficient basis for going on together into a working relationship. As the responsibility of the agency for the child must continue for the entire period of placement, it is evident that the foster-home applicant, as well as the agency, has much that is new and difficult ahead in learning to share responsibility for the child without usurpation on the part of either. Only the agency that can keep its function constantly alive and sustained may hope to come through with any large number of foster homes that succeed by chance.

The casual reader may not realize that child placement as thus described involves a new conception of the role of the agency in relation to the entire task. Ten years ago the individual social worker was the focus of attention and effort—his qualifications, his training, his grasp of psychoanalytic or psychiatric concepts, his emotional maturity, even his need for personal therapy as a prerequisite for casework. How were youngsters of twenty-one or twenty-two to be prepared in knowledge, personal development, and professional skill to carry the increasing psychological implications and complexities of social service as then conceived, and where could enough young people of such high qualifications be discovered and recruited? These were the questions that confronted schools of social work in this, the era of the psychiatric social worker.

This emphasis on the individual practitioner is a natural corollary to the assumption that the focus of agency practice is necessarily in the psychological problem presented by or found in the client who comes asking a particular service. Since this problem can in no way be predicted or understood beforehand, the entire responsibility for the development and outcome of the case in this view must rest largely with the worker who carries it, as he alone is in contact with the client. The agency becomes, as it were, a tool for the worker's use in his handling of the individual case.

The shift which functional casework has made from client's need to agency's service carries with it a new configuration in which the agency itself is the center, a vital organic whole, determining its function and sustaining its service through every worker who is identified with that service and acts as its representative with the client and in the community. This implies the presence of supervisors and executives who are themselves professionally adequate and able to sustain and develop the service of the agency through a vital relationship with the workers they supervise and with the community they serve.

This new concept of agency as the supporting matrix and controlling center of operation, working through defined structures but with imagination and flexibility, gives to the worker a less powerful but more possible spot in which to exercise whatever of individual skill he possesses. Freedom becomes excessive when the identity of agency is lost among staff members working more or less as separate individuals. On the other hand, where the agency is accepted as the greater whole of which the worker is only a part, the limitation on individual power and practice is more than compensated by freedom to work creatively within a clearly defined area of responsibility.

Only when agency is thus conceived and maintained can child placement, extending as it may over many years of responsibility for the development of a child, provide the steady, reliable background on which the foster child learns to depend despite unavoidable changes in workers and foster homes.

Three major contributions to social casework stand out as basic to the progress that has been made in child placement in the Philadelphia area during the decade following 1930. The first is a dynamic psychology of the individual which recognizes the creative nature of will and the conditions under which psychological growth takes place. The second is a clear understanding of professional helping as a process in its own right, capable of being understood and controlled in the interest of client and agency, a process that admits the dependence of all such helping on client initiative and client participation. And finally, there is a new conception of the social agency as an organic whole with a clarified function by which the casework process is stabilized and directed towards a goal valid for client, worker, and agency. On this firm yet flexible foundation, rooted in the very nature of growth, child placement has developed a philosophy, an understanding, and a practical skill worthy to be called professional.

❧❀❧

Some Specific Differences
in Current Theory and Practice

IN CONCLUDING THIS PAMPHLET, recognition should be
given to important differences in theory and in practice
that have emerged in the field of child placement comparatively recently, differences that for lack of better terms
may be characterized by the terms "functional" and "psychoanalytically oriented." The material in this pamphlet
is functionally based as a practice, and rests on a conception of psychological growth and of the nature of professional helping that, for the Pennsylvania School, had its
final theoretical formulation in the psychology of Otto
Rank. While there are numerous sources for the character-
ization of psychoanalytically oriented casework in the
literature coming from the family field, there is little published material in relation to child placement that presents
a definitely psychoanalytic approach to the detail of practice. In fact, except for the publications of the Pennsylvania
School and its graduates which have appeared within the
past eight years, there is little to be found in recent casework literature that establishes child placement on general
principles, either of practice or of casework theory. Individ-

The "Conclusion" of a pamphlet, *The Role of the Baby in the
Placement Process,* published by the Pennsylvania School of Social
Work, 1946.

ual phychiatrists and psychoanalysts have expressed opinions and have written articles from various angles on the problems of the foster child, but their contacts with child placement have usually been at long range, as agency consultants, or more intimately, as therapists for the problem child in the care of a placement agency. Their attitudes are naturally determined by their therapeutic concern and function, seldom by a direct or continuing responsibility for foster-home placement as such. They have sometimes turned to the foster home as a convenient source of environmental therapy for the problem child in his own home, and they have given advice on placement, or perhaps direct treatment, for the child who fails to adjust in foster-home care, but seldom, if ever, has any psychiatrist or psychoanalyst had the basis in experience for understanding the nature of foster-home placement as an authentic professional service in itself, capable of giving to the dependent child the very help he needs to overcome the growth problem created or increased by his dependency. . . .

It is partly because of this dearth of technical literature on child placement, that one turns gratefully to Dr. Florence Clothier, whose intimate relation to child placement through her longtime connection with the New England Home for Little Wanderers, has found clear expression in many articles that have been appearing in recent years. Dr. Clothier's psychology is psychoanalytically based, and the foster-care practice to which she addresses herself is one which places its emphasis on family history, on prolonged detailed study of the prospective foster home, and on the elaborate observation, testing, and medical examination of the child preliminary to placement, preferably in a "study home" or laboratory setup.[1] I think it is safe to say that Dr. Clothier has had little or no contact with a functionally organized placement agency, nor with casework that operates on a belief in the efficacy of its own professional helping process, as the vital medium in the whole placement enterprise. I doubt that the casework with which she has been familiar has yet developed sufficient responsibility for its own process to use its psychoanalytic orientation independently, in a placement service clearly differentiated from therapy. Therefore, while Dr. Clothier is clear on her conception of the nature of the baby and his original relation to his mother, the deductions she draws from this conception in regard to placement have doubtless been influenced by the kind of placement she has seen. From the functional point of view, the placement practice implied by Dr. Clothier's references to social work has apparently not used the very realities of its own service dynamically, in terms of a continuous, sustained process through which child, parent, and foster parent are helped to move forward constructively, within the placement situation. It seems to me important to bring out Dr. Clothier's views regarding the perils of foster-home care for young children by direct quotation, and before concluding this pamphlet, to try to clarify the differences in psychological viewpoint and consequently in the practice which it represents.

I quote first from an article on "Problems of Illegiti

[1] Florence Clothier, "The Role of the Child Study Home in Child Guidance," *Mental Hygiene,* January, 1944, p. 64.

macy" published in *Mental Hygiene,* October, 1941 (pp. 582, 583 and 584).

A warm close relationship between two human beings is far harder to break off than is a relationship not yet established in any real sense. By urging the mother to nurse her baby and by permitting a mother-child relationship to develop, we put a tremendous pressure on the mother to keep her baby. And we create a situation that will lead to the child's first trauma from the outside world, namely, the eventual breaking off of its relationship with its natural mother. The mother, who, after one to six months, gives up her baby, loses not only the product of her conception and whatever it may have stood for in her phantasy, but she also loses a baby with whose personality her own has become inextricably interwoven. Another human being's absolute dependency on her has tied her to that human being. Suckling, fondling, and care for the baby have made it more consciously a part of her than ever it was *in utero.* Compare the loss of a mother whose baby dies at or within a few hours of birth, with the bereavement of the mother who loses her baby during or after the nursing period . . .

. . . Social workers, like physicians, must be prepared to reach a decision as to what will be best for the baby and for the mother, and then to work actively toward the carrying out of that program. . . . Reaching a decision as to the future of each individual case that comes to her attention and working toward the carrying out of that decision, implies great responsibility for the social worker. Training, experience, and intuition must combine in helping her to decide for each particular client whether separation from the baby is advisable.

... It is unfortunate, that, with professional advantages on her side, the social worker has permitted overconscientiousness and obsessional adherence to casework tenets to limit rather than to extend her activity in this field.

In some cases the mature, experienced social worker will recognize, even in the prenatal period, that separation of the mother and the baby is advisable because it will inevitably occur sooner or later. In such cases it behooves the worker to formulate a tentative plan for the separation and to get in as much as possible of the preliminary work of carrying out this plan before the baby is born. This preliminary work, of course, will include casework treatment aimed at making it socially and psychologically possible for the mother to give up her baby.

There are two fundamental assumptions in this statement, one regarding the nature of casework help and its relation to the client who asks for a service—in this instance the unmarried mother—the other regarding the undesirability of permitting an experience, however valuable in itself, if its cessation will cause pain. As to the first, Dr. Clothier's reference to urging a mother to nurse her baby, as if it were accepted casework practice, goes against every professed theory of casework, functional or psychoanalytic. No trained caseworker today would deny that the client must not only be free to choose his own goal but should be helped to find it. Just how free this choice is in actual practice depends upon how genuinely the agency and its worker respect the strength and integrity of the weakest applicant, and also upon the worker's capacity to initiate and further a true relationship process in which the inner movement of the client towards a plan, not the decision of the worker, determines the outcome. For Miss Smith,[2] the help given to the unmarried mother could never be in terms of knowing in advance what she should be "induced" to do regarding her child, before or after birth. Knowledge of the practical difficulties in a mother's attempt to support a child alone, and of the unfitness of the very young or unstable girl for motherhood, may enable an experienced worker to predict the outcome in a given case, but experience should also have taught her never to let her own opinion obliterate the possibility that this particular mother may work out an unexpected solution to an apparently predetermined eventuation. Nor can she afford to forget that what each individual wants and needs, however slight his capacity, is to possess his own experience and to arrive at his own conclusion, faulty though it be. To enter into this helping process with the unmarried mother, is not to drop the reality of agency operation, nor to forego its focus on the welfare of the baby, but to utilize the limits inherent in the situation—limits of time, of money, and of practical necessities—to bring the relationship process to an outcome which is valid for client, worker and agency.

The second and even more important point made by Dr. Clothier is fundamentally opposed to the psychology of growth which underlies functional casework. Her approach

[2] Mary Frances Smith, "The Integration of Agency Service in Placement of Babies," in *The Role of the Baby in the Placement Process* (Philadelphia: Pennsylvania School of Social Work, 1946), pp. 7–41.

to pregnancy, birth, and nursing, implies fear of life itself, since all growth experience entails a continuous process of separation from the past and its love objects. To an attitude that sees only the loss and pain of this growth movement, life must indeed seem full of hazard, to be avoided by escaping as far as possible any experience, the leaving of which may be painful or traumatic. Since life begins for each of us with the most violent of physical experiences in separation and loss, it is hard to see how, with this philosophy, it could be worth enduring. It would be easier not to live at all. But the fact remains that human beings are not just the passive victims of trauma from birth to death. They do find fulfillment in experiences that are hard to leave. They can overcome the traumatic aspects of a painful parting by the discovery of unused strengths for living in the self. True, man is a suffering being, but he is also a powerful creative force, with a capacity for molding the outside world into something that he can claim as his own. What man resists, above all, is external interference with any phase of his living before he himself is ready to abandon it. It is not the leaving but the lack of control over leaving, that he fears. If he can possess to some degree the ending phase of even the deepest relationship, so that he feels as part of himself the movement toward the new, then he cannot only bear the growth process, however painful, but can accept it with positive affirmation.

It seems to me that in her feeling for the future suffering of the unmarried mother and in her desire to save the child from his undeserved fate, Dr. Clothier would render even more sterile or more traumatic, vital experiences that, however condensed in time, can and do have their own inherent value for mother and child. If I were adopting a child, I should infinitely prefer one who had experienced for a time, at least, the healing organic connection with life outside of the uterus, through the breast of his own mother, to the baby who, following the trauma of birth, has had to bridge a chasm of disconnectedness without the immediate restoration of unity which only the mother can supply. And would not any woman who had succeeded in giving her baby a good start at the breast, be better able to give him up, for adoption if need be, with the feeling that she had done what she could for her child, and at a cost to herself? Perhaps, all living is at bottom a matter of bearing the pain, in order to possess in feeling the value, of vital experience. The only irreparable trauma is to be cut off from the full development of the self in relationship, by some inner or outer compulsion.

Be that as it may, the most important practical issue in Dr. Clothier's position centers around the use of the temporary foster home as a first step toward permanent placement. Two quotations, the first from an article on "The Problem of the Frequent Replacement of the Young Dependent Child," in *Mental Hygiene,* October, 1937, and the second from "The Psychology of the Adopted Child," in *Mental Hygiene,* April, 1943, will indicate her objections to the basic procedure advocated in this pamphlet.

> The problem is that of the harm done by well-intentioned agencies and workers in moving the young child about from one home to another . . . The increasing number of professional social workers have come to look

askance upon the former casual, but permanent, disposal of dependent children. The newer, more modern method is to regard each placement as a trial or experiment. . . . For the young child who is in the process of forming object-loves, and, because of them, giving up the gratification of his own personal wishes, it is a tragedy each time he is moved from one home to another. Each such move means nipping in the bud the child's strivings to become a social being. With too many such nippings or frustrations, the child gives up trying to form object-loves and, like the infant, seeks pleasure in the gratification of his own desires without regard to society —so little to be depended upon for love, security or stability. (pp. 549, 553) . . . We all know that it is a reality situation that young children sometimes have to be moved, but when such a move is necessary it should be regarded with the same serious thought that the surgeon gives to a major and difficult operation . . . When a foster home is contemplated for the young dependent child it should be regarded by the foster parents and by the social worker as a permanent plan unless extraordinary circumstances intervene. (p. 557)

The second quotation follows:

The infant who is placed in a boarding home preliminary to adoption does live through some sort of socially influencing experience in relation to his foster mother, but, because of the very fact that the home has deeply influenced his ego development, the interruption of his relationship with it is traumatic. (p. 225) . . . Any child who is placed for adoption after a preliminary temporary placement is deprived, not only of the primary

security of an intimate relationship wih his own biological mother, but also of a completely experienced
infancy with his adopted mother. (p. 226)

In regard to the importance of the mother and the first
relationship with her through the medium of mothering,
nursing and physical care, there is no possible dispute. All
placement, particularly of the baby, must begin with that
fundamental comprehension of the child's first and most
important medium for social and personal development.
The basic issue here is rather a question of what is possible
for the child, himself, when natural mothering fails him.

The first point to be answered is that no up-to-date
foster-care agency would advocate experimental placement
of any child, except insofar as all placement has in it elements of the unknown and the unpredictable, in which it
does not differ from the natural family. One could not
deny that foster care involves the possibility of replacement, since no foster family can provide a guarantee against
illness, death, or change of circumstances that may necessitate the removal of a foster child. Also, many placed
children have parents or other relatives who introduce
change into the placement plan. The stable core of placement must reside in the agency itself and its capacity to
provide workers who, even when they change, continue to
represent the same kind of professional relationship and
service to child, to parent, and to foster parent. As one
little five-year-old reassured herself in the midst of a removal, "The Aid never sleeps, does it?" As far as is humanly possible, the responsible children's agency sets this
standard for itself and its representatives—never to sleep

where a child in placement is concerned, but to sustain the placement process for the foster child reliably as long as he needs to use it. To the child who has his own part in placement and is related to the agency worker as to one who can be trusted to see him through any placement problem, however painful, even replacement does not need to have the external, forced, and therefore tragic quality, that is implied in Dr. Clothier's account. Dependence on foster-home care is not a fate one would choose for any child, but since it is inevitable for some children, the only way to approach it constructively is to help the individual child to make of it something to which he can relate in some measure voluntarily, and which he can therefore use for himself to grow on. From the articles in this pamphlet one sees that it can happen when the will of the child and his own capacity for growth are given first consideration.

Objection to the use of the temporary foster home as a needless moving about of the baby, who suffers loss and upset with every change, is a natural one. I think any lay-man—and even Dr. Clothier is such when it comes to the actual responsibility and firsthand knowledge possessed by the placement worker—would react as she does with disbelief and condemnation. In fact, there are too many foster care agencies extent today who have never placed children through the medium of living, moving relation to each individual child and his parents. Instead, they operate on a rational plan, a scientific blueprint as it were, made on the basis of facts externally observed or obtained and imposed from the outside upon all concerned—parents, child and foster parents. To such an agency the temporary home is only a necessary evil, to be used as a stopgap when the permanent placement is not available. One could not blame them or Dr. Clothier for hesitating to put any child through one more of these forced, unrelated experiences, however well planned, which, from this approach to it, seem to be unavoidably injurious. Such placement is indeed traumatic, whether it be labeled temporary or permanent, an it is only because children have tremendous capacity in themselves to overcome trauma, to adjust to change, and to utilize whatever they can find in their environment for healing, that the average, everyday child comes through these externally planned, well-intentioned placements as well as he does. Workers are better intuitively than the theories on which they think they operate, but that is no reason for not establishing intuition on a foundation of psychological insight and conscious professional practice, capable of providing foster-home care for the unusual as well as for the average child, without the devastating experience of forced separation, as far as this is humanly possible.

It seems to me that in concentrating on the trauma of placement, Dr. Clothier has temporarily forgotten the natural traumas of the growth process itself, which lead the baby to break away from the union with his mother, in order to take on the father or some other member of the family as a step in separation and differentiation of his own ego. This is not done purely positively, just because he has completed his first experience with his mother and is ready to go on—a picture we like to believe is the true one—but because the reality of his mother has brought in painful, separating experiences, controls not of his choosing, failures to meet his most pressing demands, and perhaps a new baby to take his place. Even the most fortunate babyhood is one continuous process of meeting inner and outer change, so that although separation from earlier relationships is, in truth, the result of an inner urge to grow and develop the self independently, it is also reaction to a series of traumatic, external events from birth itself, through weaning, toilet training, walking, competing with siblings, and finally going to school alone. When one adds to this process the fact that the average parent is young and all too human, bearing within him the net result of his efforts, perhaps unsuccessful, to assimilate his own life history, one can only marvel that any child ever adjusts, much less creates a satisfactory self.

It must be that the very growth movement which every human being fears and yet longs for, essential to the life process though it be, is feared as life is feared, because to live freely is to risk death, while to refuse to move, to resist change successfully, is also to die. In other words, while man is essentially ambivalent and conflicted in regard to change, he is also an animal capable of living in a changing medium, indeed requires it for his own development. It is only on the basis of accepting the inherent dualism of our attitudes toward inner and outer movement, and of utilizing it to help even the youngest client to discover his own forward-moving direction in the midst of external trauma, that foster-home placement for the parent-deprived child becomes a tolerable profession.

The articles in this pamphlet have demonstrated far better than any words of mine, how a baby can use a temporary foster home, if it is one that has accepted its *raison d'être,* and is sustained in its service by its relation to the agency, to fulfill his needs, and how with the support of the worker, he can leave it in order to take on a home toward which he himself is moving, with some sense of his own will and choice. One needs to appreciate the fact that this is more help than the average child in his own home ever gets in realizing his own desire to separate from the breast, from the lap, from the control of his mother.

It is with this point, implied but not clearly stated in these articles, that I wish to close the pamphlet. We are accustomed to recognize that within the casework relationship the adult client responds to what is evidently for him a unique experience of being understood, of being free to express feeling even when his will meets opposition from the conditions and limitations of agency service. What we have hardly dared to affirm is the fact that even a baby, deprived of the rightful satisfactions of infancy, may benefit from a unique and vital experience seldom granted to the child in his own home. I am not suggesting that to be a foster child is preferable, but I am stating a fact when I point out that the baby who leaves his own mother and goes through a good foster home into an adoption home, with the kind of immediate understanding, firmness, and unselfish support described in this pamphlet, gets an accelerated or intensified growth experience, which, for an adult, we would not hesitate to label "therapeutic." It is the unselfish nature of the truly professional relationship, which utilizes the placement process for the fulfilment of the baby's present needs, in order to free him to experience his own part in change, that alone can hope to overcome without denial, the destructive aspects of foster home placement.

A Functional Approach
to Family Casework

THIS VOLUME, *A Functional Approach to Family Casework*, which it is my privilege to introduce, marks the culmination of an effort of many years on the part of the casework faculty of the Pennsylvania School of Social Work to clarify for itself, for its students, and for its training agencies, as well as for the profession, a point of view regarding the practice of family casework about which it has conviction and on which it undertakes to train students. This effort was necessary because within the last ten years there had gradually emerged between the classroom teaching of this School and the philosophy and practice of some of its training agencies in the family field, a difference of approach whose implications for student training could not continue to be ignored. This difference was evidenced primarily in our emphasis on the importance of the social agency and its particular function as a determinant of the casework process, in contrast to a tendency to allocate to the caseworker himself greater responsibility for determining and meeting the need of each individual client.

The first volume of the *Journal of Social Work Process*

Originally published as "Introduction" to *A Functional Approach To Family Case Work:* (Social Work Process Series; Philadelphia: Pennsylvania School of Social Work, 1944).

in 1937, entitled *The Relation of Function to Process in Social Casework,* had brought out clearly what the functional approach could mean in the practice of casework with children. At that time, the material on which we were learning about the importance of agency function as a much needed source of control in casework method was drawn chiefly from the work of the child-placement agencies of Philadelphia. The deepening comprehension of three major child-placement agencies in our community regarding the nature of their service as one long, sustained process of establishing and maintaining the functional relationships on which a child's placement depends, provided a rich stream of case material on which to learn and to teach. We had also drawn heavily upon the evidence of process as presented in the practice of the Philadelphia Child Guidance Clinic. There was, however, only a limited opportunity in Philadelphia to examine the effect of this new understanding of function on actual casework results in the family field. This lack was obscured, but also emphasized, by the almost unlimited possibilities which were opened up in the area of public assistance in Philadelphia, where supervision for the first time was being separated out and analyzed as an essential and unique process in social work, related to casework but differentiated from it by the very difference in its task and in the relationship to agency service.[1] Because of the necessity for functional definition, both of the service and of its supervision, the public-assistance agency in Philadelphia became for a time another proving ground for this new conception of function and its

[1] Virginia P. Robinson, *Supervision in Social Casework* (Chapel Hill: University of North Carolina Press, 1936).

determining relation to any process, including casework.

It was natural, therefore, that in 1938 the second volume of the *Journal,* edited by Mrs. Rose Wessel, should be devoted to *Method and Skill in the Practice of Public Assistance.* It was inevitable, also, that the interest of our casework teachers in the operation of this new and important function should sharpen their awareness of the differences that soon became apparent in case material from this source and that brought into class at the same time by students from the private family agencies. While students were impatient with the limitations of the often too rigid public assistance policies, they were correspondingly alert to the lack of clarity and direction so often characteristic of a family casework situation. They were quick to face the private agency student with a challenge as to his function. No amount of understanding and open-mindedness on the part of the teacher could prevent the conflict introduced into the work of a student thus subjected to criticism by his peers, no matter how warmly the School might be related to the training agency involved. When to this dilemma was added the teacher's mounting interest, positive though it might be, in the possibility of applying this new concept of function to the problems of family casework, it is evident that, unless the training agency was equally interested, an insoluble conflict was in the making between student practice in agency and school training in the classroom.

As our conviction regarding the applicability of a functional approach to family casework grew firmer, our teaching became correspondingly clearer and at the same time more difficult for the students in the family agency to reconcile with their field work experience. There were valiant attempts on our part, as well as on the part of those family agencies whose practice was most at variance with the School's teaching, to bridge the gap, to minimize the practical differences, to make it right for the student. Acceptance of the difficulty of reconciliation came almost simultaneously to our teachers and to the training supervisors of one important family agency when we faced the fact that the problem involved not only a difference in casework, but in supervision itself. The difference actually went all the way. It seemed clear to us that for these supervisors student supervision meant an almost indefinite period of freedom for each student to unfold in his own time and on his own terms, without the pressure of school requirements or of the crisis precipitated by the possibility of failure to meet them. For a professional school organized on the basis of requirement and achievement within a limited time, this is obviously an untenable concept of supervision from a purely practical standpoint. Furthermore, psychologically, in terms of student learning, it fails to comprehend and hence to utilize the dynamic afforded by the very nature of the training process, with its self-chosen goal of professional competence, just as, in casework practice, it forfeits the control and direction provided by agency function and policy for an anomalous personal freedom.

While a school of social work has its own professional practice and carries the responsibility for a training process based on classroom teaching and individual advising, it must depend for its immediate contact with agency casework on the field work of its students and the case material presented by them in the practice classes. In those areas where the social agencies were pioneering for themselves on a functional basis, the work of second-year students reflected truly a developing method and casework understanding which could be sustained by supervisors and teachers alike. Such a connection between agency and school is vital and mutually effective. Each learns from and is influenced by the other through the dynamics of a training process which depends equally on both. Where there is no such common basis the relationship between school and agency loses its living force and ceases to be a source of learning for those concerned.

To the keen regret of the casework faculty, this vital connection between the School and the family field seemed to be seriously impaired until, in 1939, the situation was saved for us by the introduction of a full-time program with field work, in the recently instituted Advanced Curriculum. This brought into the School senior caseworkers and supervisors from a wider geographical area, our own graduates as well as graduates of other schools, and some workers without full technical training but with experience and qualifications beyond the regular student level. Through the freedom of these responsible, mature students to try out the new functional approach with the backing of their agencies, the School again achieved a broad working contact with family casework on a level that has made teaching and learning in that field dynamic and sound.

One might well ask why the family field rather than any other should become the focus of difference in viewpoint. Some of the reasons for this are obvious. The family agency is truly the generic agency from which specific services have sprung. Its practice has set the pace for professional achievement in this country, while to it we owe much of whatever theory we possess today. Other fields, important as they are practically, have not been so significant theoretically, as far as casework method is concerned. For example, no important theory regarding casework method had ever come out of the children's field, to my knowledge, before the publication of our first *Journal* in 1937. The daily practice in this field has seemed to be the answer to all theoretical problems. Agencies have children to place in foster homes or something equally emergent and real. Even today, significant differences of opinion regarding fundamental principles in the area of foster-home placement are difficult to find in the literature. Not until the Child Welfare League of America began to include technical case material in its *Bulletin* of 1940 was there even a regular medium for publication in that field.

That the presentation of any new method in social casework should meet formulated difference of opinion chiefly from leaders who represent the method and theory that have been developed out of family agency practice is, therefore, to be expected. Because these leaders are usually not interested in family casework as a specific service, but in family casework as something generic—not so much as a method of giving a service, as a form of psychological treatment—they tend to challenge the functional point of view in general theoretical terms, without reference to the concrete material on which the theory rests. For instance, one of the criticism most commonly expressed is that the functional theory is unscientific. No one to my knowledge has ever tried to show specifically that the practice on which this theory relies is lacking in helpfulness to the client in obtaining the service for which he applies, nor that this helpfulness, where it seems to be demonstrated, is not connected with an understanding of the process involved and with a conscious, consistent use of that understanding. If by "scientific procedure" one means not so much the complete reliance on a deterministic causality as the recognition of a universality based on verified comprehension of the nature of law of the particular process in question, then this approach is scientific.

Since in our eagerness to repudiate all connection with a rigid, mechanistic conception of causality, we have allowed the epithet "unscientific" to go unchallenged— in fact, have asserted the unpredictable nature of the casework process, as far as the client is concerned—this may be the time and place to declare publicly that the functional theory of social casework, far from being unscientific, seems to us to constitute the one approximation to a scientific method ever to come out of social casework itself. Since the "law of the process" underlying casework help can be isolated and understood, provided the conditions under which it can occur are given and are subject to reasonable control on the part of agency, it is as open to observation and generalization as any other living process, when the social worker is as ready to accept the conditions inherent in his role as is the laboratory scientist in biology. The fact that the social worker, by definition, is there to help, while the primary purpose of the scientist is to observe or experiment, should give us pause in our efforts to relate social-work practice too closely to scientific procedure, but it need not prevent us from understanding and relying on whatever is universal in the process for which we are responsible.

Perhaps the lay origin of social work, its original lack of professional freedom, of professional training, and of professional responsibility, all of which persist to some extent into the present, account for its readiness to see in psychiatry and psychoanalysis, a way of helping that is better defined, more scientific, and therefore more desirable than anything social work can hope to offer of its own. The resulting tendency of social workers to rest upon the authority, even to utilize the supervision, of this more firmly grounded, better trained, legally sanctioned profession, in order to fill what seems to be a void in their own, has been the source of much confusion as to what, if anything, is indigenous to social casework. It has also often blinded both agencies and workers to the nature and potential value of their own task.

This leads to the further point which is usually raised against the functional approach—that it merely substitutes Rankian therapy for Freudian psychoanalysis. To many of the writers who present this argument, only a psychology based on the work of Freud may claim affiliation with science, and to them the charge that the functional method is unscientific appears to be substantiated authoritatively on this ground. With the same stroke, it is clear, social casework as such is again denied and only a form of psychotherapy remains. To escape from this dilemma is indeed difficult, for no answer meets the objection of the social worker to whom Freudian psychology is essential and psychoanalysis the only fundamental source

of help. The advantage given to those of us who have
learned from Rank lies in the fact that, although his own
professional practice was therapy, he did uncover the universal nature of the human being's problem in taking
help and he supplied us with a psychology and philosophy
of helping that can be used independently of therapy.
But it was only when we realized that it is the function
and structure of the social agency which differentiates the
helping that belongs to social casework from the helping
found in therapy, that we were finally freed from the necessity to confuse the two modes of helping and could
concentrate on learning to use with skill the particular
process for which we are responsible. Deep as is our
acknowledged debt to Rank for his insight into the nature of professional helping, apart from psychotherapy as
well as within it, it is no longer necessary to depend on
his experience rather than on our own. Through using
the differentiation and control provided by the nature of
social service and by the determining differences of specific agencies with specific functions, we have located and
described repeatedly in our published material what seems
to us to be a method of helping peculiar to social casework.

It follows then that this method, which is generic, will
underlie all case material that records any particular instance of its utilization. Perhaps this is the answer to
another criticism commonly made against the functional
point of view, namely, that it is a point of view, not
eclectic or ambiguous but unified and consistent in every
piece of case material, to the point of monotony. One can
only reply that this consistency is not, in our opinion or
to our knowledge, due to blind identification or slavish
imitation on the part of students and others, but it rather

bears witness to the scientific validity of the hypothesis on which we work. To say that the recorded experience of caseworkers who work functionally is not to be trusted is to cast doubt upon all case recording and all casework experience. As to the danger of the casework process becoming dull or repetitious because of its generic base, it seems to me that there is more reason to fear the complexity and infinite variety which the caseworker is expected to meet skillfully, when, as in functional casework, only the nature of the process and the function of the agency remain stable. The client, on the other hand, is free to be or to become himself, in his own way, with the help of the worker and under the challenge of the new possibilities opened up by the agency. As long as clients retain their uniqueness as individuals, no point of view can ever make casework mechanical or merely repetitious. Perhaps what is feared is that the caseworker will not be equally free, and this is true. Only the client remains on the level of personal freedom. The worker is necessarily limited by professional responsibility, but within those limits no boundary is fixed for the development of his skill and his human understanding.

Closely related to the reproach that functional casework is unscientific is the further charge that it has abandoned diagnosis and its resultant plan for treatment. This is true insofar as diagnosis and treatment are concepts taken over bodily from medicine or psychiatry, for they represent an attitude toward the client which seems to us fundamentally antagonistic not only to functional practice but to social work itself. The client, in our belief, is not a sick person whose illness must first be classified, but a human being, like the worker, asking for a specific service. He, no less than any other human being, finds it painful to put out a need that he can no longer meet independently, and to subject his will, however feeble, to the possibility of unwelcome control in obtaining what he seeks. The functionally trained worker does not take upon himself responsibility for knowing the complete personal history of every client who requests a service, but he does expect to follow every client through the conflict which he experiences in trying to use help, as well as to get all the information regarding the client's situation or previous history that bears on the giving of this service. The functional approach demands of the worker a fundamental understanding of change and growth, a deep comprehension of what it means to take help, derived from his own training experience and from a conviction that only the client can determine in and of himself what he will utilize helpfully from the services available. We understand diagnosis, then, not as a categorizing of the client's makeup, with a resultant prescription for his needs, from the viewpoint of an adjusted personality, but an attempt on the part of worker and client to discover whether client need and agency service can be brought into a working connection that is mutually acceptable. The diagnosis is made when worker and client arrive at a plan for continuing or finally terminating the contact. Diagnosis in this view leads not to treatment but to a working relationship, set up under certain determining conditions, with a purpose or plan worked out by the client and accepted as a tentative arrangement by agency. There is here no secret labeling of the personality of the client by the worker, no unshared intention to treat "a fundamental emotional problem," but a practical judgment reached through an application process in which the client has an equal responsibility. The worker carries full responsibility for agency service, for the knowledge of the problems this very service can create for the client and his family, for understanding the universal human resistance to being helped, no matter how great the need, and for the skillful utilization of time in the client's interest. But no worker knows, or should presume to try to control, the vital process through which a client experiences change in his use of agency. Nor can any worker, however skillful, determine or foresee the exact nature, direction, and depth of such change. Herein lies the freedom for creative utilization of help that escapes the foreknowledge or diagnostic acumen of the helper, however scientific his attitude, and goes beyond or even against any treatment plan laid down in advance.

It is not for the sake of widening or deepening these theoretical differences, but rather in the interest of working on the problem which the family agency presents to the functional approach, that this volume is offered. There is no ready answer to the challenge of a social agency whose purpose can be defined generally, but whose specific services cover a wide range and leave uncharted such an area of increasing demand, for instance, as that which is often called "counseling"—a term that unfortunately obscures the confusion and uncertainty into which the average family caseworker is thrown when deprived of the support and control inherent in defined services and practical procedures. That his uncertainty is justifiable is evidenced by the borderline character of many of these requests for help, which seem to be purely personal and psychological. The caseworker who tries to meet this demand is caught in a two-way fear with respect to his service—either that the client *will not* return, an indication of failure to help; or that the client *will* return and bring the worker face to face with the possibility of a worker-client relationship which feels more like therapy than casework.

There are family agencies so closely affiliated with psychoanalytic psychiatry that they do not hesitate to meet this type of application with a modified form of psychoanalysis, for which a psychiatrist may take a nominal or an actual responsibility. As this obliterates the essential difference between therapy and casework,[2] we of the functional persuasion are not content to accept as insoluble the undeniable problem of family agencies today, without an effort to locate a specific function and a casework method, even in this area of so-called "counseling."

As long as there is some tangible service which the client seeks and the agency offers, however slight it may be as compared to the psychological help he receives in obtaining it, the worker seems to be freed, equally with the client, to engage in a genuine helping process. While

[2] Although casework and therapy are alike in that both are methods of helping based on an effective relation between a professional helper and a person seeking help, they differ essentially in the degree to which the world of reality is continuously represented. The psychoanalyst and his patient tend to retire into a world of two, in which even the psychiatrist as second person seems to exist largely for the sake of the patient, except for the realistic restrictions of fee, time, and place. In social work, on the contrary, the client, however understanding the consideration he receives from an individual practitioner, remains always in a three-dimensional world, represented by the agency's responsibility, not only to the single client, but to the family and community in which his problem is expressed.

there is no doubting the personality change effected in every case presented in this volume, it is also clear that neither worker nor client departed in any instance from authentic casework practice. This is determined, it seems to me, by the pervasive presence of agency, as a background, which holds both worker and client in a larger reality. However, without actual reliance on the focus provided by some concrete service, through which agency is expressed, it is difficult for them to gear their relationship to a social casework medium. It tends to approximate the common sense-friendly or the professional-therapeutic. The functionally trained worker becomes uneasy in either situation, as it soon deprives him of the role which he can carry with skill and leaves him as unsure as the client, whose fear is enhanced by any attempt to internalize his problem but whose projection it it upon others gives no practical possibility for solution.

*   *   *   *   *   *

[The latter part of this introduction discusses the papers presented in this Journal.]

A Philosophy of Helping in Social Work

IN SELECTING THIS TITLE for a paper to be presented to a group of school counselors, I am, in fact, asserting my own

Paper delivered to a meeting of Counseling Personnel of the Division of Pupil Personnel and Counseling, School District of Philadelphia, January 8, 1947.

belief that counseling in a public school system is a kind of helping that is not primarily vocational or educational guidance, or yet a form of psychotherapy, but is rather directly related to the professional helping that belongs to functional social work.

I can well believe that the very terms social work and social worker carry negative implications for many of you, as they often do for the general public, that you will not thank me, perhaps, for putting school counseling under that heading. While I might claim fellowship with you on another basis by reminding you that teachers and professors, like preachers and social workers, are also a frequent prey to public ridicule—witness the old-maid schoolteacher and the absent-minded professor—I would prefer instead to go below the surface to a deeper connection between this common attitude toward schoolmen, ministers, and social workers and an equally prevalent reaction to all forms of professional help, even medical and psychiatric help. The professor, the teacher, represent authoritative wisdom; they correspond to the community pressure on youth, to learn in the prescribed ways. The preacher, the social worker, even the doctor and the psychiatrist, also represent authority, the authority of the good, the righteous, the respectable or normal, and the successful, to whom the sinners, the failures, the sick, the poor, the unadjusted must bend and from whom they must ask for help or healing.

There is something in human beings that instinctively rebels against accepting constituted authority or admitting need for professional help, particularly in relation to the inner man. Perhaps teachers have learned more easily than social workers the truth of this statement, because they know only too well that children resist being taught, that learning is more or less a continuous struggle. However conforming outwardly, every child with a spark of individuality finds some spot to put his resistance to school or if not school, to Sunday School or to some social institution that represents to him infringement of his inmost self and his own way of feeling or thinking or doing.

While it is understandable to most of us, who can still think of ourselves as schoolchildren or even as high school or college students, that it is natural to resist being taught, however necessary it be to learn or however sincere the desire of the learner, it is hard for most people to accept the assertion that adults in need also resist being helped just as truly as children resist being taught. How can it be that benevolence itself may provoke a desire to retreat, to refuse. Social workers have taken a long, long time to discover what seems, at least to one school of thought, to be a basic factor in offering the services of a social agency, which is that the applicant not only asks for help, he also resists taking it, unless he controls it completely.

There would appear to be in all of us some fundamental fear or distrust which makes us struggle to the last to maintain something that feels like independence and to resist admitting a need that might spell weakness or vulnerability before the helper, who apparently has the answer and therefore the power to control, to give, or to refuse. In fact, it is some necessity to maintain the self intact that proves to be the greatest obstacle to learning, to training, and to helping. One might characterize this phenomenon psychologically as the human will in its negative, resistant form, the will that is organized in struggle and conflict with the forces which threaten it, both internal and external. A child has to find himself somehow over against others, his parents, his teachers, his mates, in order to discover who he is. This can become too aggressive, too defensive for, or too repressive of, his own individuality. For all of us the balance is hard to maintain between the fighting organization of the will that we need in order to meet the daily problems inside and out, and the positive, purposeful will that is primarily for itself and not against anything. If this is true, then the first problem of helping—teaching, counseling, social casework or therapy—is to make it possible for the child who is sent or the adult who comes to a source of help to work through the layers of fear, refusal, and resistance sufficiently to accept the help that is offered, and to arrive thereby at some now unrealized positive expression and use of his own powers.

In order to profit by this insight as teacher, counselor, or social worker, one must first accept the fact that however sincere the desire to help, however obvious the need, it is not always possible in any particular instance. Either the helper has not the right service to offer or the requisite skill with which to offer it, or the person in need is unable or unwilling to use the help. True, one can compel a child to sit in a classroom, but not even the best teacher can make him learn against his will—nor can a social worker force a client to take or use a service he does not want, or whose conditions he will not meet, however great his need. To be a helper then under any guise requires a kind of discipline of self that makes it possible

to take refusal or rejection, to leave the other person free
to go his way even though one deplores the outcome.
When a child is involved, this is not easy and many of
you may even consider it wrong. A child should be taught,
should be helped, should be saved. I agree and I know as
well as you how bitter it is to admit helplessness in the
face of a child's need. Yet, I also believe that the recognition of our own limits as helpers is the first essential in
being able to help (or even to teach). That recognition
which is an end result of professional training has to go
beyond a mere verbal admission to the depth of acknowledgment of our helplessness to save another against his
will.

As a corollary to this first principle of helping, I would
add another that may seem to you too obvious or too
inherent in the first to need special mention, that is, that
child or adult, whatever his need or the contribution of
the helper, must ultimately take help in his own way,
create his own salvation out of the source the other has
provided. Hopefully, the helper can set up conditions that
are favorable, can with skill further the process; but the
actual movement which leads to a constructive solution,
although it requires the medium of relationship for its
dynamics, is finally dependent on the impulse toward
growth and the capacity for self-reorganization residing in
the individual himself.

In this connection, I should like to make a comparison
between the point of view which I represent, which as
psychology rests on the work of Otto Rank, and as social
work theory is called a functional approach, and two other
views which one may designate by the terms psychoanalytic

and nondirective or client-centered counseling. I am sure that many of you are familiar with the Freudian psychology and I understand that Dr. Carl Rogers presented his view to this very group last year.

The psychoanalytic approach to helping emphasizes the resistance of the patient to the efforts of the therapist, as does the Rankian theory, but the psychoanalyst considers this resistance to be the patient's fear of refusal, his weakness and desire to escape in the face of painful reality, and treats it as something "bad," something the patient should not have, an attitude with which the patient agrees. Rank, on the other hand, saw the resistance of the patient as an indication of the strength of will with which a human being inevitably resists what must feel like the imposition on him of a stronger will, the therapist's. In other words, Rank accepted resistance not as a peculiarly unfavorable aspect of the patient's personality but as a natural result of the helping situation, in which the therapist seems to have the patient at a disadvantage. Rogers, on the other hand, in his presentation of counseling as nondirective, or client-centered therapy, appears to have ignored the client's inevitable resistance to being helped or changed, even when he comes asking for it. Evidently Rogers hopes to eliminate this difficulty by emphasizing the passive or accepting role of the counselor and the nondirective character of his relation to the process. What he has overlooked or underestimated, in my opinion, is the impossibility of maintaining such a neutral, colorless relation which denies the very reason for which the helper is there, i.e., his desire and intention to help the client with his particular problem. Even if one could be so without will in the situation, the client would put upon the most passive helper his own need to be opposed, to have someone upon whom to project the conflict which he cannot solve alone.

Rogers' passivity reminds me of Freud's early technique of free association, in which the analyst was supposed to sit by and the patient's only task was to say whatever came into his mind. One can easily see that there would be plenty of room for resistance even in this apparently harmless requirement. Could anything be harder than to be left so free? What if nothing comes; what if the mind is blank? Perhaps you yourselves have experienced that blankness in coming to a supervisory conference. You know that you do have problems and that you are supposed to bring them to the supervising counselor. But I am willing to risk the bet that those problems tend to vanish from your mind as you enter the supervisor's office —or possibly you suddenly feel yourself overwhelmed with innumerable practical details, which you then pour out in a flood of externalities, complaints and worries. If the supervisor just sat and said, "Yes, you do feel overburdened, don't you," do you think you could respect her insight, her understanding, or her responsible relation to the job?

With Dr. Rogers' stress on the importance of the immediate relationship between helper and client, and on the present life problem of the client rather than on his historical past, the Rankian school and most psychoanalysts today would be in approximate agreement, but from the viewpoint of the experienced psychoanalyst Dr. Rogers has reduced the therapeutic process to a dangerously simple, would-be, foolproof procedure, and has removed from the helper the burden of responsibility for helping, without which he has no reason for existing. Do not let yourself be misled into thinking that there is any royal road either to being helped or to the professionally responsible role of helper. It takes "blood, sweat, and tears" as well as training.

Fortunately for me, Dr. Rogers' theory and method are directed to therapy, not to social casework. My task from this point on is to relate these basic principles of helping which cannot be separated from therapy to a conception of social casework as developed by the functional point of view. The very term *function* implies a direction and a goal, so that it could not possibly be thought of as nondirective, nor could it ever be completely client-centered, since social casework as we know it today is always related to a social organization, an agency with its own character, its own particular purposes, its conditions and limitations, and its community sanction.

Functional social work was developed originally in Philadelphia, largely through the Pennsylvania School of Social Work, the Philadelphia Child Guidance Clinic, and the child-placement agencies. The psychology of helping on which it rests is derived from Rankian theory, but as a theory of social-work practice it cannot be laid at the door of any school of psychotherapy. It has grown out of fifteen years of experience in trying to make the service of social agencies truly helpful to those who need them and are able to use them, fifteen years of learning to respect the job that belongs to social work without trying to make it psychiatric or psychoanalytic, and fifteen years of learning to train workers who are able to be responsible for what they do, as social workers representing an agency and its community, not as would-be therapists on their own.

When I first came to Philadelphia in 1918, in the period following World War I, the trend in social work was away from the sociological and social rehabilitation, toward an interest in understanding the individual. The effort was toward some kind of psychological interpretation, some diagnostic description of the client's personality or behavior problem and its causes, based on an elaborate assembling of personal and family history.

In the private family-agency of this period, there was a beginning tendency to ignore the relief aspects of their work in an emphasis on treatment of the individual through the casework relationship, regardless of the fact that the client still came for the weekly check. At this stage of development, casework had gone no farther in its emulation of psychoanalysis, also just coming into power, than to try out its technique of passivity, a kind of nondirective listening not unlike Dr. Rogers'. It was simpler to listen when one did not know what else to do and it sometimes produced results. Gradually, however, the passive acceptance for which Philadelphia was noted moved into a more active exploration and interpretation of personal history and family relationships; and here, too, the past easily became a refuge from responsibility in the present. Currently, since relief has been taken over by the public agency, the trend in family casework is toward a form of psychoanalytic treatment often called counseling, and frequently supervised directly by psychoanalysts. However, there is growing rapidly in this immediate section of the country a vigorous movement toward a functional definition of family-agency service, which the Pennsylvania School is proud to have promoted.[1]

In the field of child placement in Philadelphia with which I was associated for many years, there was a similar beginning but perhaps because of its essentially concrete, real nature, a strongly functional outcome. In those early days of 1918 in the Children's Aid Society of Pennsylvania and the Children's Bureau of Philadelphia, both of which I served as psychologist, we began to study individual children as never before. We gave them mental tests, we observed and recorded their behavior, we put them through medical examinations, we wrote up elaborate social histories, only to say to ourselves in the record, "No wonder this child behaves as he does; his father drank and deserted, his mother does not love him. Of course he lies and steals. What he needs is to be loved." Of the need there was no doubt, but how to secure love for this unlovable boy? In certain New York agencies of the period the consultant psychiatrist would sometimes put the obligation to provide affection upon the worker with her twenty or thirty other children, and her human uncertainty as to permanence of occupation. I need hardly comment that practically, even if theoretically desirable, this source of love is sure to fail. Love to be satisfying must be reliable and personal. Help from a social agency has to be professional in order to be reliable or effective.

[1] See pamphlet, *Counseling and Protective Service as Family Casework*, ed. Jessie Taft (Philadelphia: Pennsylvania School of Social Work, 1947).

In Philadelphia which was less under psychiatric influence than New York, the *foster home* tended to be the answer for child and worker. Our effort was to find by intuition or good luck, the foster home that would do the trick. If one home failed, perhaps it was not the right home, so find another, better luck next time; or perhaps it was the fault of own parents who interfered too much. Maybe we could find a distant country home where they would visit less often. Thus was allocated to foster parents almost the entire responsibility for the success or failure of placement. True, the worker visited, encouraged, interpreted child psychology, or finally removed the child of an unsuccessful placement, but there was no control. It was not until the nineteen thirties, that this trial-and-error method was transformed by a new comprehension of child placement and its meaning to child, parent, and foster parent. For the first time in its history, the Children's Aid really looked at its function and tried to become responsible for carrying it as a continuous process in time that involves the consent, the responsibility, the participation of everyone involved in its on-going. For the first time, it became clear that only the parents can give a child over for placement, that they have the power to make or break any plan of agency for the child. They discovered that child placement begins in an application process with the parent, who has a right to know what agency will expect of him and to begin to understand what he must bear in loss of parental rights if he places his child.

At the same time, the placement agency awoke to the fact that the youngest child, even the baby in arms has its own relation to placement and can fight it to the end if he so wills. Workers learned that the child's power to accept or reject foster care is as great as the parents' but that if the parent comes to genuine acceptance, the child's attitude is simultaneously affected. Also that if the child's own strength and capacity are respected, and if he is permitted to express his feelings, his fears and resistance, he may, with the worker's support, find his own way of moving into a foster home positively as something he can use for himself. With this approach, which takes into account the responsible part carried by every participant, including the rights as well as the duties of foster parents, the caseworker finds her true function as agency representative. She is responsible for keeping a placement process going, which continuously balances and rebalances the human forces that have to be integrated toward the goal of growth and development for the child through the medium of the foster home. This kind of social casework is active and directive. It is client-centered in that it exists for the sake of a service to parents who need it, and for the child whose daily living depends on it, but never for one moment does it operate by wiping out its own essential character or refusing to stand by the responsibility it carries. This is what we mean by functional casework, casework that makes it possible for the clients who seek a service to face its painful problematic aspects in order to use it constructively if they so decide. The functional caseworker needs to be as sensitive and understanding as a therapist, but what he has to know is how to carry his own job, how to make his service effective—not how to conduct therapy.

I might at this point give you case illustrations of what I mean by this description of helping in social work, but even so, it would not apply exactly to your activities in the school, and might carry little conviction beyond the interest of the story. I should like rather to discuss what seems to me to be the application of a functional theory of helping as opposed to a psychotherapeutic conception in your particular field of school counseling, leaving to you the case illustrations which you can supply far better than I.

As I understand it, the counselor in a school has a function that differs from that of teacher, principal, disciplinary, or attendance officer, and is yet so related to them that his work would, ideally at least, in no way conflict with theirs or with the necessity of the pupil to come to terms with the aspects of school life which they represent. I can appreciate the difficulty of your task, especially as you have probably come out of the teaching function. How hard it is, how long it takes to develop a new, unique relation to the school itself, as well as to the pupil. You are required to represent the rightness of schooling itself, as well as the particular school you serve, to become as much a representative of the whole school and its purpose in relation to parents and children as the principal, yet your function is not his, although he includes it in his conception of the needs to be met. While as former teachers you understand the teacher's relation to pupils only too well, as counselors you are obliged to separate from your too easy identification with the teacher's problems, in order to discover your own quite different role. Functions are truly dynamic and differentiating, one does not lead into the other easily, however closely connected. I can well believe that when you faced your first referral from some impatient teacher, and saw before you an uncomfortable, silent child who was not there to be helped with his arithmetic, nor yet to be disciplined for his behavior, you felt as helpless and without direction as the child himself. As I see it, school counseling involves a whole new vision of the social importance of school to child and parents, as well as a new comprehension of the power that parents and child exert over the educational process and its success or failure. It is on the development of the counselor's function, in my opinion, that this vision must depend primarily for its realization.

If child placement, which, however important, affects relatively few children, is to be considered social work, how much more truly is the educational process of the public school to be recognized as the most important and pervasive socializing influence in our civilization, next to the family itself in its effect upon the personality development of our children. Teachers and principals are so accustomed to the traditional working of the school and so absorbed in the problems parents and children create to prevent it from doing its utmost; problems of attendance, health, behavior, poverty, and lack of intelligence, that they seldom stop to realize the power they wield, the weight their function carries, and what a tremendous leverage is theirs, once the school learns to find a focus for utilizing this social meaning in order to meet the personality factors that create many educational problems. Indeed these problems will become open to solution, only as fast and as far as the public school learns to carry responsibility for the social forces which are inherent in its educational process and to be willing to approach education as at bottom a social service, which must be chosen and furthered willingly in some way and to some extent by the youngest child or the most ignorant parent.

It is the counselor who brings to a focus and has back of her the value that the school possesses at bottom for every child and every parent however at odds they may be at the moment. The counselor has no need to create authority or fall back on discipline. Nor does he need to become a therapist, forgetting the school in his concern for the child. Merely by virtue of his position as counselor, he represents the whole meaning of the public school system in our society. However we criticize it, however a child rebels, its validity is not questioned. There is no ordinary child (perhaps one may except a genius) who would not desire in his heart to do well at school, to be approved by teachers, to become popular with his mates, and a source of pride to his parents; no parent however indifferent, who does not feel his child's failure at school to be in some measure his own, who would not want things to be bettered, if he had any way to begin.

This is the counselor's underlying source of strength, the fact that he can safely assume that the most problematic child or parent, would, if he could find a way to move toward it, want something to be changed, some help to improve his relation to school. But that want is overlaid with fear, defensiveness, distrust of school, and disbelief in self. Often it cannot be reached through teaching or discipline, it is beyond group help. Only the individual approach, through someone who represents the school, but who has a different focus, who is free to see the child himself, as neither teacher nor principal is free, can hope to meet this situation in which the educational process is blocked by the child's inability to use it. To put it in social work terms, the client (parent or child) for some reason is no longer able to use the service of the agency or may never have been able to use it to capacity.

I realize that when I put upon the counselor an obligation to accept the school and its system wholeheartedly, I may seem to be assuming a perfection that is nonexistent. Surely the school system is imperfect, some principals lack social vision, many teachers are impatient with counseling as a form of "spoiling" or are themselves ineffective in their teaching and in their handling of group problems. The counselor may well be tempted to lose himself in identification with the child's side, to feel that the pupil is justified in his rebellion. The fact remains that unless the counselor can find in himself enough conviction about the rightness of schooling and of his school in particular to represent it as something of vital importance to child and parent, and to believe that the child has it in him to meet its conditions constructively if he so wills, he will be unable to carry the function of counselor and will be impotent to help the child to a better school adjustment. For helping rests on the inevitability of the problem to be faced which the helper represents, as truly as it depends on the helper's understanding and acceptance of the client's ambivalence, his wanting as well as his resistance.

The function of the school counselor, then, is no different from that of any caseworker whose job it is to enable an applicant who asks for it to utilize the service of his agency. Only in this case the service itself is education, which every child needs and every parent wants for his child—the agency is a large complex, perhaps over-crowded, understaffed school, its timespan covers all the years a child is growing up. The counselor is the social worker who believes in the service of his agency so surely that he is in no danger of ceasing to represent it and its conditions. He knows that these conditions are there to be met if the child is to find a happy on-going relation to school but he is not the teacher with thirty or forty children to keep in order. He is there to help the individual child to express all his bad feelings, justified or not, to face his fears, his hatreds, even of the teacher, his doubts of the counselor and the school and finally, for as many interviews as it takes, to help him also to look at his own part in his problems, to weigh his need for school, to consider what if anything he is willing to do, in order to stay there, to make things better, and how, if he so decides, he might begin. It may be that the child's problem obviously involves a parent, indeed it is hard to believe that the parent does not have a part in every case where a child comes into real conflict with the school. If the parent is brought in, the counselor's function remains the same. He is not concerned to involve or reform the parent except as the parent however fearful, threatened or defensive, is actually related to what is happening at school, and from the counselor's viewpoint is important because his participation is essential to any constructive outcome for the child. While the parent's power and rights are to be respected, as well as the child's, there need be no denial of the school's requirements. The counselor has the power given to him not only by the principal but by the meaning of school to the community. The most irresponsible parent, the most hostile or defensive one, is as sure to want the school for his child, as the child is to need it, if he is approached respectfully and with that understanding conviction.

So the school counselor, because he can stand for the school both as a goal and as a stumbling block to parent and child, is free to relate to them in understanding of the problem his service creates. Through his identification with their conflicted feelings, he can release them to a new comprehension of the school as they discover its humanity in him, and by his firm support of the school's requirements, help them to face and affirm the necessity for change in their relation to school.

I do not know whether you can accept this description of school counseling, but if I am right in my understanding of its potentiality, it needs for its practice, the same helping process that is utilized by functional casework, not the therapeutic process of psychoanalysis or nondirective therapy. Its function is not to solve the personality problems of children or their parents as such, but to try with individual consideration to help child and parent to solve school-connected conflicts which prevent a constructive use of the very service the school exists to give.

꙳

The Function of the Personality Course in the Practice Unit

[The first part of this paper covers the history of the relation of psychiatry to social work and characterizes the difference which marks the position of the Pennsylvania School in its understanding of casework as a professional process in its own right.]

FOR THIS SCHOOL, then, the solution to the problem of training professional workers for the practice of casework in a social agency, a casework that is clearly differentiated from psychotherapy, depends: first, on the recognition of a basic helping experience and process which is common to all professional helping, but is to be controlled and made specific only in relation to the particular function that determines and directs it;[1] second, on the realization that the training of students for practice in a casework agency is a profoundly potent form of professional helping, where

Paper published in *Training for Skill in Social Casework* (Social Work Process Series; Philadelphia: University of Pennsylvania Press, 1942).

[1] Jessie Taft, "Function as the Basis of Development in Social Work Processes," *News-Letter,* American Association of Psychiatric Social Workers, Vol. IX, No. 1 (1939).

psychological growth in a learning experience can be clearly realized and furthered through the dynamics of the training function in teaching and supervision.

The personality class as it operates today in the Pennsylvania School is determined, not so much by a particular psychological content or required learning in intellectual terms, as by its functional relation to the experience of the student in this learning-growth process that is essential to the development of a disciplined professional worker.[2] In the agency, the student is related immediately to his supervisor who will go with him step by step in his efforts to assimilate the function and carry out specific tasks. The supervisor is humanly as well as professionally helpful and certainly must consider and wrestle with the student as a person again and again, but always she is held not only to her responsibility to student and school as a training supervisor, but to agency and the welfare of clients with whom the student is engaged. The student is important to her, but his *purely personal* experience as a learner can never come first, nor can she be to any extent the recipient of his thinking about the relation of his past self to all this disturbing present and his efforts to gain a little conscious control through theoretical formulation.

In the casework class while the students, both individually and collectively, are the center of the teacher's interest, the focus is on their "doing," the actual recording of how they have worked with clients, their successes and

[2] This emphasis does not exclude a carefully selected reading list with fairly heavy requirements, and assumes that the student will learn to grasp the significant aspects of a life history and to recognize the psychiatric and psychoanalytic theories that determine current psychological interpretations.

failures in representing the agency, their mutual exchange of criticism and commendation, their learning about what casework is, and how to use the class and the experiences and opinions of their classmates. The casework class is vitally related to every student's individual performance, and is always in the process of helping him to evolve, out of his experience and out of related reading, a steadily deepening comprehension of functional casework. It also provides an experience in itself, a weekly testing-out of the reality of the student's efforts, not only to tolerate the differences he finds in other students, but to respect and learn from them. The casework teacher as the student's adviser in the School is responsibly related to his progress both in class and in the field. She it is who evaluates his growth in skill, in responsibility, in the actual doing of the thing he has come to learn, and, together with the supervisor, holds him to the standards set by school and agency for satisfactory work at the level where he is.

Throughout the year the casework teacher, as adviser, holds up to the student the professional ideal, the goal he has set for himself in his decision to take training. His personal problems come in for consideration and analysis only in relation to their interference with his progress as a student. When his personality pattern or his personal problem presents so serious an obstacle as to indicate a need for therapy, the School accepts the situation as one no longer compatible with its program. The School does not try to train a student who at the same time wishes or needs to put himself into another process as demanding as therapy, nor does the School undertake to give to students personal help unrelated to the professional goal. A student is never "treated" either by casework or any form of psychotherapy. Whatever growth or change or progress he experiences is the direct result of the training process itself in which the development that comes with functional learning is not only to be expected, but *required*.

How does the personality course fit into this training unit? It is the balance wheel which rights the otherwise too strong emphasis on the professional goal, the agency, and the client, The personality class, which accompanies the casework class through three semesters, is geared to the need of the student himself, his right to explore the very experience he is undergoing, and his necessity to orient himself theoretically, both in relation to his impacts with clients and with supervision. He needs to understand himself, not completely, but as he is in this meaningful learning experience, and to formulate for himself a working psychology that holds true, not only for the client, but for himself, for his teachers and supervisor alike. Thus the first personality class for the beginner is called "Attitudes and Behavior." Its purpose is to help the student to become aware of and to weather his own reactions to these new situations, to consider the various ways in which one prepares for an important change like coming into an unknown school, what it means to accustom oneself to the reality one finds, to get used to classes that are disturbingly different, and to field work that exposes all of one's ignorance, fear, and helplessness. In content, this is carried by some appropriate reading, by asking the student to write briefly on various aspects of what he is undergoing, by bringing into class material from biography and fiction on which students may analyze experiences like their own, but sufficiently removed from the personal to leave them free.

Into this class the student also brings some of his puzzling encounters with clients: attitudes he does not understand or will not tolerate; behavior he condemns or wishes to avoid. He is full of shock, surprise, disillusion with himself and the client. He has to grow into acceptance of his own emotions as vital expressions of living, in order to allow the client to feel as he feels. Here, together with others who are going through like experiences and a teacher who is able not only to accept him but to help him to go beyond these difficult beginnings, he finds that it is safe to put out in class the way he *feels* as well as what he *thinks* about what he is doing in agency and in school. There is no norm for the feelings he should have, no one has to agree with anyone else in ideas or emotions, but the student who wants to go on with training soon realizes that he has to "keep moving" and risk himself ever more deeply. The natural impulse to help, which has ultimately to be disciplined into skillful practice, may express itself in personality class in all its naïveté and in that expression move on to a deeper level of awareness and desire to change.

The personality class, then, is a focus for the personal change which the student undergoes, the process of accepting, step by step—or perhaps coming steadily toward a decision to reject—the amount and kind of self-discipline which, it is evident, will be increasingly demanded of him if he is to become a social worker on the terms of this particular school. The first semester is an experience in itself, a measured stretch of time with an ending which has meaning in the school year. The student has come through a concrete experience of beginning. By this time he is ready to decide to follow through this beginning, or to conclude that its leading is not for him. At this point, the adviser brings together the student's threefold relation to training and helps him to leave or to continue, in the light of inner and outer evidence.

The personality class that accompanies the second semester is called "Development of Personality." It is assumed that now the student is ready for a deeper plunge into the field he has chosen for himself. Hopefully he is past the upset and confusion, the unbearable newness and helplessness of his initiation. Now he wants to understand how his clients come to be as they are and above all, how *he* could have developed the many problems that the personal self presents, both to himself and the supervisor, in his efforts to relate skillfully to clients. The personality class allows him to work on this legitimate and passionate interest in his own psychology, and what it means to experience a change in the very self, as he now knows he must if he is ever to master this thing called casework.

The "Development of Personality" uses as content the developmental crises in the life history that are common to all men in our culture and are determinative of personality because they are determinative of the individual's relation to the "other"; such as pregnancy, birth, nursing and weaning, talking, walking, toilet training, the birth of siblings, going to school, adolescence, and the like. While much is required here in reading and accurate knowledge, the material is brought to life in terms of fiction, the student's impulsive feeling-reactions, the teacher's basic comprehension of human development, and bits of experience, brought in by the class from their field work or their own lives. What they learn here of human behavior and human emotions is not something to be turned upon the clients as "technique." On the contrary, the only understanding that is sought is first of all an increased understanding and acceptance of themselves in relation to others with all the weakness, strength, and fear that are there to be faced—not erased or denied but utilized; an understanding that must be absorbed into blood and bone before it can contribute helpfully to the client-worker relationship.

At the close of this second term of personality, the student who is learning has acquired some belief in internal change for himself and for clients as not only possible but necessary for living, and into the term "personality" he has begun to put vital content, a new conception of the process of becoming a self that goes back to birth, and a new appreciation of the capacity to enter into relationship with another, as fundamental to casework and to life itself. The final assignment for the term paper indicates what the teacher expects at this point:

Describe and analyze a relationship, personal or professional, between two people—preferably one in which you are one of the two participants, but at any rate one which you know intimately.

It will be helpful to consider such questions as: What brings two people together? What holds them together? What precipitates change in their relationship? What precipitates change in personal development on the part of either or both? How does such change take place and within what limits? What does it mean to become responsible for one's own part in a relationship?

While the completion of the first year is a real ending for some students, it presents a critical period of evaluation and decision for all. For those who apply and are accepted, the second year necessarily becomes another beginning, as real and as problematic as the first, but on a different level. The second-year supervisor meets a student who has completed a stage in his training, who may have known himself as a responsible worker for several months. He feels that he has left that painful first-year struggle behind him and is in no hurry to put himself back, as it were, into the learning situation. As a second-year student, he is not so ignorant, not so helpless, not so afraid as when he entered, but he *is* proud of his newly achieved professionalism. Instinctively he resists the second plunge into uncertainty and the admission of unknown areas that remain to be conquered.

As a rule the second-year casework class, with its demand for material on a higher level of responsibility, upsets whatever is false in the assurance he has built up during the summer and initiates the dissatisfaction that finally leads to the deeper growth and command of skill that second year requires. Often a student breaks through into taking help from his supervisor only ofter a long struggle to do everything himself. "By this time, I ought not to rely on my supervisor as I did in my first year," is the justification for the period of resistance that has been indicated in various ways: conference periods not kept, dictation undone, cases that seem at a standstill for no good reason, all the myriad ways in which refusal-to-learn-through-supervision may be expressed. But there is a difference. The second-year student knows something about beginnings, about resistance to learning, about his own relation to change. What he does not know and must learn in his own stubborn way, is that growth is a process not completed once and for all; that, in a training experience like this, every beginning, every ending, constitutes a crisis on which movement and reorganization take place.

It has taken us all these twenty years of experiment with the personality class to comprehend its function truly as is evidenced by the fact that we have been willing to make our second year personality course called "Patterns of Growth," an elective, and to put it in the second semester after the casework class instead of with it. The students have known better instinctively, for they have never failed to elect this course and have consistently complained about taking it in their last semester. Finally, after these years of blindness, partly due to expediency, we have come to believe that what we knew was true for first year is equally true for second. Actually, we found that the second-year casework teacher as adviser had been attempting to carry, with individual students, the burden which the personality class rightfully took over in first year. Thus there fell upon both supervisor and teacher an undue responsibility for the student's personal struggle in adjusting to second year, and an imbalance was created that from now on we hope to remedy by making second-year personality a required part of the practice unit in the first semester.

The content of this course consists of reading in psychological theory and in biography with the detailed study of several authentic life histories as presented vividly in autobiographical form. The purpose of the course is to follow through these lives patiently in detail in order to make real to students the stability of the individual's fundamental pattern in relation to change and growth crises, and to show, also, how truly he may use them for the freeing and reorganization of the ego on a new level of self-realization and creativity. Through both thoughtful and impulsive reactions, through identification, rejection, uncertain tolerance, to final serious effort to understand and bear the ways in which individuals strive for their own development, the students begin to comprehend the meaning of psychological growth as an irreversible organic process in time, and to affirm the newly won sense of a disciplined professional self that can be demonstrated in practice.

In the last semester, field work takes on more and more the character of a regular job, carrying full responsibility to agency in everything but time. Seminars in specific areas of casework conducted by lecturers from the agencies are scheduled for the first half of the last semester, along with various electives, some of them in the personality area, but the true completion of the personality casework teaching unit is reached only through the thesis seminar. Here the student takes over, to organize and put out for all to see, the evidence of his own growth, the proof of his professional competence in a presentation of his practice as it is. The thesis, then, authenticates the birth of the professional self, which has been forming over a two-year period and may now come forth convincingly. There is no student, in my experience, who does not feel that the thesis is the culminating point in his training experience, the bringing together of everything he has learned, transmuted into the precious metal of his own philosophy and practice. Through the thesis, the student begins his separation from the self that was dependent on teacher and supervisor, and assumes, as far as he is able, responsibility for what he thinks and for what he does as a social worker.

Whether one can accept the role of the personality course as described in this paper depends on one's whole conception of the essentials for training students in social casework; whether such training is conceived of as primarily external and environmental, an imparting of definite content accompanied by a relatively detached "learning-to-do" in a social agency, or whether, as in this School, one conceives of training as a unified process, a profound organic learning experience over a two-year span integrated by its purpose and direction, broadened and formalized by its connection with relevant background courses but sustained and balanced by the threefold division of the training unit and the shared responsibility of two teachers and a supervisor for the development of the student toward the professional goal.

PART VI

Final Statement of Philosophy
1949-1950

Time As the Medium of the
Helping Process

Seventeen years ago, fresh from a vital experience in taking help as well as five years of private therapeutic practice, I presented a paper at the National Conference of Social Work, in which I tried to impress upon social case-workers a new sense of their responsibility for the time element in casework practice. At that time I was much closer to Rankian therapy than to social casework but for that very reason, casework offered a challenge that I have been trying to meet squarely ever since, not to discover how therapy could be introduced into social work via casework, but to find out what was truly indigenous to casework, as such, and how it could be taught and learned from its own base, as an authentic helping medium. In the pursuit of that interest, I joined the faculty of the Pennsylvania School of Social Work, where the defining of casework in its immediate daily practice was already well under way. As I reread what I wrote about time seventeen years ago, I take back not a single word. All my experience since then has more than confirmed the viewpoint that was expressed there in somewhat philosophic terms.

Paper delivered at the National Conference of Jewish Social Welfare, Cleveland, June, 1949.

About casework at that time, however, my ignorance was genuine. This has since been remedied by a knowledge of casework practice and its determinants that comes from teaching in the Pennsylvania School, from its faculty, its students and above all from vital contacts with its training agencies. In following the changing practice of these agencies through the years, the School has learned and has helped them to learn, what it means to give help effectively through the specific function of a particular social agency.

What we have learned about the nature of social casework as the medium for giving an agency service, we have called the functional approach, or functional theory of casework. I think that I may have been responsible for that term because as editor of our first publication, I had to have something generic to call it in order to differentiate it from the casework based upon psychoanalytic theory and method and because, as a matter of fact, we had discovered that only the difference in the particular function and its setting could account for the differences to be found in the various forms of psychological helping. In every social work process, as in Rankian therapy, there is a common or generic base. In essence, all help, as we mean it, is psychological and depends upon a relationship process, whether it is expressed in the tangible form or relief, of foster home, of hospital service, or is derived from interviews alone. Whether you call the interview form of helping, supervision, counseling, casework, or psychotherapy, depends not upon the difference in the nature of the basic helping process as such, but upon its functional determinants and the way in which they bear upon the helper and the one to be helped.

Rank was in no way responsible for our understanding and use of the concept of function in social casework, but he was responsible for the discovery of the meaning and effect of ending in a therapeutic experience and for his recognition of the will, both the will of the client and the will of the therapist, neither of which can be obliterated in any therapeutic process. Not only did Rank acknowledge will as the dynamic force in therapy, but he divorced his therapeutic practice from the medical concepts of diagnosis and cure with the discovery of the basic problem that is to be found in every form of therapy—which is the unbelievable difficulty with which any human being, even the weakest, brings himself to take help. It is because of the organized will and its effort to maintain control over itself that even psychological growth as an internal organic process can often arouse greater fear than outside interference. Thus to enter into a professional helping process as the one in need is to subject oneself to fear of the helper on the one hand, and fear of internal change on the other. It is obvious that the medium of such internal change is time, and that to take help in Rank's meaning becomes nothing more or less than the deliberate use of another person in such a way as to release and further a process of psychological reorganization which is a form of growth— an irreversible, internally determined process in time.

Around this universal human problem in asking for and taking help from a source outside of the individual's control, Rank has developed his therapeutic method which, as you can easily see, is diametrically opposite to the medical diagnosis and treatment approach whereby every seeker-of-help is seen as a person more or less sick. Although it is fully admitted by everyone that no patient can be helped without his consent and cooperation, nevertheless, for Freudian practice, the emphasis remains not on the internal, self-determined growth process to be released with the aid of the therapist but on the diagnostic conclusion and plan whereby the therapist will determine and direct the experience that he sees as essential if the treatment is to result in a cure, or in as much of a restoration to normal as he conceives to be possible for a particular individual. Thus there devolves upon the helper the role of chief actor in the therapeutic drama. His is the delicate responsibility of weighing in advance the potential strength as well as the present weakness of the patient; his the decision as to the level of treatment, the degree of transference, the goal to be reached and the method to be used. The therapist, as Rank describes him, assumes a less authoritative but no less demanding role, since he conceives of himself as an assistant ego, not a medical authority, one who will permit the patient to discover what strengths he has or can develop; but, even more, who will support him as he learns to bear and take responsibility for his human limitations, his weaknesses.

To carry such a helping role, is no less arduous since however correct the diagnosis, it cannot result in a plan; however desirable the therapist's goal for the patient, it will not determine the result, which is arrived at not primarily through the therapist's knowledge and direction, but by the growth process which is released in the patient according to his ability to take the help he needs and the therapist's skill in making himself available. This means that, however skillful or able the therapist, the amount or degree or, if you like, the level of the help given must in the last analysis depend, not upon what he might desire to give, but upon what the patient is able to take under the circumstances and at that time. It must be the patient who creates the new relation to life, not the therapist. A role thus limited in the exercise of knowledge, power, and creativity seems to me to be naturally difficult for a man and particularly for a man with medical training. To become an assistant in an organic growth process comes more naturally to the woman, but the fact remains that for any would-be helper, learning to carry the role of assistant requires a discipline of the self, of the will, in favor of the other, that comes only after long training and with deep purpose to enter into another's growth process helpfully. To become willing not to know everything about the patient in advance, to enter into the dynamic interplay of the therapeutic process without trying to predict or control the outcome, is as exacting and responsible a discipline as exists in the world today. It requires a skill that is immediate, that operates in the present on a knowledge, not merely of causes, but of process and of one specific process —that is, an intensified psychological growth process under relatively controlled conditions, such as may obtain in social casework, in supervision, in psychotherapy. To avoid misunderstanding, let me say here categorically that Rankian therapy is not client-centered or nondirective in the sense that the therapist passively reflects the feelings and reactions of the patient. Rank based his therapy on the acceptance of the therapeutic process as a battle of wills, but a battle through which the patient may finally conquer in becoming responsible for the projection of his will upon the therapist, since the therapist has not entered into the conflict to overcome the patient, nor to force upon him his own psychology.

Perhaps the core of the difference between Rankian and Freudian practice lies just here, in the different conception and evaluation of time; whether one conceives of it as the therapist's time or the patient's time—as an analysis of the past or a new utilization of the present. This, in turn, depends upon one's understanding and acceptance of the human will, its creativity and its necessity to project itself upon other wills and upon the social and physical environment. To live, we must put ourselves out into and upon our surroundings; we must, if we are to survive, find the answers to our needs, in parents, in friends, in being able to conquer the spatial world in which we are placed. Science, even psychological science, is primarily based on projection, a learning to understand and to control, as far as possible, the outside forces, including social forces. We want to know what causes behavior in order to control it but ordinarily we think of it as the behavior of others, not our own. In fact, so essential is it to gain control through projection, that introspection has always been suspect in psychology, since at worst it savored of the morbid or at best was subjective and unverifiable. The mental hospital provides the picture of our efforts to get at mental illness through every possible external approach before undertaking actual psychological measures. Even now, shock treatment provides an almost irresistible out for the far too busy hospital psychiatrist. In psychoanalysis, however, there has been a unique mixture of treatment that recognizes the helping relationship as present, in its reliance upon the transference, but projects upon the past the causal determinants of the patient's neurosis and tries to bring them into the present as the explanation of the immediate relationship. Even the transference is thought of as a carry-over from the past and is more or less deprived of its present reality although it is recognized as essential for the treatment actually taking place.

Here you have the past introduced into the living present to disguise it, to mitigate its immediacy, and to act as an external or, if you will, spatial medium on which to project the present conflict. The revolutionary contribution of Freud seems to me to be not so much the discovery of the causal relation of childhood experience to the neurotic problems of the adult, but rather the dawning recognition of the transference relationship as the basis of effective treatment. Here for the first time in the history of man is the beginning of an understanding of professional helping, of the possibility of utilizing man's ability to enter into a relationship as a means of relieving his emotional distress. But for Freud himself, as for his followers today, the transference relationship, however essential, was potentially dangerous. It was acceptable only insofar as its impact on the therapeutic relationship could be softened or diverted. In a recently published translation entitled *An Outline of Psychoanalysis,* Freud says, "It is the analyst's task to tear the patient away each time from the menacing illusion, to show him again and again that what he takes to be new real life is a reflection of the past.[1]

[1] Sigmund Freud, *An Outline of Psychoanalysis* (New York: W. W. Norton, 1949).

Here it seems to me is a statement of a fundamental difference between Freudian and Rankian therapy, between the diagnostic and the functional, between a psychology of cure and a psychology of helping. The question is how far can we face and use for helping the medium of time, as present, which is in truth the only kind of time we are actually experiencing. How far are we impelled by our need to project and control spatially, into a displacement of the present process upon a completed, static external past which it is actually impossible to reach, as such, except as we bring up memory content to carry the too immediate willing and feeling aroused in the present moment of experience? We can hardly avoid admitting that the help the patient receives comes not from his reliving of an unhappy past but from the fact that he finds courage to live and feel differently in the present. If the therapist can trust the organic nature of the growth process of which he becomes a necessary but transient part, he will trust also its inevitable direction out and away from the source of help, once that help has been genuinely accepted. The transference, if it can be understood in its present meaning as the natural and necessary projection onto the therapist of the patient's willing and feeling, will be accepted as the patient's reality of the moment, created by a form of relationship that he has never before experienced. His unreasonable efforts to escape the help he sought, by trying to use the customary controls found in family and friendly connections, will fail in the face of the therapist's maintenance of his role as helper, not friend, family, lover, or God. Unable longer to resist the truly unselfish understanding and response of the therapist, the patient, in spite of his fear of encroachment, may finally yield, not to the therapist, but to his own will to unite, to accept the therapeutic situation as his own. The more complete and full this climax of acceptance, the more immediate will be the indications that the direction of the process has changed, that the beginning movement is over and the movement toward separation has begun. The middle phase lasts no longer than it takes the therapist to recognize and the patient to admit that the struggle with beginning is finished but that the equally important and absorbing problem of how to leave what one has taken, remains to be discovered.

To help the patient to leave in relation to this organic growth movement, rather than in terms of the content covered, is to utilize to the full the momentum of his impulse to separate from the helper in the interest of a newly developed self which craves to test itself in the real world. While the movement toward ending is clearly the patient's, he cannot be expected to know it for himself at every moment as the therapist should. For the patient this movement is full of doubts and fears, of guilt and grati- tude, of alternating feelings of helplessness and power. Only the therapist whose personal self is, hopefully, not involved in this struggle to separate can provide the ob- jectivity and firmness required for setting the actual day and hour of ending. It is this separation phase of a helping process that presents the greatest difficulty for the therapist and for the patient. It has to be ended sometime—the question is how to end it so that the patient gets all the momentum possible from his struggle to affirm his readi- ness to leave, in the face of his guilt for deserting the therapist, and his fear of becoming so responsible for himself. For Rank, this inner growth movement of the patient provided the index for the termination of the therapy but the actual day and hour he set with the patient some time in advance, thus providing an external reality around which the patient's wanting and not wanting could be focused.

It is not easy for anyone to be consistently sure that the end of a vital experience is of his own choosing. Always there comes a day when it can be felt as imposed, a death sentence, an attack, a rejection, a desertion. Even the force of the organic impulse toward individuation can be repressed, obscured, or confused by outer pressures or by fear of an inner movement that cannot be completely foreseen and planned for and that may lead us into danger or what seems too much self-dependence. If it were not that the therapeutic relationship becomes oppressive in its emphasis upon self and its unsuitability for normal human projection, the therapist would find it even more difficult to help the patient to separate. Actually, the patient comes to crave outside reality which not only permits but responds in kind to his need to project. If the therapist, himself, is free of vanity and willing to be abandoned, if he is not caught by his own fear of finality but can trust the life process, the patient will achieve his greatest gains, in fact will clinch the entire experience through his mastery of the ending.

The failure of therapists and social caseworkers alike to grasp the dynamics of the ending phase of helping and their almost universal reluctance to take responsibility for setting an ending, is due, I believe, to the extreme difficulty of working in a time medium as such, not only because of the unnatural internalization but because it bears instant witness to the passing of life itself. I can find no better statement of the nature of the problem than in a poem by Edith Henrich, entitled "Space and Time."[2]

> Man is an animal at home in space;
> The earth and sky are beautiful to him;
> Imagination presses at the rim
> Of all horizon for a farther place.
> He fits his wings to climb as eagles climb;
> He fetches constellations in a mirror
> But time escapes him; time is unleashed terror:
> He is an animal obsessed by time.
> He has no instrument to hold it with except his
> counted pulse, his measured breath.

The passing present of relationship, on which every helping process depends, is a present of immediate, living experience, which both helper and helped would fain remove a little into the safer past, the remote future or the objectivity of intellectualization. In fact, there must be some kind of content whatever the source, to carry the present meaning. It does not matter as much as we like to believe whether the focus is on family history or current reality problems, provided the therapist keeps his awareness of content as a vehicle for present willing and feeling related to the therapeutic situation, and himself yields to the limitations of a process in which he plays a minor though essential part.

To understand the problem that time creates for every human being one has to realize the life-death meaning that

---

[2] *The Quiet Corner* (New York: William Sloane, 1946). By permission of the publisher.

self-consciousness can put into the passing moment, which, however brief, contains the enigma of all living. As Kierkegaard puts it: "Such a moment has peculiar character. It is brief and temporal indeed, like every moment; it is transient as all moments are; it is past like every moment in the next moment. And yet it is decisive and filled with the eternal. Such a moment ought to have a distinctive name; let us call it the Fullness of Time"[3]

Not only the patient but the therapist also must learn to take the moment for its positive value, its beauty, its satisfaction and yet be willing to let it become the past. Not only the patient, but the therapist, must learn to bear the fear, the pain, the doubt, and disillusion of this moment without pushing it into the past unadmitted or using it to deprive the coming moment of its unique character. How does anyone learn to bear the loss, the separation, that every moment implies and at the same time find courage to affirm the value of the moment that follows? There would be no solution to this problem if it were not for the fact that time is only a name for the inmost nature of man, his own medium, which can sustain as well as confound him. It is his own element if only he will yield to it instead of fighting it. However, the fact remains that the fear of a life process that we do not control, although we can interfere with it or further it, is very great, while the capacity of the individual to create outside of himself in a spatial world that promises ever greater mastery seems almost limitless.

The basic task of helping then, provided the helper

[3] *A Kierkegaard Anthology,* ed Robert Bretall (Princeton, N.J.: Princeton University Press, 1946), p. 161.

himself is in some possession of the solution, is to provide a unique relationship experience in which the time medium is heightened or exaggerated by limits deliberately utilized, so that the one who needs help may overcome his fear of living sufficiently to experience his own unrealized capacity for using and leaving the helper, for yielding deeply to the need of the other and as a consequence finding the self that can go on without him. In such an experience it is possible to affirm the passing moment as right, to feel it as the very reflection of the self, to bear more or less courageously its pain, its fear, its guilt as well as its fulfillment and its on-going. On the other hand if the momentary relation of patient to therapist is partially denied and the historical past or even the present reality problem is made the focus of the therapist's projection as a form of externalization, the time process is necessarily obscured and may even be ignored. In which case the patient may only have acquired in his past or in his present environment another area on which to place responsibility for himself. Moreover if the time is prolonged over the years, the dynamic of ending is lost. The analytic hour can become habitual, a way of life, or merely the setting for an unacknowledged and hence unending will contest. In the recent recognition by psychiatrists of the value of shorter periods of treatment as effective for therapy there is hope that time will begin to be used more consciously just as the current reality problems of the patient have begun to be recognized as equal in importance to his infantile traumas.[4] Even the value of altering the time

[4] See Franz Alexander and Henry Morton French, *Psychoanalytic Therapy* (New York: The Ronald Press, 1946).

form, in the spacing of hours as a means of controlling the transference, has been acknowledged. However, the final step, which would see in time not merely a means of added control by the therapist but a vital medium for the self-discovery of the patient, has yet to be taken.

As a therapist, in former years, I learned to use time this way, to go with the patient's movement and to bring him to an ending for which I took responsibility, although he may have had a certain amount of choice as to the day or week. It is possible, if one is willing to use a relatively brief period, if one can hold to the role of helper and if one can accept the transference for its meaning and value to the patient, to give help within this rarefied two-person situation. But since I have discovered how much more can be accomplished in a setting that relates more directly to the reality in which both helper and helped must live, I sometimes wonder why anyone would choose to practice what might be called, "pure therapy."

It was the Pennsylvania School and the conventional block of time called the semester that taught me another use of time and a deeper sense of the power of the function and the social agency as instruments for helping. Perhaps only a person who had worked alone in an office without the backing of any professional group could appreciate the relief that a supporting agency gives, with its reality value for helper and helped. A school that trains students for social work is as much a social agency as a family society, but it is also related to education with the accepted time limits of quarter, term, semester, year. It was a revelation to me to see the use that every student makes of these limits, when the school itself appreciates their importance in terms of beginnings and endings. No allowance is made, because it would be practically impossible, for the individual differences that students present, as to rate of learning, maturity, emotional capacity, intellectual ability. While classes are arranged in sections according to age and previous experience, the length of time required for graduation is the same. Yet what each student undergoes within this arbitrary time form, if he can use it at all, is as truly a growth experience in learning as if it had been geared to his individual pattern. How does this happen, how is it possible that many different supervisors, with as many students, should be able to carry on a training process that must fit into an externally imposed time structure and arrive at a common goal? At least it must be common enough for credit to be given. If you had seen this incredible process come through for as many years as I have, if you had been the adviser of students whose individual differences could hardly be greater, and had seen the growth movement in each one attain a new level of development individually appropriate but with something generic too, perhaps you could begin to believe as I do, that everyone has the capacity to gear himself to the time that is available for him, provided only he accepts it, wills it, does not fight it as imposed.

It is interesting to note that supervision, the one form of professional helping that is clearly indigenous to social work in functional determination and development, has seldom been confused with casework or psychotherapy since the earliest period of its brief history. Yet every student who has learned to give help, through having ex-

perienced what it means to take it in the supervisory relationship, will testify to its powerful influence. In order to
carry responsibility for its own operation, an agency necessarily puts limits of some kind on the otherwise endless
time process which any supervision might become. The
acceptance of a conventional probationary period for new
workers, or for unsatisfactory workers, the periodic evaluation process as a basis for promotion, the norms arrived
at as a measure of what to expect from a first, second, or
third year of supervision in terms of worker performance,
the status of senior worker, all bear witness to the effort
of the agency to structuralize the time medium, to insert
lesser beginnings and endings, through which progress
may be measured, arbitrarily perhaps for any particular
individual, but validly in terms of agency experience and
purpose.

Supervision as it has developed in social agencies is then
the least controversial of the helping processes in that social work on the whole has not depended upon psychiatry
or upon psychoanalysis for supervisory form and content.
In fact, quite the reverse. Psychiatry in the training of
its students and beginners has had something to learn
from social work as some psychiatrists have freely and
generously acknowledged.[5] Even the differences introduced
by a Freudian versus a Rankian psychology can be discerned here only by those who find their basic concep-
tions of help too different to be harmonized even in a
process as concretely determined and functionally limited
as that of agency supervision. When, however, it concerns

[5] Frederick Allen, "Training in Child Psychiatry," *American
Journal of Orthopsychiatry*, XVI, No. 3 (1946).

the structures and procedures developed by agency for giving service to the client, who is an outsider, the area of uncertainty and the difficulty of defining responsibility are tremendously enlarged, while the method of helping carried out by the individual worker becomes the center of conflicting theories and practice. As long as the client's need can be met in some tangible form, the agency has an anchorage that keeps it within its own social work bounds. However, when family relationships or individual maladjustment divorced from tangible need, form the bulk of client demand, then there is no escape from looking at the nature of the service required to see whether it belongs to social work or to psychiatry; and if to social work, whether the social agency can become truly responsible for giving it or whether it must rely on another profession for defining the service and for supervising the worker. In my experience, such a divided responsibility does not work. I believe that either the psychiatrist should become truly responsible for administering the social agency whose worker he supervises or that the social agency should carry full responsibility for any service it undertakes to give. If it is not equal to a counseling service, why should it feel impelled to offer it?

The agency that operates on a psychoanalytic psychology will have its own decision to make regarding the training that will be required of its workers if they are to become psychotherapists, and of its administrative staff if they themselves, not a consulting psychiatrist, are to be responsible for offering psychotherapy as an agency service. It is to the functional agency that I would speak, for its problem is less complicated, however difficult, and that problem is to learn to take the same degree of responsibility for helping within a time medium that it took when the help was externalized in space.

It was not many years ago when some of the training agencies of the School began to recognize the importance of the time factor even in rendering tangible services. Practical necessity, perhaps, made limited time acceptable in giving money, once maintenance relief was taken over by the public agency. The psychological nature of a helping process, focused on the giving of temporary relief with a condition as to its use, became clear to these workers who had the courage to stand by the time limit. It was not easy, even with considerable support from clarified agency policy, but it was possible and workers gained conviction as they saw what it meant to a client to struggle with and overcome the conditions of the help he had requested. It was in this same period that application was developed as a process, which also required a time structure in order to make a client's initial request a genuine decision to try to use agency. I think it is fair to attribute this elaboration of beginnings to the functional viewpoint which is based on the premise that everyone fights the help he seeks unless he controls it pretty completely, and that a helping process consists largely in the gradual overcoming of the initial fear and resistance to any help that affects the self. When the counseling case first came into prominence apart from concrete services, I well remember the thinking and experiment that went into an attempt to put time structure into the application. The first tendency had been to accept the applicant for marital counseling on the basis of one interview. Experience soon proved that the client might be counted on to return for one or two interviews, but seldom remained long enough to accomplish anything. Putting in a limited but required period during which to develop the meaning of his request and what it would ask of him in order to use this form of service, introduced real process in the very beginning that gave the applicant a basis for choice and worker and client a basis for decision. While various factors entered into the defining of this application period and gave body to the process, such as fee, necessity for regular appointments, the ultimate involvement of the partner, it was really the utilization of a defined time form that lent new control and effectiveness to what had been a losing effort to help without the old supports.

Beginnings are hard enough, particularly for clients, but they do not hold the same degree of apprehension for worker or for agency. In my opinion, functional agencies have understood and taken genuine responsibility for application structures and have made it possible for workers, with the support of agency experience and conviction, to utilize their skill to the utmost in this initial phase of helping. It remains for the functional agency to take possession of its responsibility for a time-structured leaving process that is uniform enough for workers with supervisory backing to use with assurance. A worker who on his own would not have what it takes to determine an ending, or the conviction to hold to it in the face of client resistance, can be sustained by agency's affirmation that the time structure has proved to be right for the majority and useful as far as it goes for any client who can accept it. True, a given client may not get all the help he will ever need, or all that would be possible at this time ideally, but there is comfort and justification in the knowledge that what he gets, under such conditions, is at least helpful. It will not hurt him if the time limits have been determined by agency policy, not imposed or ignored by a well-meaning but unskillful worker. There is a general fear on the part of caseworkers that time structures will restrict their desire to be flexible and to move with the clients. The opposite is true, provided the time forms adopted by agency have grown out of experience and conviction and are subject to change as continuing experience may indicate. We labor under the illusion that there is an objective measure of the amount of time that a given client should have and that the hastening or the postponement of an ending date in terms of client reaction to it will somehow lend flexibility to an inevitable termination. Actually the flexibility we crave does not rest on freedom to alter the structure but rather on freedom from having to alter it, so that we may be flexible in meeting the client's efforts to find his own relation to the given. Only thus will he discover that he has within himself that which can enable him, not only to bear the ending as a partial dying but, in overcoming the fear inherent in this separation, to gain a new relation to time as the medium of the life process itself.

❧❦

A Conception of the Growth Process Underlying Social Casework Practice

SINCE ALL PRACTICE in a helping profession, whether it be labeled casework, counseling, or psychotherapy, depends at bottom on the practitioner's conception of growth and personality development and his ability to utilize that conception in his role as professional helper, it would seem that any experienced caseworker could express easily and at a moment's notice the psychological basis on which he operates and which he believes he actually uses to help the client. I yield to no one in the degree of conviction that characterizes my belief about how one helps—and through years of teaching a good deal of that conviction gets theoretical expression—yet when brought face to face with the problem assigned to me in this paper, the task seems almost insuperably difficult. I ask myself why this should be. It is not because I am hesitant or doubtful about my own point of view and its validity; rather it seems to me to be a resistance to putting into words living experience, which can never be accurately represented verbally. One's very fidelity to a scientific standard reacts against the distortion that words inevitably entail,

Paper presented at the National Conference of Social Work, Atlantic City, April, 1950.

not only in their failure to represent a moving relationship process but in the unpredictable response they elicit from the reader.

In the interchange of the classroom, where the teacher's intimate relation to each student in the training process underlies theoretical discussion, where the immediate experience of the student with his client or with his supervisor makes vivid every psychological concept, the understanding of growth and change, of personality development and the helping relation, is a gradually deepening result of a vital process which keeps concepts, theories, and ideas from congealing into sterile systems, from becoming something one learns from an outline or a book. Only in such a living experience does any student learn to understand and accept his own growth process as well as how to enter into the growth process of a client helpfully.

Because it seems to me that to return to the origin of human growth—in the uterus, at birth, and through childhood—is a story so familiar to most of us that it may fall on ears deafened by repetition, I have tried to examine the assumptions about the nature of personality growth and change that underlie the training process with which I am in daily contact and for which I carry responsibility, in relation to the oldest and most experienced student group in the University of Pennsylvania School of Social work.

The median age of this advanced or third-year group is usually nearer forty than thirty. A good many years of social work experience, in addition to the degree of Master of Social Work, are represented, ranging from casework through supervisory, to administrative and teaching practice. In the current class are two students whose practice assignment is in teaching, six who carry supervisory and administrative responsibility, and eight who are in regular field-work placements. Two of the latter are teachers of social work on leave of absence. Yet the focus of the class is casework, and the material for discussion is obtained primarily from the current practice of class members. How can a teacher possibly bring such a diversified group together so that they will finally experience community of process in the movement of the class, as individual psychological growth?

It does happen—and it happens year after year in spite of an incredulity that the teacher experiences with every beginning. Can it really be true? Is the kind of learning that implies growth change in the self actually to be expected, even to be required, of these already developed, professionally organized individuals?

For me there is only one answer to this question. To believe in the client's capacity for growth, through the helping process of casework, requires the kind of conviction that stems from the worker's own experience of growth through some form of professional help. Only a training process that is geared to the expectation of psychological growth, or, if you like, to the development of a professional self in the student, can be counted on to provide the basis for such conviction. Therefore, the conception of growth that underlies the practice of casework must, in my opinion, also underlie the training for social casework. If we differ at one spot, we must differ also at the other.

There was a time, not too long ago, when we tended

to assume that the personal change resulting from a psychotherapeutic experience was equivalent to the change produced by training and therefore could be translated into casework or supervisory skill directly. We have had to learn that, however valuable as a basis for training, no personal psychotherapy of itself is preparation for the giving of any specific form of professional help. Never would one expect the client to be transformed into the caseworker by the fact that he has developed a new use of himself through casework help. While the basic growth process may be identified in the client who has used help, it is qualitatively and quantitatively different from the change that may be expected when the development of a professionally skillful self becomes the consciously chosen goal of the helping process that we call training for social work. Even casework skill cannot be transformed into supervisory skill, nor can caseworker responsibility be equated with supervisory responsibility, without an intervening developmental process.

Therefore, in basing this discussion on an analysis of the concept of growth that underlies training for social work, I am resting not only on an assumption about the essential connection between taking help and giving help but on the meaning of growth itself and its relation to change. The growth on which training and casework depend is first of all a capacity of the human organism, dependent on the original impulsive organic matrix and on the direction inherent in its every manifestation. Growth on any level results in change, but change, which can be undone, is not necessarily growth, with its spontaneous, irreversible movement toward fulfillment and integration of the organism's potential for development.

To believe in the possibility of giving help or of being helped in any fundamental way, one must believe in the existence of a natural impulse toward better organization of self, which, however blocked or confused, provides the basis for a new orientation to living, once a situation is encountered which can disrupt the habitual pattern and release, for the formation of a new integration, the underlying growth tendencies. That psychological growth takes place in normal, as well as in extraordinary, life situations is taken for granted. Our problem as social workers is to discover how our social services may operate to provide such growth-producing situations for the individual who has not been sufficiently freed in the natural course of events to use himself effectively or to his own satisfaction. Similarly, the training school has the task of providing for the would-be social worker a growth-producing experience which will establish the conviction necessary for the skillful giving of professional help. To believe in the possibility of growth for the client, one has to have known the release of growth in the self, through help consciously sought and professionally controlled.

We who are dedicated to a professional utilization of natural growth have discovered certain essential aspects of the psychological growth process on which we depend for providing a helping situation. First, we know that, however important the physical environment for maintaining life, psychologically the only reality for man is other men. Whether he knows it or not, man develops whatever of selfhood he achieves through his social relationships. The self, in so far as it is a self, is social in character, and reflects its use of other selves in its developing organization. The baby's first use of "no" registers his beginning differentiation of himself from his parents. From the moment of birth, if not before, he climbs, as it were, by the putting out and taking back of needs and wants upon those who are available for his use.

The two basic needs that form the two poles of the psychological growth process are the need for dependence upon the other, as it is first expressed in the oneness of the uterine relationship, and the opposing need for the development of self-dependence as the goal of the movement toward adulthood. The two are never divorced in living, and it is on their essential conflict and interaction that we rely for the dynamic that keeps the individual moving to correct the imbalance that exists and must exist at any given moment in his use of himself. In any case, whether it be to satisfy a hunger that only the other can meet, or to experience the security that only self-development can give, the individual reaches his particular self-formation through his movement in relationship, the putting out and taking back of his projections upon those who are or have been important to him. Discarded parts of the self are left behind in abandoned relationships, while expanding goals are reached through newly achieved connections.

Because this use by the individual of his social environment is equally true for everyone constituting the environment, each human being is both the actor and the acted upon. The baby begins using what he finds in mother and father as actively as his developing organization permits, but it is equally true that, infant though he is, he too must bear, and begin to react to, his parents' projections upon him. We tend to think of the parents as almost totally responsible for the beginning self of the child, but it is well to remember that the child creates the parent in his own image as truly as the parent creates the child. Seldom do we ever arrive at an adulthood that can remove our basic projections on parents sufficiently to see them as human beings like ourselves.

It is to be expected, then, that very early in his career, the individual will develop his own organic pattern for meeting the critical experiences of birth, with its beginning and ending, and all the vital connections with the mother that follow. So manifold and complex are the factors that determine this pattern, such as the inherited constitution, the intra-uterine experience, the particular kind of birth and its relation to the particular makeup of the infant, as well as all the variables that follow, that one can never speak of causes but only of the fact that a characteristic pattern seems to result for a particular child, a pattern that is to be discerned in the child's way of beginning and ending, or of refusing to begin or end, in the earliest relationship to his mother. Thereafter this pattern will be identifiable in all the growth crises that occur in the natural course of events, modified by developing social relationships but never changed so completely as to alter the identity of the individual. He will always retain his peculiar and individual way of meeting growth changes—in other words, of beginning or ending, of uniting and separating, of emphasizing primarily self or other.

Does this mean, then, that repetition is the basic fact about human behavior and that to talk about psychological growth is a waste of breath? The only answer we as social workers could or would bear is that, regardless of the fact of pattern, and the apparent compulsion of the individual to perpetuate his own original way of meeting life, his impulse toward growth and change, his hunger for self-development and creative expression, are equally real. If there were not in the client, the patient, the student, and in us all some unrealized potential for spontaneous psychological growth and a creativity that may be directed toward the achievement of a more inclusive, better integrated self, all our talk about helping or learning would be of no avail.

This characteristic pattern, which begins to form itself from the moment of birth, is in truth no mere automatic or mechanical reflex; it is, from its inception, the expression of whatever of organization the infant self is able to achieve in feeling its own needs and struggling blindly for fulfillment. The pattern becomes the actual structure of the self and is backed by all the energy of the organism as far as it can be held within the limits of the conscious ego.

My objection to the word "ego" is that it either seems static and harmless or by implication harbors the taint of something one should not be or have. Even "self," with its ethical connotations of selfish or unselfish, is too passive a word to carry the forces that are first brought into some kind or organization to protect the baby from external threat and to express, as actively as he can, his internal necessity. I feel the need for the word "will" to carry, on all the levels of growth, the controlling and creative forces that make the child hard to train and every individual hard to help.

In the child, that ever-active will is more apparent in the capacity to resist, to refuse, than in its power to choose positively, to create. Perhaps for all of us even as adults it is easier to know what we do not want or will not have than to move positively toward the self-chosen goal. This is what is meant by the originally negative character of the will, which gets organized primarily in opposition just as consciousness grows on the necessity to meet problems.

If all threat came from the outside, the problem of psychological growth would be simplified. Actually, the living forces of the physiological organism do not come into the control of the consciously felt and relatively integrated self easily and naturally, and never completely. They are as much of a problem for the individual as the forces in the environment, indeed far more of a threat, since he can in no way escape them and they represent the inevitable life process that leads not only to a desired maturity but, finally, to death. They are the very source of his individual life, but because he cannot know and control them completely he fears them, and denies, represses, refuses, or resists in a necessity to hold on to whatever of self has been achieved. Only at points of growth crisis, where the pressure for further development becomes strong enough to overcome the fear of change and disruption, is the ordinary individual brought to the necessity of enlarging his hard-won integration. Genius seems to belong to another order—where the overwhelming necessity to create goes beyond all refusal or purely negative ego control. In trying to state the internal aspects of growth, I leave out for the moment the persons in the environment on whom or by whom growth crises are precipitated, but always these relationships are effective in the formation or modification of ego structure and in the acceptance or rejection of the underlying life forces by the individual will.

The possibility of providing for the individual in need an artificial growth-releasing situation is, in my opinion, the epoch-making psychological discovery of our era, a discovery that may yet be found to be more momentous for the future of civilization than the unlocking of the forces in the atom.

We cannot, of course, ignore the fact that religion and education have laid the groundwork for both group and individual helping and will continue to create channels through which socially desirable goals are advanced, but neither church nor academic school possesses the secret of the professionally controlled helping situation as it is found in social work and psychiatry.

In spite of fundamental differences, I think all schools of thought might agree on the significance of the professional character of casework and psychotherapy. For the individual, who from birth has never known any but personal relationships as his medium for development, suddenly to find himself able to project upon a person who is there for him, not using him for counterprojection, must in itself be felt as profoundly new and different, fearful perhaps, even in its potentiality for release. Only genuine necessity, a need too deep to be ignored and beyond the individual's capacity to meet on his own, will enable him to overcome the initial fear that the first touch of this unknown one-sided relationship can arouse.

Perhaps agreement would also go so far as to stress the

fact that, in the relative absence of counterprojection by the helper, the individual may go further in experiencing his own growth impulses than he could ever do when conditioned at every turn by the other's continuous need and use of him. Only when the essential social medium can be weighted in his favor by the professional controls of social work or therapy is the individual freed to discover and take over his own projections as well as to feel his own spontaneous movement toward self-development.

Yet another principle necessary for the successful utilization of a professional helping situation would probably be accepted by all of us, at least verbally; that is, that the situation must be chosen by the individual. Only if he wants the help offered through a particular service will it be possible for the helper to function. Thus growth itself, as far as it depends upon professional relationships, can be refused by the very person who needs it most. We may know in general how the growth process can be released through professionally created conditions, but no one will ever be able to control in actual practice the way in which the particular individual will respond. He can be forced or induced to come, perhaps, but his constructive utilization of the situation rests always on his own determined and persistent effort or, as we say mildly, "he must choose it," often making of that choice a simple intellectual weighing of alternatives.

Now I can no longer avoid the areas of disagreement, the spots where the functional and non-functional part company, if they have not already done so. For, in my belief, this growth as we know it, in terms of personality development, is a stormy, painful affair, which is not to deny that we want it more than anything else in life. Nothing produces the depth of satisfaction that movement to a new level of integration affords. No love relation, however fulfilling, can outweigh the joy of a new-found self, nor can the love relation compensate entirely for the self-development that it may hinder.

The basic need of the individual, after all, is not pleasure but more life, to make more and more of the underlying energy accessible for integration, to go with the life process instead of fighting it, and to find and use his own capacity for relationship and for creativity, however slight. Pleasure, or better said, satisfaction, attends the active, successful expression of the organized will; it is a by-product, not a motive or an end in itself. On the whole, pleasure is a word for little satisfactions, the enjoyment of moderate projects that involve not too much of the self, nor too important issues.

This leads me suddenly to training as we know it in the Pennsylvania School, where reliance on the nature of the growth process as I have described it characterizes our conception of learning and determines the structures we utilize.

One criticism of this conception of training is frequently voiced in the question, "Does learning have to be painful?" or in the assertion, "The Pennsylvania School makes learning painful." The answer to the question is that the kind of learning that rests on growth change as essential can never be made painless. Personality development, directed toward a goal, is a costly process and, in answer to the accusatory statement, is impossible to impose on anyone. The pain will be tolerated by the student only when it comes out of his own struggle to reach a goal that he has chosen and must choose again at every step.

And only as he experiences a kind of satisfaction in self-discovery that is paramount will he gain the conviction to sustain him in his course. The definite, known-in-advance time limits that give training its underlying characteristic structure also contribute to support the student in his purpose.

There is no one person in the training process to represent the helper. The helping function is dispersed and, in the Pennsylvania School, may be said to be carried by three persons, each of whom has a vital role to play: the adviser, who is also the teacher of the student's practice class, and is finally responsible for being related to his progress at every point; the supervisor, who is not employed by the School, but carries on student training within his regular job in an agency, and is geared to School time structures and standards through a sustained relation to the adviser; and the teacher of the personality class, who is concerned with helping each student to examine his own reactions to the training process, the positive and negative aspects of his own will and the feelings that attend it.

It is clear that this triangular distribution of the training forces gives to the process a character quite different from casework, from supervision, and from therapy. In one sense the student is subjected to far more powerful pressures than the client or the worker because he is related so intimately to three helpers. On the other hand, these helpers are truly there for him, insofar as he has entrusted to them the responsibility for his professional development. In other words, he has asked for the kind of pressure to reach a training goal that a school of social work represents. Moreover, in their common understanding of the training problem, and in their ability to differentiate their respective roles, they offer a unique opportunity for the student to use one helper to reach the others. His problem can be broken down and its too total quality mitigated by the fact that he is not confined to one source. In addition, the student has the stimulus, the support, and the comfort of the group process, in classes that are bound together by a community of goal and training experience. Nowhere is this group support more essential than in the case of the advanced student.

The applicant for the advanced curriculum differs from the first-year applicant in that he comes as a trained worker, supervisor, executive, or teacher, whose purpose is deep-seated and consciously arrived at. Usually he is a graduate of another school. He has some awareness of what he is undertaking and has counted the cost financially and in terms of personal and professional inconvenience. He would not apply if he were not aware of a lack in his professional skill. He knows in the abstract that it will be hard to become a student again, but he has little conception, nor can he be given it in advance, how great will be his resistance to the concrete experience of being supervised, or how deep the pain of realizing the "not knowing" and "not being able." For, even in the case of the advanced student who comes with previous training and substantial experience, the School's basic understanding of fundamental learning as requiring psychological growth will be maintained.

Therefore, from the point of application, the student who enters the advanced curriculum accepts, as far as he can beforehand, the School's expectation of change in his professional self as already organized, but he is hardly prepared for the kind and degree of fear and resistance that will begin to emerge in terms of his own particular pattern as he feels himself threatened by the training situation. The more he brings of ability, experience, and professional purpose, the harder he finds it to let himself become sufficiently disorganized to entertain the new and to use the help the supervisor is so ready to give. As a rule the classes and the teachers are less disturbing. Resistance in one form or another tends to focus on the practice, where lack of skill cannot be rationalized. There is no need to manufacture pain; one's obvious failure to give the help the client is seeking is sufficient cause.

I am reminded of one gifted student in the advanced curriculum, whose previous experience as a successful student-supervisor for another school made it unusually hard for her to take on the student role. Her strong denial of the resistance she had known so well in her own students kept her from using the agency supervisor to whom she was assigned for casework practice. She held out for a good six weeks of the first semester and seemed incapable of feeling, much less expressing, any really strong negative to a supervisor whom she admired and respected. But she was not learning and she knew it, for no one realized more keenly than she how lacking in helpfulness was her work with children and foster parents. The time pressure inherent in the semester, which is utilized to the full by teachers, students, and supervisor, began to make itself felt. Conferences with the adviser clarified the problem and left it firmly on the student. If she could not, she could not. The School would have to accept it, but unless she could give in to a real use of supervision, there would be no learning process for her. For this particular student, able to see anything theoretically, suffering from her own failure to work skillfully, and guilty for the loss to her clients, the crisis came suddenly and in an explosion that amazed her no less than her supervisor. She described it later in writing:

> However, in one conference all my fear and all my rage exploded into words, into anger at my supervisor and at this (learning) experience in which I felt myself caught. In the heat of the battle I had to realize that it was my battle—no one was fighting me. I had to see how fearful I was of this situation which I could not control: how I feared what the other person might do to me, if I did not control him . . . I cannot recreate this experience without marveling at the amount of pain there was in it for me, and yet apparently it was the only way in which I could make a beginning. It was truly a beginning, too, for in sharing in this tremendously negative way all my own fears and anger, I had somehow put myself into the relationship and could recognize what was mine. I could see my supervisor as herself without my negative projections and myself as myself. . . .Now I could know, too, with what passion and force a person can resist the help he is asking.

One may well ask: But is it legitimate or even possible to put mature, experienced social workers through such an experience? The answer, and the only answer, is that no one "puts them through." If learning is to be other than an intellectual consideration of ideas, if it really demands a change in the already organized professional self to permit a new development of skill in helping, then it will be resisted as intensely as it is sought but it will be lived through for the sake of the gain to the very self that was able to hold out against it. Age is no barrier, up to a point. Psychological growth seems to be just as possible, as real, and as satisfying to the student who has left forty well behind as to the student in his twenties. In fact, I cannot recall in my experience any advanced student whose learning was blocked primarily by age. Every student, advanced or beginning, will meet the training situation, as we know it, with fear however disguised, and with resistance however subtly expressed. Until that beginning phase is over, and some yielding to the need for help takes place, there will be no taking in of the new, and no change for the better in practice. There follows the characteristic form of the growth process as one finds it in all forms of professional helping, a yielding to the need for help, an unburdening of the self in projection, and gradually a taking back into the self, with new tolerance and responsibility, the parts that have been deposited upon others.

The original resistance to help seems to be based on a rejection of need for the other, as dangerous and unjustifiable weakness. "I should be able to do it myself" is the typical explanation. Only when the fear of this need is overcome and the incapacity of the self to progress alone is admitted, does the positive phase in the process dominate the picture. Then, pleasure in the strong, sustaining relationship, with the supervisor and through him with the agency, is matched only by an unbelievable improvement in practice and, simultaneously, by a sense of change in the self. This typical growth cycle is repeated in lesser swings and on different levels as the mid-term and semester time limits introduce new beginnings and endings. With every repetition the student's capacity to understand and bear his own pattern increases. Finally, it is the time structure of the school year as a whole that brings the training process through to an ending with a thesis based on the student's development in practice, to carry the separation experience and to give expression to the newly integrated professional self. Only those who have seen students move through this learning experience can know with conviction how joyful and rewarding is this final evidence of professional development.

The training structure that can utilize this conception of the psychological growth process for vital learning is not easily developed or maintained. It implies the kind of living organization that makes a social agency truly an instrument for giving help, based on a oneness of purpose and a common understanding of training and of learning conceived as necessarily involving the whole self of the student. Above all, it rests upon a sustained relationship between school and training agency, as it is expressed in the shared concern of every adviser and supervisor for the student, whose training depends on the genuineness and effectiveness of their relationship. The school's understanding of what it costs the agency to take students, its basic identification with the service the agency gives and its way of giving it, must be balanced by the agency's trust in the school and its training and by its experience of value received through student supervision and school connection. Only thus can the manifold differences that must arise in this complex interrelationship between school and agency, between student, supervisor, and adviser, become the dynamic that vitalizes the training process and makes possible the attainment of its goal—the achievement of a reliable professional self for every student.

PART VII

❧

Retirement and the Biography
of Otto Rank
1950-1960

◆✦◆ THE FIRST FEW MONTHS of retirement after commencement in June, 1950, brought a sense of release and freedom from routines and obligations. There was time for travel, for reading, for music, for painting. But more important, and all too soon, the long slow process of separation from institutional connection and support and from a full professional life began to be realized. For the first two years, from 1950 to 1952, Dr. Taft and I served as consultants on the Doctoral Council of the School, a wholly unsatisfactory arrangement for us who were used to full-time functional responsibility, during which time it became clear that only complete separation from the School would be right and would give its faculty the chance to develop their own positions and choose their own leadership.

In the fall semester of 1951 Dr. Taft was asked to give a course on Rank for a few faculty members and advanced doctoral students, an opportunity which she welcomed and which gave her great satisfaction. It was during the work on this course and with the sense of time at her disposal that her obligation to the Rank materials packed in a trunk and a steel cabinet in the basement of the School began to seek a way to discharge itself. A first step in this direction was to find a translator for the materials in German script, especially Rank's early daybooks and the correspondence between Rank and Freud, for she was unwilling to let any material go out of her possession until she

345

knew what it contained. Through the University of Pennsylvania a translator was obtained whose knowledge of German was satisfactory but whose unfamiliarity with Rank's content and vocabulary necessitated her concentrated work on these translations to accompany the translator's. In a letter to a friend she says, "I can almost read German script now." In the summer, in Vermont, through the Marlboro School of Music, she found a fortunate connection with Mrs. Herman Busch, wife of the cellist, who was at home with German script and could render it into modern German type, but not into English.

From the beginning she had the invaluable help of Anita Faatz, who for purposes of this project became known as "researcher." She took over the major role in finding the library where the Rank collection might be deposited for safe keeping, and for the use of qualified research workers. Expert assistance and advice were given generously by the librarians in the three libraries that Miss Faatz visited: the Library of Congress, Princeton, and Columbia.

By January, 1957, after a visit to the Columbia University Library and a talk with Mr. Roland Baughman, Head of Special Collections, Dr. Taft had no further doubts about the placement of the collection in the care of that library. Her decision, with a description of the collection and the reason for the choice of Columbia, is stated in her own words in her letter to Mr. Baughman written on January 15, 1957.

> In consequence of my conference with you on January 14, I have decided to present to the Special Collections Division of the Libraries of Columbia University a collection of letters, papers, and manuscripts of Otto Rank,

a Viennese psychotherapist and onetime associate of Sigmund Freud, which were deposited with me at the time of his death on October 31, 1939. These were later made over to me in a legal paper signed by his second wife, Estelle Buel Rank (now Simon) executrix of the estate.

This collection consists of: (1) a group of early materials, written 1903–1905, before he met Freud, among them four daybooks, a notebook of poems, a notebook of dreams, the manuscript of *Der Künstler;* (2 correspondence between Freud and Rank during the years 1906–1924 covering the controversy over *The Trauma of Birth,* the book on which Rank finally severed his connection with Freud. In this section there are some 40-odd letters, handwritten, from Freud to Rank and typed copies of letters from Rank to Freud, also a few letters to and from Ferenczi; (3) copies and some originals of the circular letters by members of the inner circle, Ernest Jones, Abraham, Eitingon, Ferenczi, Rank, and Freud, during the years 1920–1924; (4) original handwritten manuscripts, first typed copies, notes and corrections of Rank's major works; (5) Rank's own listing and comments on his writings and publications up to and including 1930, with references to reviews and sources; (6) I shall also include a nearly complete collection of his major publications in German and where possible in English translation. In addition to this material I possess 150 or more handwritten letters from Dr. Rank covering the period of my acquaintance with him, 1926–1939, which I intend to add to the above collection at a later date.

I have selected Columbia as the most suitable repository for this collection, because it was to New York that

Dr. Rank came in 1924 as the first Viennese psychoanalyst representing Sigmund Freud to practice in the United States, and because he returned to New York repeatedly as analyst and lecturer and finally chose New York for his permanent home in 1934 as the city which symbolized for him the America he had come to love. I believe also that Columbia offers a unique center for the proper use of this material which it will make accessible to the scholars and research workers who are qualified to use it. The choice of Special Collections, rather than medical or psychiatric libraries is determined by the fact that Rank was not a psychiatrist, nor was his interest primarily psychotherapeutic, despite his contribution to that field. His major work relates as well to literature, folklore, art, philosophy, and the development of civilization itself.

As to the conditions which I may put on this gift, first it is my desire that the library should be as unrestricted as possible in its judgment as to proper use. However, there are two conditions which seem to me to be essential: one, the collection shall remain the Otto Rank Collection and shall not be dispersed; two, the chronological organization made by Rank for the particular letters that give a picture of the relationship between Freud and Rank and between Rank and other members of the inner circle ending in Rank's separation from the group shall be maintained in the form in which he left them.

An article written at Mr. Baughman's request was published in Columbia Library Columns. The spring of 1957 was spent in preparing the Rank material for mailing—fourteen boxes in all—an arduous task.

In the meanwhile, simultaneously with this work of

preparing the material for Columbia, her effort to translate the daybooks and the Freud–Rank correspondence continued, and the problem of what use to make of these
materials absorbed her. Two letters to Anita Faatz written
in the fall of 1954 indicate her relation to this problem.
September 28, 1954, soon after her return from Vermont
she writes:

> I don't know how long I will last. I can't seem to get
> myself back to editing until I am ready for it—and I am
> apparently not ready, judging by the resistance, but I
> have only a letter or two at the end of Part. B to finish.
> How I wish I had completed it at Deer Run.

Later in the fall—November, 1954—at work on the
Freud–Rank letters her dilemma continues:

> I shall write Anna Freud as soon as you are about
> through with this copy to ask if I may send her the letters
> for her consideration. While I don't yet know what I'll
> try to do with them exactly, I'd like to know that I
> could before I put too much into trying. Probably I'd
> write Knopf or someone else to see if there was any
> interest, but no use to do that unless I have the consent.
> So the next step is to try out the Freuds and Ernest Jones,
> and the second, to reach Ferenczi's estate.

By 1956 in spite of ups and downs in daily living, including two hospital experiences in 1955, her relation to the
Rank project had deepened almost imperceptibly until it
was clear to her that she was going to write something out
of her own knowledge of Rank. By the summer of 1956 in
Vermont she knows what she is doing. A letter to Anita
Faatz on August 12, 1956 states this clearly.

This will feel like a voice from the tomb, for I have indeed been buried in what I am trying to do, altho it occupies at most, 3 hours—2½ or 2—daily at 10, including Saturday and Sunday. I seem to be pretty totally absorbed, even when I am actively engaged and have apparently put it out of mind. It does not worry me or keep me awake nights. I sleep like a top but something is withdrawn from the usual projections. If Virginia were not so identified and so actually helpful with the typing. I don't know what we would do. When she isn't typing she's at the cabin painting all morning. It's a rarely helpful arrangement of which only she would be capable . . .

I am actually at page 60, plus a preface of 7 or 8 pages. . . .

The hard part—*The Trauma of Birth* and separation from Freud and the letters come next—perhaps no harder than the years from Paris on. Anyway I'm in for trying what seems to be a biography as far as I have some direct access to it, without asking people which I'll never do— it's my version of Rank and that it will remain. . . .

August 28, 1956, just before leaving Vermont for Flourtown, this continues:

I will be obliged to say something to my Flourtown friends when I get home to account for my business. What amazes me daily is that I do this—never before have I written this way—continuously and objectively. Just shows, you never can tell. . . .

How I wish I thought the Freuds wouldn't hold me up. At any rate there is no note of hostility to Freud and there won't be for I don't feel it. Jones is my problem but I try to restrain myself. . . .

I am so one track that it is hard for me to attend to food. I think I may stop working today or tomorrow—

I have brought Rank up to 1926 when I went to New York for analysis. It's a good stopping point.

Discussing this new way of writing which continues to amaze her she asked me to add a footnote to her letter to Anita to say, "tell her I have learned to partialize and that makes what I am doing possible after a lifetime of being able only to do everything whole."

In the winter of 1956–1957 she settled down in Flourtown to the hard work of including the people who must consent to the publication of Rank's letters to them and correspondence developed with Ernst Freud, with Ernest Jones and Dr. Michel Balint, executor of the Ferenczi estate. There was revision to do when Jones' third volume of his biography of Freud appeared in 1957. Of this problem she writes on October 22, 1957:

> As you may imagine I have been through a pretty hard time—trying to contain Jones inside myself and not let him ruin my book, as well as to find the right way to include him for he can't be completely ignored. . . .
> I have now gone over every word from start to finish with a too critical mind but I rejoice to find that I have no fault to find with Part I or Part IV. I can't see how I ever did the latter—it's beyond me.

She was delighted when she saw the manuscript typed in final form. Eager as she was by this time to get it to a publisher, she was able to listen to a point of criticism that Miss Faatz made—at first impatiently, but as she thought it over she wrote:

> I want you to know that I went over the spots you brought up and changed all of them. You were perfectly right. That last bringing in of social work and all the

rest was nonsense. I must have been too tired to care. So I just crossed it out and left the sentence to stand on its own. Now aren't you glad you stuck to it? I'll bet you were tired and so was I. And there's a kind of ending in it that you must feel too—even if you are glad to be free of it.

In looking for a publisher, the first thought was Knopf, where she had had a connection by correspondence since his publication in 1935 of her translations of *Will Therapy* and *Truth and Reality*, a connection which had been recently reactivated by Knopf's publication of a Vintage Book of some of Rank's writings entitled *The Myth of the Birth of the Hero and Other Writings*. The firm gave the manuscript courteous consideration but, as was to have been expected, did not find it within its field of interest. The summer of 1957 was spent in waiting for consideration from another publisher. When the waiting period seemed unjustifiably long she asked that the manuscript be returned. The happy inspiration of the Julian Press came to her in the fall of 1957. Her letter to its publisher dated January 6, 1958, describes the beginning of what was to be a most positive experience with Mr. Arthur Ceppos and his wife and assistant, resulting in the publication of the book on June 20, 1958:

Thank you for your prompt reply to my letter of December 29. I am glad that you know enough about me to take me on faith, at least for the moment.

For my part, I know very little about your company except for the Progoff publication[1] and a volume *Gestalt*

[1] Ira Progoff, *The Death and Rebirth of Psychology* (New York: The Julian Press, 1957).

Therapy[2] whose subtitle "Excitement and Growth in the Human Personality" struck me as unique in a field which seems so often to deny the possibility of anything but change in the human psyche. The list of titles on the back of the cover is my only other source of information regarding your work. However the little I know seems to warrant a belief that Rank's philosophy has some inherent connection with your interests. Consequently I am sending you my manuscript by parcel post.

After the work of translation was done, I wrote this manuscript in one continuous process over a six months period and finished it about March, 1957. The appearance of Dr. Ernest Jones' third volume on Freud with its final disposition of Rank and his work as the end result of cyclo-thymia forced me to some revision of Part II. I am aware that I may need editorial help in reducing some of the quotations of Part I, or possibly in eliminating some material of Part III, but on the whole, the manuscript must be taken for what it is or not at all. I have no interest in the result of publication in money terms, nor would I want extensive publicity, but I would like to be assured that the limited audience of analysts, clinical psychologists, and social workers, as well as artists who are related to Rank's work in *Art and Artist* would be circularized effectively.

If, after you have seen the material, you are sufficiently interested to want to discuss it, I could come to New York for an appointment.

Hoping that a publisher's idea of "a reasonable time" will approximate my own.

---

[2] Frederick Perls *et al., Gestalt Therapy, Excitement and Growth in the Human Personality* (New York: The Julian Press, 1951).

The pre-publication announcement of the book brought many gratifying responses from professional associates and former students. The book itself, jacket, typography, and content, was a delight to her. She did not expect much from reviewers, but in spite of this she was not prepared for the first review that appeared prematurely before the publication date in *Time* magazine. In no sense of the word a review of the book and with no knowledge of Rank's contribution, it picked up Jones' picture of Rank and headlined the word "sick." Dr. Taft saw it first at her birthday dinner, a miserable occasion for the three of us who had the welfare of this book at heart. Questions about this review were the first reactions to the book to reach us when we reached Vermont for the summer.

Appreciative letters from professional colleagues, former students, and friends, balanced to some degree the reaction to the *Time review*. One letter written on June 26, 1958, by Marjorie Mohan Turville, an alumna of the School who graduated twenty-two years ago, is of particular interest as it touches the little understood question of influence. It is quoted here with Dr. Taft's answer:

DEAR DR. TAFT:

You have undoubtedly heard from every graduate of the Pennsylvania School who subscribes to *Time!* Also undoubtedly, the others will not have felt the need to send you carbons of their letters to *Time*. My only feeling as I enclose mine is that you may be interested, amused a bit, to hear from someone who has been completely separated from professional activity since the day the degree was awarded twenty-two years ago.

The appearance of your wonderful and needed book

does give me an excuse to let the teacher know what a good child I have been to remember for so many years what she taught me and to prove it with the carbon. Actually, the review, if it could possibly be rated as such, is incidental—I knew when I saw the first ad in *The New York Times* that I would have to write you, and then I wrote a paragraph of a letter when I had read only to the end of the second paragraph of the Foreword. And then I decided I was being a bit precipitous!

My point is that beyond the tremendous professional value of your book and your great personal accomplishment in producing it is a public value. I could never say that my reactions are representative of the *general* public. No one who has been touched (marked? branded?) by the Pennsylvania School can ever settle comfortably into being "general public"—we probably wouldn't want to, really, even though we frequently suspect that living in the world is simpler for the untouched! But there still remains a public for a book on Rank, for your book on Rank. There are people like myself who are convinced, of their own experience, that the Rankian philosophy creates the most valid approach to people and the most useful therapy. There are people who have had psychiatric help of one kind or another and have developed a valid interest. . . .

This is a small public, I know, and a kind of special public. But it may show you that there are numbers of people who are grateful for the kind of help toward thoughtful understanding that your book provides.

And may I add my personal congratulations on your wonderful completion of a very tough job, my personal pride in your publication of the book, and my own profound gratitude.

July 5, 1958

DEAR MRS. TURVILLE   (vividly remembered as Marjorie
                     Mohan, whom I can still see as
                     she looked 22 years ago)

Indeed I have not been flooded with carbons, only one,
in fact, a single inimitable paragraph like your own. I
only wish that *Time* had the sense to publish both. Too
bad that *Time* which stole a march on the publication
date of June 20, should be the widely read magazine it
is for the general public. Already, even here, I have been
met with references to it, and strangely, with interest or
with curiosity, and no conception of why I might object.

I find it hard to express the kind of satisfaction your
letter gave Miss Robinson and me. It is good to find that
someone out of professional practice since graduation
can still present the essence of a philosophy of helping
that touched her twenty-two years ago. I doubt whether
any current practitioner could do it as well. As for your
writing, it has the touch of continued practice—you are
no novice. . . .

I hope that you will not mind, that I have sent copies
of your letter to my publisher. He is a rare man who has
personal conviction about Rank that leads him to risk
losing money. We hope for a review in *The New York
Times Book Review* that will be respectful if not lauda-
tory. With warm greetings.

Other and more serious reviews than the one in *Time*
appeared, but few indicated any real knowledge of Rank or
an appreciation of the purpose and point of view of the
author. She acknowledges one that was especially gratifying
to her in a letter to Dr. Frederick Allen, psychiatrist, until
his retirement director of the Philadelphia Child Guidance
Clinic.

I am so glad that you consented to review my book for the *American Journal of Psychiatry* where it might so easily have been misinterpreted and for the authoritative backing your second review will give to the Alumni and students who read the *Journal of Social Work Process*. Second, I am deeply grateful that you have stated accurately what the book consists of and what it tries to develop. I am surprised to find how unusual it is to get a real review of a book. . . .

In the year following the publication of the biography of Rank, Dr. Taft and I became involved in the organization of our papers as the School of Social Work was celebrating its fiftieth anniversary in 1959, and I had been asked to prepare a paper on the history of the School in its first fifty years. This paper was presented to an Alumni Colloquium in June, 1959,[3] an occasion which brought great rewards to Dr. Taft and myself, as well as a realization of strain from which we had to recover in an idle and happy summer in Vermont. Dr. Taft delighted in the citation which was given her at this Colloquium by the Alumni Association in which it was acknowledged that "Much that comprises the strength and distinction of the University of Pennsylvania School of Social Work originated in her thinking, teaching and writing.[4]

On our return to Flourtown, in the fall of 1959, Dr. Taft began to consider the organization of her papers. She began work on this project actively in January and finished, with

[3] Virginia P. Robinson, "University of Pennsylvania School of Social Work in Perspective: 1909–1959," *Journal of Social Work Process*, XI (1960), 149.
[4] The full citation appears in *Journal of Social Work Process*, XI (1960), 149.

her papers from 1913 on in chronological order, on March 25, 1960, a date noted in her line-a-day diary. She kept an active file of reviews and reactions to her biography of Rank and correspondence relevant to her concern for Rank's contribution. Several letters have been selected for inclusion in this volume as they show the persistence of her concern for Rank to the end of her life, letters that are as characteristic of her relation to herself and to the person to whom she writes as are her formal papers.

With Dr. Fay Karpf,[5] a social psychologist and Rankian psychotherapist who practices in California, she had over many years, continued a correspondence focused on their interest in Rank. In June, 1959, Dr. Karpf writes:

> I am writing at this time to ask you some questions about Rank's use of the Time Limit in therapy. I am surprised at the confusion of views about the matter. I have been asked about his procedure in this regard and since I do not want to be dogmatic and base myself on my own impressions merely, I naturally turn to you. I would greatly appreciate your views regarding the subject.
>
> For example: what was Rank's position, after he separated from Ferenczi, about "irrevocable" termination? Did Rank ever use the Time Limit to set a definite ending (like 3 or 6 months) at the outset of therapy? It is my impression that he was quite flexible in this regard

[5] Dr. Fay B. Karpf is the author of two pamphlets on Rankian therapy, and a book, *The Psychology and Psychotherapy of Otto Rank* (New York: The Philosophical Library, 1953); also a summary article, "Rankian Will or Dynamic Relationship Therapy," in *Progress in Psychotherapy*, eds. Jules H. Masserman and J. L. Moreno (New York: Grune & Stratton, 1957), XI.

and that he arrived at a decision only after a period of study and consultation with the patient. That, however, is not the view many people have, including Alexander. I am also of the opinion that the "irrevocable" part was chiefly the contribution of Ferenczi.

I am most eager to get your reaction to the above. Also, I am wondering whether there is somewhere an authoritative statement on the above questions which could be decisively cited, other than the passages on end-setting in *The Development of Psychoanalysis, The Birth Trauma,* and the chapter on The End Phase in *Will Therapy*.

I hope it will not be too troublesome for you to answer the above questions. If you have not completed your article for the Collier Encyclopedia yet, perhaps you will wish to consider including an appropriate statement on the subject. I am sure people would be interested in such a statement which could settle the matter once and for all.

Dr. Taft answered as follows (June 20, 1959):

Your letter arrived when we were in the midst of the final week of the 50th anniversary celebation, the Alumni Colloquium. Much as we appreciated the warmth of response from former students and the consideration of faculty for our comfort, we had to accept the difference that age makes in capacity to endure even the most wanted contacts. I am seventy-seven this week and while I do not seem too different to those who see me at a distance I no longer have the endurance. Miss Robinson has been under a more prolonged strain beginning with an honorary degree from the University in February which certainly proclaimed their cordial acceptance of the present school under Dean Smalley. It ended with a paper on the history of the School which she had finally organized into something that could be read in an hour and a quarter. Quite an achievement for a fifty year span as was her ability to keep her voice clear. The meaning it evidently had for the Alumni present was reward enough but afterwards we were pretty well worn out.

So much for the School. The Collier article on Rank has been accepted after a second writing to add 800 words to the 300 originally specified. I don't know when the Encyclopedia will be published.

Now for your questions which I do appreciate as an honor. How rare it is to be asked a real question!

I wish I could refer you to a direct quotation from Rank but I think the fact that there is none is in part an answer. Never would anything be "irrevocable" or rigid for Rank and for a person with his lightning-like response, even he could not foresee the exact way in which a therapeutic process would be terminated. The only aspect that remained fixed was his comprehension of the nature of the process, however varied in different individuals. From the first day, he would never lose sight of the inevitable development from a gradual acceptance to a gradual withdrawal. He trusted his relation to the patient to utilize the dynamic to the best advantage of the particular person. I would doubt that he ever set a definite time limit in the beginning. He might, as he did in my case, accept without argument the time I insisted I had, and simply agree to try. But when I had reached the point of giving up control he set an ending just enough different that it broke up my pattern. It was I who tried to limit in advance, not Rank. I am sure that there were for him as many ways of setting an ending as there were individuals with varying needs and patterns. My own belief, and I think Rank would agree, is that anyone uses the time he has if he knows it is all he has, provided he is not handled arbitrarily by an opposing will. As Rank says, it has to end sometime, the actual date is as good a point to fight on as any, provided the patient has genuinely experienced the leaving process.

For me, the therapeutic process is never a once and for all time affair and it was not so for Rank. One can use differing periods of time for all one is capable of at a particular level of development. I speak for the relatively normal people of the kind I worked with. I do not know how Rank handled the really sick ones but am sure it would be on the same fundamental understanding of the therapeutic process. It is too bad for psychiatrists like Alexander to assume that Rank began a therapy by explaining about the birth trauma or by setting up a firm ending. Nor did he ever claim that birth is the cause of the neurosis as he is generally supposed to have done. But psychiatrists, like others, believe what they want to believe. Nor did his later feeling for *will* wipe out his understanding of the biological matrix.

Have you seen a new book by Ekstein and Wallerstein, *The Teaching and Learning of Psychotherapy?* It is interesting to see medical men begin to honor supervision and even to recognize the contribution social casework has made to this process.

This long essay hardly gives you a satisfying answer to your question. I hope that you will forgive my inability to do better.

In the fall of 1959, Dr. Karpf forwarded to Dr. Taft a paper by Dr. John M. Shlien of the University of Chicago Counseling Center—at Dr. Shlien's request—given in a symposium of the American Psychological Society on length of time in therapy. Dr. Taft replied to his paper on October 2, 1959 as follows:

I was surprised to receive a recent paper of yours from Dr. Karpf who wrote that you had asked her to forward it. It sent me to my files where I found your letter of September, 1956, suggesting a meeting to discuss Rank and enclosing a copy of a report on some research on time limited therapy. I regret that I was, at the time, not used to retirement and was trying hard to be truly retired so that I was quite unwilling to engage in professional controversy however friendly.

There is too much that I would say to you if I started, as I have found by trying. Just let me express my appreciation of your truly fine-grained, sensitive understanding of time and time limits and venture to wish that you could trust yourself more and use research less in your further investigation of the therapeutic process.

I am enclosing the last paper I wrote before retiring when I still had practice under me.[6] I think it unlikely that you would have come across it. It gives the basis for my final conviction about the value of time limits. It was so much more visible in the school situation than in the purely therapeutic relationship.

Please don't feel any obligation to comment on it. It might just answer some of your questions about my point of view.

Dr. Shlien made use of her letter and the paper that she enclosed in the mimeographed Discussion Papers[7] of the Center, with the following introduction:

[6] "A Conception of the Growth Process Underlying Social Casework Practice," 1950.
[7] Vol. V, No. 15 (October, 1959).

At the last APA meetings, I gave a paper (in a symposium on "length of time in therapy") heavily based on the theory of Jessie Taft. Dr. Fay Karpf, a friend of Otto Rank and Jessie Taft, was on the symposium, and I asked her to forward a copy of my paper.

As you know, I was deeply influenced by Taft, as were many of us here, not only in regard to the research on time limits, but also ideas about growth, the role of the therapist, emphasis on immediate experiencing. The letter of reply is rather precious to me, and I reproduce it here, with her "last paper before retiring" because it may have something to say to all of us—about time limits, with which we have not yet finished; about concepts of growth; perhaps about practicum training and personal therapy; other things.

In answer to Dr. Shlien's letter seeking to make an appointment with her when he might be in Philadelphia and inviting her to Chicago to speak to the Counseling Center staff she wrote on December 8, 1959:

You should have no difficulty in understanding what Rank meant by *will*. But you may live to regret your success.

I shall be glad to try to see you about January 30th, weather and health permitting. If you can give me notice in time, I can arrange to meet you in Philadelphia at the University of Pennsylvania School of Social Work, 2410 Pine Street, where we could use an unoccupied office. Flourtown is hard to get to and takes time, also an office would feel more suitable for our purposes.

As to the time limit, the immediate situation would probably determine it for both of us and maybe would suffice for the entire future so let May and June rest for the present.

Your very kind invitation to come to Chicago would have been a welcome challenge twenty years ago, but no longer. At seventy-seven one is not always so mobile, so professionally eager. But I am surprised and pleased to find that I still count with a group of psychologists like yours.

Perhaps you and I might go over the two cases, if we meet in January, sufficiently to satisfy some of your questions.

A correspondence developed with Jack Jones, a writer engaged in a psychological study of modern totalitarian phenomena who had sent her his article entitled "To the End of Thought" in which he acknowledged the value of Rank's contribution. Three letters from her in response to his are very characteristic and very revealing of her attitudes. When he wrote that he had been commissioned to review her biography of Rank for the magazine *Modern Age* she responded on February 23, 1959,

Your letter surprised me—first that you should want to review my book and second that such a solemn quarterly as *Modern Age* seems to be should be interested enough to publish it. . . .

Your "Bohemian" newspaper is equally foreign to me. My background of philosophy comes from many years ago. My real experience is related to social work where I had an opportunity to teach freely and to train graduate students preparing for social work as you will see if you really read my book. I am a realist and my impatience with argument is great. . . .

I found the responses to your article very difficult reading but no one could doubt their sincerity. I marvel at your patient and skilful response to them.

Hoping that you will not find my book too unreward-
ing for your purposes . . .

When Mr. Jones sent her his review of her book she
replied (March 17, 1960):

It was most kind of you to permit me to read your
review of my book. What a bad time you had with
Modern Age. However, I have to agree with their editor
that it is late to be printing a review, especially in view
of the declining public interest in psychoanalysis. I think
even Freud's name has ceased to be headline news and
Rank is relatively unknown even after much of the active hostility has ceased.

In my opinion, Rank will someday be discovered, but
it will not be via my book, which is far too feminine,
or if you will, based too much on an interest in actual
helping, to reach the rational, scientific mind.

I appreciate your sympathetic account of my book and
agree with your criticisms. The latter are inevitable from
any but a social caseworker's point of view. Even the
analysts do not understand. But I did exactly what I
intended to do, no more, and no less. No one could be
less fitted to write a definitive biography than I am. I
intended only to show a psychological growth process
that endured to the end. Since I had no other firsthand
material, I utilized the personal letters as evidence of a
man who maintained his human relationships over the
years when he was written off by Jones and others as
psychotic. I would under no circumstances have con-
sulted the opinion of others. I wrote only what I knew
in and for myself.

As to the importance of his relation to social work,
he gave to a limited group of social workers the secret

of helping. But it is not understood except by those who have felt its effects. It will never be popular; it is too hard to live up to. As to the value of social work for Rank, you are right. It served to sustain him when he stood completely alone and he found challenge and interest in the problems of helping which caseworkers presented to him.

Your review indicates to me that my book was coincidental with your need to express yourself about Rank. Why not write a completely independent article. Good luck to it, if you do.[8]

On April 9, 1960, to a letter enclosing articles from *Liberation* she wrote:

I think you must be one of those rare humans who really answers. I do appreciate your thoughtful consideration not only of me but of your own reviewers.

It is clear that what you have written on the underlying meaning of communism is extremely provocative. I found all three articles in *Liberation* really interestting, altho by the end of the third, I found myself entangled in masculine (?) argumentation. Beyond a point, I am too much woman to accept the external, rational approach. Only the internal is genuine and real for me. However, despite your rationalistic skill, you sound like a very nice person.

I shall send a copy of your letter to Mr. Arthur Ceppos of the Julian Press, altho I doubt his present interest in my book which probably lost him money. Unless he contacts you, I see no purpose in your writing to Sir Herbert Read. But I thank you for the offer.

[8] Mr. Jones took her advice about the review. It was published in article form as "Otto Rank—A Forgotten Heresy," *Commentary*, September, 1960. His book is to be published by Horizon Press.

You are right that Rank's greatness went far beyond the therapeutic for he had all of the born intellectual's necessity for theory and universality. Nevertheless, through therapeutic experience, he alone seems to have grasped the basic and inevitable ambivalence of will and impulse, the need for continuous rebalancing, and re-integration at every level of development. You overstress the negative side of separation—it is also the means of liberation to self and creativity, the essential of growth. It could never stand as a closed system so long as life is life. But I see I am going theoretical too.

I am as ignorant of *Commentary* as I was of *Modern Age* and *Liberation,* but in any case I wish you better luck with your review this time.

In all of these letters written in the last year of her life there is frank expression of her realization of the handicaps of age, which she felt to be increasing and had no desire to live with indefinitely. Death, she felt, would be preferable to a protracted old age if one could only choose the way. Happily for her—she was active in the garden, pruning roses, transplanting chrysanthemums on an early spring day in April, when a stroke came without warning. Though her right side was paralyzed, she was fully conscious and speech returned quickly. For the period of six weeks in the hospital she was herself, concerned for my welfare to the end. As usual when she was ill she did not want to see people, and now she did not want cards or flowers except for her own roses in June bloom, sensitive to the burden it put upon her in her inability to respond to these good wishes immediately. She was acutely aware of the problem of the hospital in the midst of a reconstruction program and with limited nursing service, but determined to take the situation as it was in a semiprivate room. At first a strong impulse to recovery gave her strength to cooperate with the physiotherapist, to get out of bed with his help, to begin to practice using her left hand. This impulse exceeded her strength when a new patient came to occupy the other bed in her room, a woman who had never been ill before, immobilized with a sudden heart attack. Characteristically, Dr. Taft responded to this woman's bewilderment with her usual impulse to help and in this effort she knew her own weakness and the loss of her essential helping self. Her first heart attack followed. It was then she yielded to my urgency to let me find a private room for her and from this moment I am sure she knew with relief that the end was near. From that time on, in a private room with her own nurse, she waited with great patience through the daily round of hospital routines as strength, energy, and interests diminished day by day. On June 7, 1960, a lovely summer day, she woke to tell the nurse what a good night she had had, but in the effort to move breathing became difficult. "I am dying," she said—and her breathing ceased without pain or struggle.

Her own words from *The Dynamics of Therapy* express better than any words I can find, her attitude towards death.

"Is it not possible that much of what we call the fear of dying is largely the guilt for not having lived? Death, which is present in every moment of living from conception to the grave, must surely be a natural process too if not imposed from without."

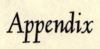

Appendix

Chronological Bibliography
of the Writings of Jessie Taft

TO THE EXTENT that it has been possible to make it so, this bibliography is a complete list of the writings, translations, and editorship of Dr. Taft. Over the years she kept a copy of each of these articles or papers, in a file uncluttered by duplications. From her collection, and from a list prepared by her in recent years, the titles of all items could be identified as the starting point for the preparation of the bibliography. Later search in the indexes of periodicals and proceedings for articles that might have been overlooked resulted in no substantial additions to the list.

What has been added from library sources is the detail of publication that traces the history and development of a given piece of writing and shows where it can be found.

1913 *The Woman Movement from the Point of View of Social Consciousness*

Dissertation submitted to the Faculty of the Graduate School of Arts and Literature in Candidacy for the Degree of Doctor of Philosophy (Department of Philosophy), University of Chicago, 1913. First published by the Collegiate Press, George Banta Publishing Company, Menasha, Wisconsin, 1915, paperbound. Reprinted in 1916 by the University of

371

Chicago Press, No. 6 of Philosophic Studies under the direction of the Department of Philosophy, of the University of Chicago.

1916 "Is There Anything the Matter with Your Child's Mind?"

> *Housewives League Magazine* (about 1916). *Reprint* (undated) issued by the Mental Hygiene Committee of the State Charities Aid Association.

1917 "Fortifying the Child Against Mental Disease"

> Read at the Capitol District Conference of Charities and Correction, Albany, March 28, 1917. *American Education* (September, 1917), p. 12. *Mental Hygiene,* I, No. 4 (October, 1919), 614, abstract from *American Education.*

1917 "How Can We Safeguard the Child Against Mental Disease?"

> Read at the Annual Meeting of the Medical Society of the State of New York, Utica, April 26, 1917. *New York State Journal of Medicine* (November, 1917). *Publisher's Reprint.*

1917 "Mental Pitfalls in Industry—and How to Avoid Them"

> *Medicine and Surgery* (September, 1917), p. 679. *Publisher's Reprint.*

1918 "The Limitations of the Psychiatrist"

> *Medicine and Surgery,* II (March, 1918), 365. *Publisher's Reprint. Mental Hygiene,* II, No. 4 (October, 1918), 656, abstract from *Medicine and Surgery.*

1918 "Supervision of the Feebleminded in the Community"

> Read before the Mental Hygiene Section of the National Conference of Social Work, Kansas City,

May, 1918. *Proceedings* of the Conference (1918), p. 543. *Reprint* from *Proceedings. Mental Hygiene,* II, No. 3 (July, 1918) 434. *Canadian Journal of Mental Hygiene* (July, 1919), p. 164. *Reprint* (1922) by the National Committee for Mental Hygiene.

1919 "Qualifications of the Psychiatric Social Worker"
Read before the Mental Hygiene Section of the National Conference of Social Work, Atlantic City, June, 1919. *Proceedings* of the Conference (1919), p. 593. *Reprint* from *Proceedings. Mental Hygiene,* III, No. 3 (July, 1919), 427. *Reprint* (1920) by the National Committee for Mental Hygiene.

1919 "Relation of Personality Study to Child Placing"
Read before the Children's Division of the National Conference of Social Work, Atlantic City, June, 1919. *Proceedings* of the Conference (1919), p. 63. *Reprint* from *Proceedings.*

1919 "What the Social Worker Learns from the Psychiatrist about Her Problem Children"
The Modern Hospital, XIII, No. 2 (August, 1919). *Publisher's Reprint.*

1919 "The New Impulse in Mental Hygiene"
The Public Health Nurse (October, 1919), p. 805.

1919 "The Neurotic Girl"
Read before the International Conference of Women Physicians, New York, October 18, 1919. *Modern Medicine,* II, No. 2 (February, 1920), 162. *Publisher's Reprint. Mental Hygiene,* IV, No. 2 (April, 1920), 436, abstract from *Modern Medicine.*

1920 "Methods of Observation in the Seybert School for Child Study."
Cooperation (January, 1920), p. 6.

1920 "Problems of Social Case Work with Children"

> Read at the Mental Hygiene Section of the National Conference of Social Work, New Orleans, April, 1920. *Proceedings* of the Conference (1920), p. 377. *The Family*, I, No. 5 (July, 1920), 1. *Reprint* from *The Family*. *Mental Hygiene*, IV, No. 3 (July, 1920), 537.

1921 "Mental Hygiene Problems of Normal Adolescence"

> Read before the Mental Hygiene Division of the National Conference of Social Work, Milwaukee, June, 1921. *Proceedings* of the Conference (1921), p. 355. *Annals of the American Academy of Political and Social Science*, XCVIII, No. 187 (November, 1921), 61. *Reprint* from the *Annals*. *Mental Hygiene*, V, No. 4 (October 1921), 941.

1921 "Individualizing the Child in the School"

> Read at the meeting of the National Association of Visiting Teachers at the National Conference of Social Work, June 27, 1921. *The Family*, II, No. 9 (January, 1922), 208.

1921 "Some Problems in Delinquency—Where Do They Belong?"

> Read at the Annual Meeting of the American Sociological Society, Pittsburgh, December, 1921, before a Round Table on "The Delinquent Girl," sponsored by Mrs. W. F. Dummer of Chicago. *Papers and Proceedings of the American Sociological Society*, XVI (1922), 186. *Reprint* from the *Proceedings*.

1922 "The Social Worker's Opportunity"

> Read before the Mental Hygiene Division of the National Conference of Social Work, Providence,

Rhode Island, June, 1922. *Proceedings* of the Conference (1922), p. 371. *Reprint* from the *Proceedings*. *The Family*, III, No. 6 (October, 1922), 149.

1922 "Setting the Solitary in Families"

Mother and Child (April, 1922), p. 155

1922 "The Need for Psychological Interpretation in the Placement of Dependent Children"

Read before the Pennsylvania State Conference of Social Work, York, 1922. *Pamphlet* (undated) issued by Child Welfare League of America.

1922 "Mental Hygiene and Education"

Read at a meeting of the Educational Committee of the Chicago Woman's Club (Fall, 1922). Unpublished.

1922 *Some Undesirable Habits and Suggestions as to Treatment*

Pamphlet written for the Bureau of Children, Department of Public Welfare, Commonwealth of Pennsylvania, Bulletin No. 4 (November, 1922); reprinted by the Department (March, 1929). *Reprint* (ninth printing, 1941) by the National Committee for Mental Hygiene.

1923 "The Placing of Children Who Are Difficult to Adjust"

The Family, IV, No. 2 (April, 1923), 39. *Reprint* from *The Family*.

1923 "The Relation of the School to the Mental Health of the Average Child"

Read at the National Conference of Social Work, Washington, May, 1923. *Proceedings* of the Conference (1923), p. 394. *Mental Hygiene*, VII, No. 4

(October, 1923), 673. *Reprint* (1923) by the National Committee for Mental Hygiene.

1923 "Progress in Social Case Work in Mental Hygiene"
Read at the National Conference of Social Work, Washington, May, 1923. *Proceedings* of the Conference (1923), p. 338.

1923 "Bringing Up Children, A Problem in Mental Hygiene"
Iowa Children's Home Herald, XXVIII, No. 11 (October-November-December, 1923), 4.

1924 "Turn Good Intentions into Channels of Objective Achievement"
School Life, IX, No. 5 (January, 1924), 113.

1924 "Work in Its Relation to Mental Health"
Read at the Annual Meeting of Woman's Foundation for Health, New York, January 18, 1924. Unpublished.

1924 "Essentials of a Mental Hygiene Program for Philadelphia—The Present Situation—What More is Needed?"
Read before the All-Philadelphia Conference on Social Work, April, 1924. *Hospital Social Service*, X (1924), 78. *Publisher's Reprint.*

1924 "The Use of the Transfer Within the Limits of the Office Interview"
Read before the Division on the Family, National Conference of Social Work, Toronto, June, 1924. *Proceedings* of the Conference (1924), p. 307. *The Family*, V, No. 6 (October, 1924), 143. *Publisher's Reprint.*

1925 "Early Conditionings of Personality in the Pre-School Child"

Address at Schoolmen's Week, University of Pennsylvania, March 27, 1925. *School and Society*, XXI, No. 546 (June 13, 1925), 695. *Publisher's Reprint.*

1925 "The Re-education of a Psychoneurotic Girl"
American Journal of Psychiatry (January, 1925).

1925 "Sex in Children"
The World Tomorrow, VIII, No. 10 (October, 1925), 299. *Publisher's Reprint.*

1925 "Mental Hygiene and Social Work"
In the volume entitled *Social Aspects of Mental Hygiene* (New Haven: Yale University Press, 1925), p. 125.

1925 "The Effect of an Unsatisfactory Mother-Daughter Relationship upon the Development of a Personality"
Read at a meeting of the American Sociological Society, New York, December 27, 1925. *The Family*, VII, No. 1 (March, 1926), 10. *Publisher's Reprint.*

1926 "The Relation of the Child's Emotional Life to His Education"
Read at a meeting of Friend's Education Association, Coulter Friend's School, Philadelphia, March 6, 1926. Unpublished.

1926 "The Mental Hygiene of Adolescence"
The Westonian, XXXII, No. 2 (Spring, 1926), 4.

1926 "The Relation of Psychiatry to Social Work"
Read at the New York City Conference of Charities and Corrections, May 12, 1926. *The Family*, VII, No. 7 (November, 1926), 199.

1926 "The Uses and Limitations of Mental Tests"
Children's Aid News, No. 15 (April-May-June, 1926).

1926 "Closed Doors and the Key to Them"
> *The Survey,* LVI, No. 12 (September 15, 1926), 613. *Publisher's Reprint.*

1926 "What It Means to Be a Foster Parent"
> *Progressive Education,* III, No. 4 (October-November-December, 1926), 351. *Publisher's Reprint.*

1926 "The Adjustment of Our Emotional Lives"
> *Hygeia,* IV, No. 12 (December, 1926), 673. *Publisher's Reprint.*

1927 "The Function of a Mental Hygienist in a Children's Agency"
> Read at the National Conference of Social Work, Des Moines, 1927. *Proceedings* of the Conference (1927), p. 392.

1927 "The Home Has Lost Its Halo"
> *The Survey,* LIX, No. 5 (December 1, 1927), 286.

1928 "Adolescence"
> *Children* (February, 1928), p. 9.

1928 "The Spirit of Social Work"
> Read at the All-Philadelphia Conference of Social Work, March 8, 1928. *The Family,* IX, No. 4 (June, 1928), 103.

1929 "Concerning Adopted Children"
> *Child Study* (January, 1929).

1930 "The Parent's Relation to the Problem of Adjustment"
> Read at the Third Conference of the Chicago Association for Child Study and Parent Education, February, 1930. Published in *The Child's Emotions, Proceedings of the Mid-West Conference on Character Development, February, 1930* (Chicago: University of Chicago Press, 1930), p. 384.

1930 "The Catch in Praise"
Child Study, VII, No. 5 (February, 1930), 133.

1930 "A Consideration of Character Training and Personality Development"
Mental Hygiene, XIV, No. 2 (April, 1930), 326.

1930 "Discussion" of paper by Otto Rank, "The Development of the Emotional Life"
Read at the First International Congress of Mental Hygiene, Washington, May 5–10, 1930. *Proceedings of the First International Congress on Mental Hygiene* (New York: International Committee for Mental Hygiene, 1932), II, p. 142.

1930 "A Changing Psychology in Child Welfare"
The Annals of the American Academy of Political and Social Science, CLI (September, 1930): *Postwar Progress in Child Welfare*, p. 121.

1930 "Do Social Agencies Contribute to Parent Education?"
Read at Biennial Conference, National Council of Parent Education, Washington, November, 1930. Unpublished.

1931 "Bringing Up Children"
Child Welfare League Bulletin, X, No. 7 (September, 1931).

1931 Review: Otto Rank, *Die Analyse des Analytikers und seiner Rolle in der Gesamtsituation* (Leipzig und Wien: Franz Deuticke, 1930).
The Psychoanalytic Review, XVIII, No. 4 (October, 1931), 357. *Mental Hygiene*, XV, No. 4 (October, 1931), 845.

1932 "An Experiment in a Therapeutically Limited Relationship with a Seven-Year-Old Girl"

The Psychoanalytic Review, XIX, No. 4 (October, 1932), 361. Reprinted in *The Dynamics of Therapy in a Controlled Relationship* (1933, 1937).

1932 "The Time Element in Mental Hygiene Therapy as Applied to Social Case Work"

Read at the National Conference of Social Work, Philadelphia, May, 1932. *Proceedings* of the Conference (1932), p. 368. *The American Journal of Orthopsychiatry,* III, No. 1 (January, 1933), 65, with revised title "The Time Element in Therapy." Reprinted as Part I of *The Dynamics of Therapy in a Controlled Relationship* (1933, 1937).

1933 "Living and Feeling"

Child Study, X, No. 4 (January, 1933), 105.

1933 *The Dynamics of Therapy in a Controlled Relationship* (New York: The Macmillan Company, 1933; 2nd ed. 1937.

To be republished by The Dover Press, paperbound, in 1962.

1933 "The Adopted Child"

The Delineator, CXXIII, No. 3 (September, 1933), 12.

1934 "Rank's Contribution to Education"

Review: Otto Rank, *Modern Education* (New York: Alfred A. Knopf, 1932). Unpublished.

1936 Translation: Otto Rank, *Will Therapy: An Analysis of the Therapeutic Process in Terms of Relationship* (New York: Alfred A. Knopf, 1936).

Translator's "Preface," Translator's "Introduction" entitled "The Discovery of the Analytic Situation."

1936 Translation: Otto Rank, *Truth and Reality: A Life History of the Human Will* (New York: Alfred A. Knopf, 1936).

Translator's "Preface."

1937 "The Relation of Function to Process in Social Case Work"

Appeared as the "Introduction" to the *Journal of Social Work Process,* I, No. 1 (November, 1937), Pennsylvania School of Social Work, Philadelphia. Reprinted in *Training for Skill in Social Case Work* (Social Work Process Series; Philadelphia: University of Pennsylvania Press, 1942).

1939 Editor: *Social Case Work with Children, Studies in Structure and Process.*

Journal of Social Work Process, I, No. 3 (December, 1939); Pennsylvania School of Social Work, Philadelphia. Editor's "Introduction."

1939 "Function as the Basis of Development in Social Work Processes"

Presented at the meeting of the American Association of Psychiatric Social Workers, National Conference of Social Work, June, 1939. The *News-Letter,* Vol. IX, No. 1.

1940 "Otto Rank" (Obituary)

Mental Hygiene, "Notes and Comments," XXIV, No. 1 (January, 1940), 148.

1940 "Comments" on *Social Case Work in Practice (Six case studies)* by Florence Hollis, Family Welfare Association of America, 1939.

In "Reader's Forum," *The Family,* XXI, No. 6 (October, 1940), 203.

1940 "Foster Home Care for Children"

The Annals of the American Academy of Political and Social Science, CCXII (November, 1940): *Children in a Depression Decade,* p. 179. *Publisher's Reprint.*

1941 "Comment" on "The Underlying Philosophy of Social Case Work" by Gordon Hamilton.

Paper delivered by Miss Hamilton at the National Conference of Social Work, June, 1941. Comment unpublished.

1941 "The Use and Development of Field Work Opportunities for the Training of Visiting Teachers—under the Auspices of the Private Agency."

Presented at the meeting of the American Association of Visiting Teachers, Atlantic City, June 3, 1941. Unpublished.

1942 "The Function of the Personality Course in the Practice Unit"

In *Training for Skill in Social Case Work* (Social Work Process Series; Philadelphia: University of Pennsylvania Press, 1942).

1942 Review: Otto Rank, *Beyond Psychology*

Mental Hygiene, XXVI, No. 4 (October, 1942), 663.

1943 "Introduction of Grace Marcus at Summer Institute of the Pennsylvania School of Social Work"
Unpublished.

1943 Editor: *Day Nursery Care as a Social Service* (Philadelphia: Pennsylvania School of Social Work, 1943); paperbound.
Editor's "Introduction."

1944 Editor: *A Functional Approach to Family Case Work* (Philadelphia: University of Pennsylvania Press, 1944).

Editor's "Introduction."

1945 Translation: Otto Rank, *Will Therapy and Truth and Reality* (2nd ed.; New York: Alfred A. Knopf, 1945), in one volume.

1946 Editor: *The Role of the Baby in the Placement Process* (Philadelphia: Pennsylvania School of Social Work, 1946); paperbound.

Editor's "Introduction"; "Conclusion: Some Specific Differences in Current Theory and Practice."

1946 Editor: *Counseling and Protective Service as Family Case Work: A Functional Approach* (Philadelphia: Pennsylvania School of Social Work of the University of Pennsylvania, 1946).

Editor's "Introduction"; "Discussion" (of "The Gold Case, A Marital Problem," by M. Robert Gomberg); "Conclusion."

1947 "To the Editor"

In "Reader's Forum" *The Family*, XXVIII, No. 2 (February, 1947), 73. This was an answer to an article by Helen Ross and Adelaide M. Johnson, M.D., *The Family* (November, 1946), p. 273.

1947 "A Philosophy of Helping in Social Work"

Read at the meeting of Counseling Personnel, Division of Pupil Personnel and Counseling, School District of Philadelphia, January 8, 1947. *The Bulletin,* National Association of School Social Workers, XXII, No. 3 (March, 1947).

1948   Editor: *Family Casework and Counseling, A Functional Approach* (Philadelphia: University of Pennsylvania Press, 1948).

Editor's "Introduction to Part I"; "Introduction"; "Discussion" (of "The Gold Case, a Marital Problem," by M. Robert Gomberg); "The Fox Case, a Problem in Referral" (Case by Celia Brody); "Conclusion."

1949   "The Dane Case"

Social Work, A Quarterly Review of Family Casework, London, VI, No. 3 (July, 1949), 316.

1949   "Time as the Medium of the Helping Process"

Delivered at the Jewish Conference of Social Work, Cleveland, June, 1949. *Jewish Social Service Quarterly,* XXVI, No. 2 (December, 1949), 189.

1950   "A Conception of the Growth Process Underlying Social Casework Practice"

Presented at the National Conference of Social Work, Atlantic City, April, 1950. *Proceedings* of the Conference, (1950), Part II: *Social Work in the Current Scene,* p. 294. *Social Casework,* XXXI, No. 8 (October, 1950), 311. Reprinted in *Principles and Techniques in Social Casework* (New York: Family Service Association of America, 1950), p. 247.

1957   "The Otto Rank Collection, and Its Relation to Freud and Psychoanalysis"

Columbia Library Columns, VII, No. 1 (November, 1957), 18.

1958   *Otto Rank, A Biographical Study Based on Notebooks, Letters, Collected Writings, Therapeutic Achievements and Personal Associations* (New York: The Julian Press, 1958).